Old Age and Political Behavior

A Publication of the
Institute of Industrial Relations
University of California

Old Age and
Political Behavior
A CASE STUDY

FRANK A. PINNER, PAUL JACOBS
AND PHILIP SELZNICK

Berkeley and Los Angeles, 1959
UNIVERSITY OF CALIFORNIA PRESS

UNIVERSITY OF CALIFORNIA PRESS
BERKELEY AND LOS ANGELES
CALIFORNIA

CAMBRIDGE UNIVERSITY PRESS
LONDON, ENGLAND

© 1959, BY
THE REGENTS OF THE UNIVERSITY OF CALIFORNIA
LIBRARY OF CONGRESS CATALOG CARD NUMBER: 59–11315
PRINTED IN THE UNITED STATES OF AMERICA

Foreword

In 1950 the Institute of Industrial Relations received a sizable grant from the Rockefeller Foundation to conduct a five-year interdisciplinary study of the problem of aging in an industrial society. The plans for the study were formulated under the leadership of President Clark Kerr, who was then director of the Institute, and his associate director, the late Lloyd H. Fisher. The separate studies which eventually emerged as subdivisions of the over-all project dealt with the economic status of the aged, the politics of the aged, the relationship of physiological and psychological age to chronological age, the social and psychological aspects of aging and retirement, employer and union policies toward the older worker, and retirement policy under Social Security legislation. The responsibility for guiding the project in its final stages has fallen chiefly to Dr. Margaret S. Gordon, now associate director of the Institute.

The present volume, one of the books emerging from the study, represents the combined efforts of a political scientist, Frank A. Pinner, now at Michigan State University; a political journalist, Paul Jacobs, of The Fund for the Republic and *The Reporter* magazine; and a sociologist, Philip Selznick, of the University of California, Berkeley.

Ever since the years of the Great Depression, when Dr. Francis E. Townsend organized "Old Age Revolving Pensions, Inc.," California has been a center of political activity on behalf of the aged.

During the last decade or so, the organization led by George H. McLain, which forms the focus of the present study, emerged as the most powerful pension movement in the state. As the authors point out in chapter vi, McLain is now endeavoring to broaden the geographical base of his organization to nation-wide dimensions. Whether or not he succeeds in this effort, the findings of the present study, particularly as they bear on the characteristics and attitudes of the thousands of aged persons in the McLain movement, will be of widespread interest.

Arthur M. Ross, Director
Institute of Industrial Relations
University of California

Acknowledgments

WE have had much help. In naming but a few of those who gave advice and coöperation, we remain conscious of our indebtedness to many others. Among the latter are the more than three thousand pensioners who answered our questionnaires and opened their doors to our interviewers.

We gratefully acknowledge the support we received from the Institute of Industrial Relations, University of California, which sponsored the study. We feel particularly indebted to Margaret S. Gordon, Associate Director of the Institute, for her untiring help. Thanks are also due the Center for Advanced Study in the Behavioral Sciences and the Bureau of Social and Political Research, Michigan State University.

Our association with Lloyd H. Fisher, whose untimely death occurred while the study was in progress, will be long remembered.

Charles Perrow and Gertrude J. Selznick contributed much by helping to draft sections of the manuscript. We were also greatly aided by Bennett Berger, Roselyn Levenson, Carol Herndon, and Sheldon L. Messinger; we extend our thanks to all. Stanford Seidner's statistical assistance was invaluable, and Roger Marz also gave much help in quantitative analysis. Genevieve Rogers, editor at the University of California Press, deserves special thanks for her patience in dealing with a difficult manuscript. Reinhard Bendix and Norman Jacobson read the manuscript and gave us the benefit of many helpful suggestions.

We are indebted to Charles Schottland, Director of the California Department of Social Welfare at the time of this study, and to the Welfare Directors of the seven participating counties for giving us access to a sample of Old Age Assistance recipients. John Henderson, of the California Department of Social Welfare, gave us much valuable advice.

We wish to express our deep obligation to George McLain,

Chairman of the California Institute of Social Welfare. He was most generous and coöperative in giving us access to the Institute's files, meetings, and staff. In drawing samples of Institute members and in many other ways, we had the active help of George McLain, Jr., and of many members of the Institute staff.

While gratefully acknowledging the aid of so many, we impute errors to none but ourselves.

F. A. P.

P. J.

P. S.

Contents

ix

List of Illustrations

Chapter I | Introduction

THIS study is born of a concern that the great increase in the number of old people may bring about unforeseen and troubling changes in the life of the community. The vision of a future containing a great many idle, dependent people suggests the possibility that a powerful, homogeneous bloc of aged may arise. There are even vague fears that this group, whose status in society has been greatly altered, may be led by opportunists and irresponsible persons who will lay rude hands on the democratic process.

Democracy cannot prosper unless the citizens are bound into their society by a complex, many-stranded network of social ties. The individual takes part in society in a variety of ways—through his job, his friendships, his family, and his organizational memberships. He has more than one stake in society; and his actions in one area of social living are controlled and tempered by their effects upon his other social relations. Thus, when acting as a parent of school children, a citizen is mindful of his roles and interests as a neighbor, as a taxpayer, and perhaps as a personal acquaintance of the chemistry teacher. By his many contacts with others, by the diversity of the interests he shares with them, and by the necessity of striking a balance among his own often contradictory interests, the citizen is inhibited from joining monolithic and uncompromising groups. Democracy relies upon the high degree of differentiation and the interdependence of groups in society as

1

a system of checks and balances operating upon each group and upon each individual.

New social groups entering the political arena are often composed of individuals whose social ties are neither numerous nor varied. Whether they are workers in a new factory town or migrants just arrived from foreign lands, members of new groups are likely to be poor in social relatedness. As a result, the suspicion may arise that the new group will be uncontrolled in its demands and ambitions, and uncontrollable should its members acquire a measure of power. If the separate status of the new group is long maintained, suspicions tend to deepen; and at times the segregated group becomes available for irresponsible political action. City bossism may be cited as an example of the corruption of democratic processes which can result from exploitation of the political potential in segregated groups. There is a *prima facie* case against segregation of any sort if the social structure is to sustain a democratic political system.

These considerations frame the political problem raised by the emergence of the aged as a new social group. Are the aged—and especially those subsisting on government pensions—becoming an increasingly segregated group in American society? Do they develop their own values and attitudes, their own forms of political, social, and religious expression—all dominated by the central life experience of old age and, for many, of relative poverty? The emergence of old-age movements during the past two decades seems to suggest that something of this sort is occurring. How far has the process of segregation gone? How serious are its implications?

This study[1] deals with the California Institute of Social Welfare (CISW), a political pressure group composed chiefly of recipients of Old Age Assistance. The organization, between 65,000 and 75,000 members strong at the time the study was made, has within its ranks approximately 20 per cent of the aged on California's public welfare rolls. Its leader, George McLain, came to the attention of Californians in 1948, 1952, and 1954 as the sponsor of initiative-referenda for the revision and liberalization of programs

---

[1] The leadership, membership, activities, and history of the organization were studied during the period 1951–1954.

of public assistance to the aged. In 1949 a particularly vigorous political battle was fought centering on McLain and his organization. With the support of the California Chamber of Commerce, the legislature called a special election for the purpose of repealing a constitutional amendment which McLain had sponsored and which the voters had adopted in the 1948 election. Californians have had ample occasion to encounter the name of George McLain, although few of them have any acquaintance with his Institute of Social Welfare.

Pension Movements in California[2]

California has been, for more than a century, the recipient of large numbers of migrants. During this period the economy of the state has changed from mining to agriculture to service industries and manufacturing. Beginning with the Gold Rush days of 1849, the state's history has been marked by the rapid growth and decline of popular movements such as vigilantism, Kearneyism, and the anti-Oriental agitation which appeared toward the end of the nineteenth century. Up to the earthquake and fire of 1906, San Francisco was the most rapidly growing and tumultuous of California's cities, and most of the state's social movements originated there. During the last half-century, Los Angeles has become the focal point of immigration; virtually every California social (or religious) movement got its start in that city.

The early 'thirties saw the rapid growth and subsequent decline of the Technocrats, the Continentals, and the Utopians. During the same period, the EPIC ("End Poverty in California") movement developed as part of Upton Sinclair's campaign for the governorship of the state. At the heart of the EPIC program was the concept of "production for use"; the state was to rent idle factories and put idle hands to work producing goods that were actually needed by the population. Sinclair's program also contained an old-age pension plan. The activities of the EPIC movement con-

---

[2] The discussion of pension movements in California is based on the following sources: Robert E. Burke, *Olson's New Deal for California* (Berkeley: University of California Press, 1953); Bill E. Fitzgerald, "Pension Politics in California," unpublished master's thesis, University of California, 1951; Charles E. Larsen, "The Epic Movement in California," unpublished master's thesis, University of California, 1945; Winston and Marian Moore, *Out of the Frying Pan* (Los Angeles; De Vorss, 1939).

sisted primarily in holding meetings and in selling and distributing EPIC literature. After Sinclair's defeat at the polls the movement rapidly subsided.

Dr. Francis E. Townsend's organization, originally labeled "Old Age Revolving Pensions, Inc.," entered upon the scene at the peak of the EPIC campaign. Dr. Townsend, a retired physician from South Dakota, moved to California and was for a time involved in a series of unsuccessful business ventures. His original plan called for a monthly pension of $200 to every citizen above the age of sixty, to be financed by a tax on all business transactions. This program was presented as more than a proposal to help the old people; by increasing the buying power of a substantial segment of the population, the plan was designed to stimulate business activity and thus restore full production and employment. The Townsend clubs which mushroomed rapidly seem to have been most attractive to the middle and working classes. The club members engaged in a great deal of social activity and helped spread the *Townsend Weekly* and other Townsend literature. Over a period of time the Townsend plan underwent several modifications. In 1944, having long since passed their prime, the Townsend clubs finally succeeded in placing on the ballot an initiative calling for a monthly pension of $60, but the proposition was defeated. This was the last gasp of the Townsend movement as a political force. In 1948 the Townsend clubs failed to secure enough signatures to qualify another pension initiative.

The movement popularly known as "Ham and Eggs" has, during the fifteen years of its existence, been known by five different names: California Pension Plan (1936), California Life Retirement Payments Association (1938), Payroll Guarantee Association (1942), California Bill of Rights Association (1948), and Pension and Taxpayers Union, Inc. (1950).

The Ham and Eggs plan was built around such slogans as "Twenty-five Every Monday" or "Thirty Every Thursday." The program was to be financed by the issuance of one-dollar warrants to be used as legal currency. These were to be amortized over a year's time by their bearers.

By 1938 the Ham and Eggs movement came under the control of Willis and Lawrence Allen. Between 1938 and 1950 the Allen brothers and their lieutenants were able to qualify four initiative-referenda; a fifth initiative did not muster the required number of signatures, and a sixth was ruled off the ballot. All the initiatives which reached the ballot were defeated by the voters.

McLain's organization is, in a sense, an offshoot of Ham and Eggs. During the campaign for the 1939 proposition, the most vigorous campaign ever fought by the Allens, McLain was their state organizer. After the defeat of this initiative, McLain left the Allens and organized the Citizens' Committee for Old Age Pensions, the forerunner of the present California Institute of Social Welfare. Contrary to the practice of his predecessors, McLain has never sponsored a full-fledged pension plan designed to make basic changes in the economic structure and the legal framework of the state. Rather, all his activities have centered on attempts to amend the existing welfare legislation.

Some interesting parallels may be suggested. The meteoric nature of all these early movements is apparent. The Utopians were able, in 1934, to attract 50,000 people to a meeting, although neither the group nor the particular meeting had received any attention in the newspapers. Both the EPIC and the Townsend movements grew within a few months from a handful of men to crusades enlisting the support of hundreds of thousands of people. The written word—Sinclair's pamphlet "I, Governor of California and How I Ended Poverty" and Townsend's weekly newspaper—was their prime mobilizing agent. Radio broadcasts for Ham and Eggs over an obscure station brought a deluge of mail and a steady stream of financial contributions. By 1938 some 175,000 persons were sending thirty cents each month to the Allens as membership dues. In the same year the Allens were able to submit to the secretary of state the largest list of names ever to appear on an initiative petition—789,000 signatures. Only 187,000 were needed at the time to qualify the initiative. The success of all these movements leaves little doubt that vast reserves of political energy were available to the political entrepreneur.

These results were achieved without the hard work of recruiting and organizing that usually goes into the building of a political machine, a union, or a business organization. EPIC and Townsend clubs sprang up everywhere in the state before headquarters had made even the first contacts in local communities. The Utopians and Ham and Eggs got along entirely without local clubs, relying simply on the members' faithful attendance at mass meetings or, as the new medium developed, regular listening to the radio. Because of the extreme looseness of the organization and the haphazardness of communication, members had no opportunity to participate in decisions. Instead, decision-making was centered in headquarters. For the same reason, the movement provided little opportunity for the growth of a competent secondary leadership. Rival organizations occasionally sprang up, led by erstwhile or would-be leaders of the groups from which they had split off.

Three strains are distinguishable in the pension movements and their forerunners: populism, the belief in mechanical panaceas, and salesmanship.

As the campaign techniques of the pension organizations became more elaborate, money income to cover overhead and yield profits became increasingly urgent. The Utopians and EPIC had been content with moderate membership fees, but the ambitious Allen brothers inaugurated the technique of making unceasing appeals for contributions. The Allens also were the first to introduce business principles into political campaigns by requiring that each promotional activity defray its own cost.

Because they combined so many different traits—socialistic and business-minded, moralistic, and hardheadedly technical—the movements have played an ambiguous role in California politics. The party regulars, in both the Democratic and the Republican camp, have looked dubiously upon the leaders of the pension movements. Yet, in view of their strength, politicians have not been able to ignore them. Frank Merriam, the successful Republican candidate who ran against Upton Sinclair, may have had Townsend to thank for his election. Democratic Governor Olson was elected with the help of the Allen brothers—and found later that he had assumed a rather embarrassing political debt when the Allens threatened him with a recall election and forced upon him the special election of 1939. Democratic politicians have more frequently accepted the support of the pension movements than have Republicans. It is doubtful, however, that these alliances are a result of political sympathies. California has been dominated by the Republicans since the Civil War. The Democrats have dispensed little state patronage and have received very little organized support. Democratic candidates could ill afford to refuse the support of pension organizations whose members—or customers—were to be found in communities throughout California.

In the Ham and Eggs movement the combination of populism, salesmanship, and the peddling of mechanical panaceas reached its culmination. From the graveyard of populism and progressivism the Allens exhumed the demands for cheap credit, increased money circulation, and the control of banks by the state. From the arsenal of Technocracy they got their critique of the price system and the idea that social reforms could be achieved through some device such as self-amortizing warrants. From the field of salesmanship came their emphasis on merchandising techniques.

It is possible that this peculiar combination of beliefs and attitudes could have been successful only in the period of the depression and the years following it. At any rate, McLain's movement, while still showing traces of Ham and Eggs philosophy, has tended to adopt the tactics of a pressure organization defending the interests of a particular and hence limited constituency. The work and propaganda of the organization have been concerned chiefly with Old Age Assistance legislation within the framework of federal and state systems. McLain demands justice for his "oldsters" within the existing institutional system, not a new system meant to inaugurate the reign of justice for all, including the aged. What was, in Ham and Eggs, the essential content of the movement has, in the California Institute of Social Welfare, become a less serious ideology to rationalize concrete economic demands.

Political Structure and Agitation

Movements such as we have described seem to grow most vigorously in the soil of recently settled or socially unstable regions. Political parties have been notoriously weak in California; they do not have at their disposal well-established machines, faithful electorates, and financial resources earmarked for political activity. Since the political forum is not preëmpted by the parties, movements which are more or less nonpartisan in character can from time to time capture blocs of votes for particular causes.

Since there is little party control over those elected to public office, pressure groups do not have to compete with party loyalties and commitments in order to gain access to legislators. Thus an organization like the California Institute of Social Welfare, combining the techniques of the mass movement and the pressure group, is able to thrive in the climate of California politics.

The great mobility—geographical as well as social—of California's population accounts in part for these political conditions. To be successful, political parties must have a territorial base. Precinct organization can thrive only where neighborhoods are fairly stable; the rapid turnover of populations in most urban centers of California thwarts the effective political organization of neighborhoods. Homogeneity of neighborhoods—according to ethnic origin, social class, religious affiliation, or income—is also helpful in party work. Similarities among the householders in a neighborhood help the party workers in formulating demands and programs which can unite a large number of persons. In California, neighborhoods tend to be less homogeneous than in the more tradition-bound cities of the East and Midwest.

The weakness of political parties belongs to California's frontier heritage. The conditions of frontier equalitarianism and of unceasing immigration created opportunities, early in the state's history, for the monopoly of political power by predominant economic interests. Toward the end of the nineteenth century, the importance of rail transportation for California's economy led to the control of the state's politics by the Southern Pacific Railroad. Against this power monopoly there arose, toward the end of the nineteenth century and in the beginning of the twentieth century, a variety of movements of the Populist and progressive type. The movements and their often idealistic leaders were intent upon breaking the dominance of the "Southern Pacific machine"—giving the state government "back to the people" by instituting methods of direct democracy which, they hoped, would once and for all end power monopolists and corruption.

The results of these movements can be read today in the constitution and the statutes of the state. The constitution can easily be amended by simple popular majorities. The governor lacks any real legislative initiative. Since his power of appointment is extremely limited—a large number of executive and judicial offices are elective—the governor is hampered in maintaining discipline within his own party.

The attempt to give the government "back to the people" has led to severe restraints upon political parties as instruments of political control and to the predominance of pressure groups on the political scene. As in many other states, restraints upon political parties have been written into the laws governing California politics. A political party has very little leeway in developing its own organization. The composition of the party's county committees and of the state central committee, as well as the modes of electing and appointing the members of these bodies, is prescribed by the constitution. The governing bodies of the parties thus constituted are rather large and unwieldy. Consequently, the official organs of the parties provide very little leadership, and the actual political leader is often hidden from public view.

Political party activity has been seriously hampered also by the practice of cross-filing, which obscures party identities in the minds of voters. All candidates are permitted to file in both the Democratic and Republican primary elections, if they are able to gain the endorsement of a certain number of qualified voters. Most commonly, the candidates of both major parties file for candidacy on both primary tickets; and it is not unusual for an election to be decided in the primary when a candidate wins the nomination on both tickets. Until 1954 the candidates' party affiliations were not shown on the primary ballot.

Since political parties have given their candidates only weak support, politicians have looked to interest groups for help. The first campaign of most legislators tends to be a series of desperate improvisations, but support from interest groups is usually forthcoming once a man has spent a term in the legislature. First campaigns are usually fought with insufficient means; so it is not very common for an incumbent to be dislodged by an aspiring candidate. Pressure group support thus perpetuates legislators in office. Short-term offices in the legislature tend, in fact, to be held for rather long periods of time.

Since parties have little control over their candidates, they are virtually incapable of affecting legislative votes. In the face of the strong pressures exercised upon them, most state legislators are incapable of maintaining an independent position. Politics thus resolves itself into a series of bargains among representatives of pressure groups, who form ever-shifting coalitions by trading the votes which they influence in the legislative assemblies.

A further political device that limits the effectiveness of political parties is the initiative and referendum. The use of these instruments of direct legislation by the people makes it possible to go over the heads of established political leadership. Typically, the initiative-referendum has been used by interest groups and movements, while the political parties remain uncommitted. The success of the initiative-referendum usually depends upon broad appeals through mass media to an undifferentiated mass of voters rather than upon intensive campaigns calculated to elicit the support of specific groups within the voting public. Political parties, whose efforts must be devoted to securing local support for their candidates, are reluctant to adopt rigid positions which might help some candidates while hurting others.

The techniques of mass mobilization, such as those employed in referendum campaigns, are the most important weapons in the arsenal of movements. This is to be expected, for movements frequently stand for policies which find little or no support among established social groups. Indeed, the absence of such support and the resulting difficulty of furthering objectives by concluding alliances with other groups are commonly the very reasons for the existence of a movement.

Deviant Leadership and the Social Base

We have suggested that a loosely structured political environment is congenial to popular agitation, based on direct appeals to the electorate, carried on apart from established channels of community organization and leadership. Such an environment gives a certain freedom to the political entrepreneur. But he must also consider his constituency, which may impose its own restraints upon him. Given a clientele made up of the aged poor, what sort of politics will arise? Will there be an orderly appeal by responsible representatives of a competent and self-restrained constituency? Or will an irresponsible, uncontrolled element enter the political arena?

It is necessary to consider, first, whether a dependent old-age population itself is likely to produce a characteristic leadership and mode of action. Are there any clues to the probable political role of a constituency made up of the aged poor? Some answers are provided by a general understanding of organizations and leadership, with particular reference to the experience of other dependent and isolated social groups.

The social base of an organization is the broader group toward which the organization is oriented and from which it draws its members and support. Where a clear-cut social base exists, as in the earlier relation between the American Federation of Labor and the craft-organized skilled workers, the personnel and methods of the organization tend to reflect the social characteristics of the constituency. Analysis of the social base can reveal a great deal about the pressures that play upon an organization and the role it assumes in the community.

Ordinarily, the relation between an organization and its social base is clear and straightforward. Members and leaders are drawn from the constituency, whose interests and attitudes they reflect with reasonable fidelity. Most of the many thousands of business, professional, and recreational clubs and societies are fairly homogeneous in this sense. While there is always some difference between the larger group of those eligible and the smaller group of joiners, and a further difference between rank-and-file members and their leaders, these differences are relatively small.

When leaders, members, and constituency are socially similar, the likelihood increases (though it is not insured) that the policies and actions of an organization will conform to the aspirations and interests of the social base upon which it rests. The social responsibility of a leadership group depends greatly on the nature and quality of the ties which bind it to its special constituency and to the larger community.

The critical issue in the relation between leaders and led is dependency. Who can act without taking account of the other? When we know who is dependent on whom, we also know who is *free* of whom, and from this we can gauge a leader's ability to pursue his own course unchecked by contol from below. Three of the more important elements that affect the relative dependency of leaders and led are the distribution of skills, the availability of alternative leaders, and the acceptance of risks.

Leadership of large groups requires a wide range of technical abilities: oral and written expression, the making and executing of decisions, and negotiations with outside groups. When the followers are poorly equipped with such skills they become dependent upon their leaders. The greater the imbalance in the distribution of skills, the easier it is for leaders to become self-perpetuating and potentially irresponsible. In many groups the lack of political competence reflects a low cultural level. If a group does not include enough people who have the requisite organizational skills, it may look elsewhere for leaders. When this occurs, a price must be paid in added dependency.

Followers are most independent of their leaders when they can easily turn to alternative individuals and groups capable of assuming office. The leaders are held in check by the realization that they can be replaced. But the availability of alternative leaders depends on the strength and diversity of the existing interested groups. In narrowly defined segments of the population, such as an occupational or an interest group, social organization is often weakly developed. As a result, there may be few organized elements and little opportunity for leadership to develop or to be sustained. In such situations, dependency on existing leaders is likely to be great.

If the members of a group are relatively weak and exposed to attack, yet wish to engage in joint action, they tend to be dependent on those who are willing or able to take the risks. And they often accept subordination despite undemocratic practices and the personal corruption of leaders. If the activity is deemed necessary, yet few are willing to undertake it, a leadership vacuum develops. This opens the way to men who, while providing the minimum service required, will exploit the opportunity for their own ends.

These are not the only conditions that contribute to the dependency of followers and clienteles. They are especially important, however, in the emergence of *deviant* leadership. A leader may be considered "deviant" when he is not representative of his members in social background or aspiration and when he is not accepted as an entirely respectable member of the community at large. Typically, such leaders arise and are accepted when a dependent, low-status constituency organizes for action vis-à-vis a dominant majority. The history of racial minorities and of the labor movement shows how and why this phenomenon occurs.

After emancipation the American Negroes were faced with the need for concerted action. They could not simply withdraw into geographical and social isolation. The ties that bound them to the white community and white aspirations were too many and too strong. As a dependent and subordinate group emerging into self-consciousness, the Negroes needed leaders who would undertake the task of communicating with the dominant majority. Yet the Negro community did not have its own strong institutions, established leadership, and orderly channels of action. In its early days the National Association for the Advancement of Colored People depended greatly on the sponsorship and support of sympathetic whites. This leadership, though unrepresentative, was not "deviant" in our sense, or exploitative; it followed a code set by the community of white philanthropy, religion, and social idealism. Yet the institutional weakness of the Negro community, combined with dependence on the whites and an atmosphere of fear, created opportunities for direct access to the population by demagogic and opportunistic leaders. The latter could readily compete with the more responsible leadership provided by the small group of educated Negroes.

The accommodative leader, who often played the role of "fixer" for the Negro community, was a ready target for accusations of dishonesty and self-seeking.

The Southern Negro leader—not being allowed to state and follow a clear ideological line but doomed to opportunism, having constantly to compromise with his pride and dignity, and never being allowed to speak upon the authority of the strength of an organized group behind him but appearing as an individual person trusted by the adversary group before him—does not have the sanctions ordinarily operating to preserve the honor and loyalty of a representative leader. The temptation to sell out the group and to look for his own petty interest is great. He thus easily comes to justify the common suspicions around him by becoming a self-seeker and opportunist.[3]

The demagogic protest leader, such as Marcus Garvey, was more markedly exploitative. And the educated Negro leader was unrepresentative because of his social background and the opportunity he had to detach himself from the Negro community and its fate.

The significant point is that a relatively uncontrolled and potentially irresponsible leadership was a natural outcome of the dependency, isolation, and weak institutional development of the Negro community up to recent years. A like development should be expected among other groups in similar circumstances. And indeed, this appears to be so.

The history of the labor movement, also, has been marked by deviant leadership. Here again we see a subordinate segment of the population coming to a new self-consciousness and attempting concerted action. On the whole, trade unionism did not base itself upon a preëxisting organization and leadership; there was a drive for new organizations and new leaders. A leadership vacuum appeared in many places, offering opportunities for reformist and socialist intellectuals, for IWW organizers, and for racketeers. Communist influence in the CIO during the late 'thirties and 'forties is directly traceable to the leadership vacuum in a number of industries organized by the CIO. With increasing stability, including firmer links to and acceptance by the larger community, the opportunity for deviant leadership has declined.

These experiences suggest that a dependent social group attempting concerted action is vulnerable to political exploitation. In such groups, leadership skills are poorly developed; and this is aggravated by the special need for intermediaries to deal with dominant and unfriendly institutions. The weakness of social organization means that alternative leaders are not readily available; and this too is aggravated by the special risks that are required of those who expose themselves as representatives of the subordinate group.

These conditions are present also among the aged, and particu-

---

[3] Gunnar Myrdal, *An American Dilemma* (New York: Harper, 1944), pp. 774 ff.

larly among the aged poor. As a segment of society the aged are weak, not only in consciousness of kind but in social organization. They have no stable, regenerative leadership or established institutions. Rather, the aged constitute another as yet dependent and subordinate group. To the extent that concerted action and leadership are required, we may expect the characteristic vacuum, with its attendant costs.

The Old Age Assistance Program[4]

The individuals whose interests McLain's program purports to advance constitute approximately 30 per cent of all Californians aged sixty-five and over, a total of 273,000 persons.[5] The average age of these people is 75.6 years. Considerably more than half of them are women—61.7 per cent. Only 4 per cent of the pensioners are Negroes and 1 per cent are of Mexican origin.[6] The average pensioner has resided in California for 30.9 years; only 12.1 per cent of the recipients have lived in the state for less than 10 years.[7]

---

[4] This section describes the situation of the old-age assistance recipient in California during the period 1952–1954, when most of the data discussed in later chapters were gathered. Recent changes in the law are indicated in footnotes 9, 10, and 11, below. The term "pension" is anathema to many Californians who believe that it refers only to a grant to which the recipient has legal title, as distinct from an "assistance" payment. Webster defines "pension" as "a payment regularly made to any person, as by way of subsidy, gratuity, etc." This is the meaning given the term in everyday speech. The distinction between "pension" and "assistance grant" seems to have more emotional and political than legal and economic significance. Under existing federal and state legislation, Californians have, under certain conditions, a "right" to Old Age Security payments. Payments unlawfully withheld can be recovered through legal action. In this study, the terms "Old Age Security" and "aid" will be used interchangeably with "pension," and the term "recipient" interchangeably with "pensioner."

[5] State of California, Department of Social Welfare, *Preliminary Statistical Release*, August, 1952, mimeographed.

[6] In the total population of individuals sixty-five years and over, Negroes and Mexicans constitute 6 per cent each. Since both groups tend to be economically depressed, it is somewhat surprising that they are underrepresented among pension recipients. One possible reason for this discrepancy is that the Negro and Mexican populations include a large number of persons who arrived in California in one of the recent waves of migration; for this reason they are unable to satisfy the residence requirements which would qualify them for public assistance. A rather high proportion of the migrants of Mexican origin have not acquired United States citizenship and are disqualified on this ground.

[7] From unpublished statistics, State Department of Social Welfare, Bureau of Research and Statistics, typescript, April, 1952.

California's Old Age Security (OAS) program was adopted by the state legislature in 1935. The act establishing the program amended the legislation governing assistance to the indigent aged and made the state program consonant with requirements of the federal Social Security Act. The three main differences between Old Age and Survivors Insurance (OASI—Social Security) and Old Age Assistance (OAA)[8] are the following: (1) OASI is a program based on contributions by employers and employees; OAA is noncontributory; (2) eligibility for OASI benefits depends on the number of years the claimant has contributed to the program, his age, and the wages he has been earning at the end of his occupational career; in OAA, eligibility and the size of the grant depend on need; (3) OASI is administered directly by the federal government; OAA is administered by the states.

By adopting the necessary amendment to its welfare legislation, California became eligible for federal grants-in-aid which cover part of the administrative cost and part of the payments to the aged. The federal Social Security Act specifies the conditions with which a state must comply in order to receive federal aid. These federal rules relate chiefly to uniform administration of the program throughout the state, and establish minimum standards for determining the eligibility of applicants.

Under the Social Security Act, the federal government assumes half of the adminstrative cost of the program. The federal government, further, contributes four-fifths of the first $25 and one-half of any amount between $25 and $55 of the average grant made by the state. The remainder of the expenses of the program is divided between the state and the counties; the state pays for six-sevenths and the counties for one-seventh of these amounts.

Under the federal law, the state must either administer the program directly or must supervise the administration by the counties and be responsible to the federal government for uniform administration. In California the administration of the program is in the hands of the county boards of supervisors who appoint the personnel to administer the program. The State Department of Social Wel-

---

[8] "Old Age Security" (OAS) is the title given in California to the same program which the federal government describes as "Old Age Assistance" (OAA). In our text we refer to the California program as OAS and to the corresponding federal program of grants-in-aids as OAA.

fare sets policies for the administration of the program in accordance with the Welfare and Institutions Code; and it supervises the program through its own personnel and by requiring regular reports from the county directors of social welfare. This administrative scheme is a holdover from the days when the counties bore the major portion of the cost of relief and had a fairly free hand in setting policies. It is often argued that this arrangement keeps the administration of the welfare programs closer to the people, but its opponents feel that it makes for uneven interpretation and application of the program from county to county, and results in administrative complications.

In most counties an applicant's first appointment is with an "intake" worker, who explains to the client that, in order to be eligible for OAS, he must be a United States citizen, and must be at least sixty-five years of age or within sixty days of his sixty-fifth birthday. He must have resided within the State of California during the entire year preceding the application, and have been a resident of the state for at least five out of the last nine years. He may not own real property the assessed value of which is greater than $3,500. His personal property, such as money in the bank, stocks and bonds, an automobile, jewelry, and furniture (of such value that they may be regarded as investments), may not exceed $1,200; or, if the client and his spouse are both assistance recipients, their combined personal property must be less than $2,000. (Both real and personal property are counted to the extent that they are unencumbered.)

The intake worker usually draws the client's attention to two other important features of the program. One of these is "relatives' responsibility." The client is informed that his spouse and all his adult children living in California will have to be contacted for the purpose of determining whether they can contribute to his support; their contributions (usually small) depend on their income and obligations, and in many cases no contribution is demanded of them. The other important feature of the program is that the amount of money which the client may expect from the government depends on his needs and income situation; it is not a flat grant.

At this point the client is asked whether he feels he can qualify for assistance. Some clients, realizing that they do not have the necessary residence or property requirements, decide not to apply. A very few decline to apply because they do not wish to have the Welfare Department ask their children for a contribution.

If the client signifies his desire to apply, the intake worker makes a preliminary determination of eligibility, fills out the necessary papers, and has the client sign the application. Many intake workers inquire into the specific reasons which have led the applicant to request assistance at this time. This is done in order to determine whether the applicant is in a critical situation requiring immediate attention, or whether there are special problems which should be taken into consideration in processing the case. Clients occasionally misinterpret this question as an unwarranted intrusion into their private affairs.

After the client has signed the application, he is informed that his case will be handled thereafter by a field worker who will visit him in his home. The client should have ready certain documents: proof of age, nationality, and residence; and bank statements, checkbooks, and other evidence of income and assets. He must report to the welfare office any change of address or of income, including income from occasional work, or any reduction or increase in his needs, for example, a temporary reduction of needs for food and housing if he resides with his children during a lengthy visit. The law also requires that the client be informed that he has a right to appeal any decision of the social worker or the welfare office, and that in case of appeal a decision will be made by the state referee. Since the prospect of litigation tends to upset the client, it is generally necessary to reassure him. The mention of the appeal procedure sometimes helps to make the client sensitive to the legal aspects of his situation.

Under the Welfare and Institutions Code, the application must be followed promptly by a home visit; this ordinarily occurs within thirty days. The field worker usually begins by reviewing the client's eligibility and examining the documents which the client shows to prove it. The social worker must ascertain that the assessed value of the applicant's property, less "encumbrances of record," does not exceed $3,500.[9] In California the assessed value of property is usually about one-quarter of the market value. The

---

[9] In 1957 this maximum was raised to $5,000.

full amount of any part of a loan against the property still due is deducted from the assessed value in order to determine whether the respondent's property exceeds the prescribed limits.

If the field worker has satisfied himself that eligibility can be established, he obtains the information needed to calculate the client's grant. In relatively simple cases this can be done immediately, in the presence of the client. In more complicated cases, the amount to be paid to the client is determined in the office after further investigation.

The amount of the grant is determined by the client's needs, his resources, and the legal limitations on the amount that can be granted. The total value in dollars of the client's regular resources in cash or kind is subtracted from the total amount of his needs. If the result is $80 or less, this constitutes the recipient's grant; if, however, the result exceeds the state maximum of $80, the client can receive only $80. In rare instances, counties supplement grants out of their own funds, but the state never contributes to any portion of a grant in excess of the legal limit of $80.[10]

In calculating the client's budget of needs, the social worker uses a schedule of "basic allowances" and "maximum excesses allowable" established by the State Department of Social Welfare. The table (p. 20) shows the schedule in abbreviated form. A recipient who has no resources other than OAS is limited to the basic allowances listed in the first column of the table. If additional resources are available, they can be utilized to meet excess needs. However, the additional allowances for excess needs may not be larger than those listed in the second column. Other excess allowances can be made for certain items not listed, such as transportation[11] and moving costs, laundry, telephone, debts, medical

---

[10] During its 1955 session the California legislature increased the maximum grant to $85. In 1956 a further raise to $90 was adopted as a result of an increase in federal grants. Since 1957 a new and somewhat complicated formula has been employed. The basic grant is $89. A pensioner may receive additional aid up to $16 if he has special needs (e.g., medical care, special diet, laundry, home repairs) and if his income from other sources is less than $16.

[11] In 1956 the transportation allowance was increased to $6 and an allowance of $3.50 for education and recreation was added. Since 1957 the budget has included a further allowance of $4 for remedies not prescribed by a physician. Increases in the total budget are usually handled by adding allowances for new expense items, not by increasing the amounts allowable for already existing budget items. Because of the method used in computing grants, an increase in existing allowances would not always work to the advantage of the recipient.

BASIC AND EXCESS ALLOWANCES IN OAS BUDGETS, 1954

	Basic allowance	Maximum excess allowable
Food..........................	$28.50	$21.40 (for restaurant meals)
Housing		
For individuals................	15.00	25.00
For couples...................		35.00
Utilities.......................	6.30	11.50
Clothing.......................	7.70	
Household maintenance and		
replacements...............	4.50	
Transportation..................	4.50	10.50
Incidentals.....................	13.50	
Total OAS grant...............	$80.00	

expenses, nursing or rest-home care, special diets, dental care, eyeglasses, and hearing aids.

In order to establish the client's budget of needs, the OAS worker adds to the basic budget any excess needs which he may have found to exist. He then determines the client's resources by adding the dollar values of all income or benefits in kind regularly received by the client. The most common resources are: Old Age and Survivors Insurance (Social Security) benefits; contributions from responsible relatives and voluntary contributions from family and friends; income from stocks, bonds, rented property, or part-time work; the value of occupancy of a house owned by the recipient; and the value of any contributions in kind received. The value of occupancy of a home owned clear of encumbrances is $3 for the first $500 of assessed value and an additional $1 for each additional $500 of assessed value, up to a maximum of $9 per month.

Once the client's grant is established and passed by the board of supervisors or its representative, the client is informed of this action by a form letter. Henceforth he will receive his pension check at the beginning of each month. Once every year the recipient's eligibility is reinvestigated. If there is any change in the pensioner's financial situation, he must report to the social worker. If, during a given month, he has earnings from occasional work, he must report these so that they can be deducted from his next assistance check. Only earnings of "negligible importance" which "offer no security" need not be deducted.

The rules governing the program thwart any efforts of recipients to help themselves or of relatives to help their aged family members beyond the required minimum contributions. The pensioners cannot realize any gain from productive work; nor may relatives help to improve the recipients' situation by occasional gifts. All such earnings and contributions must be deducted from the assistance checks. Thus the financial requirements of the law help to maintain and accentuate rather than reduce the pensioner's isolation from both society and his family group.

The CISW Program

The entire program of the California Institute of Social Welfare has been developed by McLain as a response to the Old Age Assistance law and its administration. The measures proposed by McLain and endorsed by his members refer to specific sections of the law and specific kinds of administrative behavior; they do not call for radical changes in laws and institutions or for revolutionary innovation. The most radical, perhaps, of McLain's demands is the elimination of any kind of means test; according to McLain's views, every citizen should be entitled to the old-age pension.

Although, to insiders as well as outsiders, the demand for a general old-age pension seems to be at the core of the McLain program, no serious step has ever been taken by McLain to achieve this end. To realize this demand, either the federal Social Security Act would have to be amended, or the State of California would have to cease operating its old-age program under existing federal laws and finance the pensions without federal grants-in-aid. Obviously, neither of these changes could be easily achieved. Even so, it is significant that McLain has made no real move toward pensions which people would receive "as a right." This demand has remained mainly a topic for speeches in meetings and on the radio. McLain's inaction on this point suggests a lack of involvement with basic "pension philosophy." And indeed, very little of the utopianism of former pension movements remains in the Institute of Social Welfare.

The initiatives McLain has been able to place on the ballot provide the best review of the content of his program. The important proposals contained in these initiative constitutional amendments are shown in the table, which indicates that, over a period of time, the CISW has tended to abandon its political demands in favor of more strictly economic ones.

PRINCIPAL CHANGES PROPOSED IN INITIATIVES SPONSORED BY
THE CALIFORNIA INSTITUTE OF SOCIAL WELFARE

Issue	1948 Adopted, but repealed in special election of 1949	1952 Defeated	1954 Defeated
Increases in grants	Maximum grant raised from $65 to $75 ($85 for the blind).	Maximum grant to reflect cost-of-living index, but never below $75.	Maximum grant to be increased from $80 to $100.
Added or increased benefits		a. Health benefit up to $25 per month. b. Funeral benefit up to $150.	
Liberalization of eligibility rules	a. Eligibility age lowered from 65 to 63 years. b. Personal property limitation raised from $600 to $1,500.	Personal property limitation raised from $1,200 to $1,500.	
Legal guaranties	a. Size of grant and eligibility rules written into state constitution. b. OAS obligations are "first lien" on all state funds. c. Advisory board, to be appointed by state director; hears appeals of clients from rulings of local and county authorities.	Size of grant and eligibility rules to be written into state constitution.	Size of grant and eligibility rules to be written into state constitution.
Relatives' responsibility	Eliminated.	To be eliminated.	
Administrative changes	a. State instead of county administration of program. b. State welfare director made elective (2-year term).	State instead of county administration of program.	
CISW control of program	CISW trustee elected first state welfare director under new regime.		

Chapter II	The Spokesman

ANY social movement in its early stages is unstable, fluctuating in membership, poorly integrated with the social order. The weaker the internal cohesion of the group, the more dependent will it be on ideology, dramatic action, and a forceful, colorful leader to provide a focus of loyalty and a sense of common identity. It is not surprising, therefore, that a movement based upon the aged poor should be held together by the energy and personality of a single spokesman.

The Son

Origins.—George H. McLain was born in what is now Hollywood on June 24, 1901. He first achieved public notice in 1933, when he organized and led a group of unemployed. Of his background and life up to that time very little is securely known. In interviews, McLain appeared reluctant to discuss his childhood, saying he remembered little of it. Information garnered from interviews has been supplemented by brief unpublished autobiographical sketches from his political tracts, and remarks by McLain reported in the press or recalled by persons who have known him.[1]

The picture that emerges from these fragments is vague, sentimental, stereotyped, and idealized, but its import is clear. Mc-

---

[1] This chapter is based in large part on the direct experience of one of the authors, who maintained close personal contact with the Institute for about two years and conducted interviews with McLain and members of the staff.

Lain's is no Horatio Alger story. On the contrary, the image evoked is that of the eminently successful son of a respectable, well-to-do family, shocked into seriousness and altruism by sudden hardship and a rude world. The story has slightly aristocratic overtones which are quite at variance with the public image of McLain as a man of tumultuous action rather than quiet nobility. Considering American attitudes, the aristocratic overtones are understandably faint: McLain describes himself with pride as having been "the money-making son of a self-made wealthy father," and stresses his business background, which has "kept the solid ground of realism under my feet." Nevertheless they are there: his boyhood playground was "the broad acreage of my mother's family home, now covered by the paved streets, the buildings and homes that are Hollywood." He tells us that as a child he lived in a "high-class" Hollywood district. Whenever information is specific and concrete, its status import is clear: his father was one of the first men in Los Angeles to own an automobile.

The official facts project an image of a nonmarginal man: "I am a fairly typical American." McLain claims four generations of Tennessee Baptist ministers on his father's side and, in the genealogical new world of California, membership in "an old California family of four generations of natives of Los Angeles County." A grandfather is said to have been one of the first three white settlers in the area.

From a political point of view, McLain's ethnic background is well-nigh perfect. In unpublished notes for a biography of Mc-Lain written in collaboration with a member of his staff, it was said:

> Springing as I do from Scottish, Irish, and English ancestry on my father's side, to the blood of these stalwart freemen was added the influence of my mother's family, the example of her father who gave up a career in the German diplomatic service because he could no longer accept the repressions and restrictions on individual freedom enforced by the Imperial Government.

The image of his parents suggested by McLain offers a familiar picture of the ancestry of idealistic men of action. His mother does not figure prominently in McLain's reminiscences. Her heritage is described as distinguished and vaguely aristocratic. The only

other recorded remark about his mother is that his religious training began at her knee. His father, "a successful paving contractor
who helped build Los Angeles," plays the central role in McLain's
reconstruction of his past. Of poor but honest forebears, the father
is the self-made man, representing energy and practicality. In this
way the blend of idealism and hardheadedness, of altruism and
"know-how," is accounted for.

The depression.—By the time McLain was nineteen he was
married, the father of a son, and head of his own household. He
points out, somewhat defensively, that this was perhaps his major deviation from the typical at that period of his life. At about
the same time he became a partner in his father's business, and
in his early twenties was already earning several thousand dollars
a month. The autobiographical notes describe a rosy dream and
a rude awakening: "I had no worries—life was beautiful and full
of promise. I had a job that absorbed my full energies. G. T.
McLain and Son was laying miles of paving, and laying it right.
My father and I were a perfect working team with complete trust
and confidence in each other. There was not a cloud on the hori-
zon. . . . Then came 1929—1930—1931." McLain's followers
have come to know very well the story of his father's business, its
collapse in the Great Depression, and the subsequent indignities
to which the father was subjected. The autobiography presents
a cliché-ridden but effective and moving account of the period:

I saw an immense productive machinery creak protestingly to a stop. I
saw businesses, large and small, collapse; industrial plants boarding up their
windows; farms seized; millions of unemployed; while government stood by
and wrung its hands. The tragedy of it was that individual effort was pow-
erless, men who had labored to effect economy and efficiency in business
were swept down in the vortex along with the inept and careless. Like a
mighty river in spate, a tide of economic breakdown swept through the
nation leaving destitution, diseases, and despair in its wake for thrifty and
prodigal alike. My father grew old under the strain and when he finally
turned the key for the last time on the business he had developed, he was
broken in health and strength. And I must stand—heartbroken but helpless
—along with millions of others, seeing a man who had devoted his life to
the development of his state and his country forced to turn to that state for
assistance in his time of need.

His father expected to receive from the state a "small but adequate
monthly payment which could have been applied for and granted

with decency, fairness, and at least a modicum of dignity." Instead, the law required that application be made to the county, to some "minor watchdog full of that self-importance which is the badge of little people."

After months of waiting, months of investigating, months of baring all his personal and family affairs, months of questioning and cross-questioning, what did the county deign to allow him? Having reduced him to the status of beggar, the county threw him $18 a month! Then they discovered that he was a Christian Scientist and took $5 off of his $18 because he didn't need medical care! Thirteen dollars a month after subjecting a man almost eighty years old to an inquisition that unquestionably shortened his life.

When he saw what was happening to his father, when he saw "applicants treated like mendicants," McLain tells us, "my heart burned within me." Although Roosevelt's program soon improved relief for the aged, its administration remained, in California, in the hands of the counties. "I still saw county welfare bureaus used as political tools in the hands of local politicians." He realized that "no one was going to help the needy unless the needy made their voices heard, not in thousands of small plaintive cries but as one strong voice."

He had, McLain says, "already become interested in organizing groups within the democratic framework, groups of citizens to voice their needs and wants." (In 1933 he organized an unemployed voters' group and ran for mayor of Los Angeles.) However, his sympathies "turned more and more to the needy aged group."

The fact that McLain was only forty when he entered the pension movement, and is still young in comparison with his constituents, has invited speculation concerning his motives. On the generally sound theory that vigorous political activity has some source in self-interest, and in view of the fact that McLain is himself not a pensioner, the assumption is often made that his self-interest is of a less than justifiable kind. To counter this, McLain supplies an idealistic and "psychological" reason for his devotion to the pension movement and his emotional attachment to the aged.

The heartaches and harassment that my father was subjected to rankled in my brain, and I resolved that I would do *everything* in my power to save other mothers and fathers from being subjected to the same things. Every time I go to one of our meetings, I see in the old gentlemen in the audience the face of my own father, whom I loved so dearly. So you can understand why I am willing to work ALL NIGHT, if necessary, to bring about *decent conditions* for the elderly and blind of our State.[2]

McLain presents himself as the avenging son determined, at least symbolically, to restore dignity and honor to his father. The aged are the fathers and mothers of a nation, to whom the youth owe all they have. In the hundreds and thousands like his father who thronged the relief offices—"men and women reduced to destitution through no fault of their own"—

I saw the hands that held the plow that broke the plains; I saw eyes that had looked on the vision that was America and called it good; I saw stooped backs, bent from tilling the fields, planting the trees and vine slips that had grown into California's great agricultural wealth; I saw men with faces weathered by sun and wind while they tended the flocks and herds to make America's mighty livestock industry; businessmen, manufacturers, lawyers, doctors, housewives who had mothered the nation's youth. Now that youth had turned its back on them in their need, saying, "The country you built is now ours, we may dole out enough of its goods to keep you alive but we do it solely out of our generosity, not because we owe you anything."

The sign over CISW headquarters reads: "Through these portals pass the builders of a Nation. . . . They shall not be forgotten."

Whatever the motives that brought McLain to the pension movement after his other forays into political and organizational life, certain fragmentary materials do suggest personal characteristics that seem to fit the role of pension leader. Perhaps most important is McLain's concern over social status. His father's and his own loss of status during the depression evidently rankled; and in his reminiscences he seems to be concerned primarily with the affront to dignity and self-respect imposed by public assistance officials and regulations. This background, taken together with the type of propaganda he has emphasized, suggests a way of looking at the world in which social esteem and self-respect are of great importance, and in which being deprived of these values is a painful experience. If we are right in concluding (see chap. iv) that aged pensioners are also much concerned over loss of status, then

---

[2] Albert Q. Maisel, "The Pension Preacher: He Wants to Be President," *Look*, vol. 14, no. 3 (January 31, 1950), p. 21. Quoted by permission of *Look* Magazine and the author.

it makes sense to suppose that within this group McLain's personal dispositions found a ready response.

There are other personal characteristics that help to make sense of the mutual dependence of McLain and his constituency. An apparent difficulty in getting along with people who are not cast in the role of members of an audience probably has had much to do with McLain's lack of success in dealing with conventional political groups. He has been a "loner," not only out of ambition for quick political gains, but also because he has found it hard to absorb the spirit of adaptation and bargaining that characterizes organizational life.

The Seeker

During the decade 1931–1941, and before the Citizens' Committee for Old Age Pensions was formed, McLain ran for public office five times and was connected with seven organizations, four of which he formed and led himself. In these early years, McLain seems to have had strong political ambitions, and to have regarded his organizational efforts as primarily a means of obtaining electoral support. However, his numerous campaigns for office failed, most of them dismally.

First experiment.—The story of McLain's political and organizational experimentation begins during the depression and with the unemployed.[3] Newspaper reports give two versions of the loss of his father's contracting business. One clipping from an unidentified newspaper of July, 1932, has it that in 1931 he "would not pay off certain parties to divert engineering contracts to his company. Work nevertheless found its way to his concern and finally the 'screws' were put on the firm of G. T. McLain and Son. This meant only one thing: financial ruin." In another account, also unidentifiable, the persecution theme does not appear, and his failure is attributed solely to the depression. "The depression mowed him down. His home was foreclosed upon. He went through voluntary bankruptcy and found himself in the ranks of the unemployed."

---

[3] Newspaper reports and propaganda material quoted up to the end of 1933 are from a scrapbook made available to us for microfilming by McLain and filed in that form in the Bancroft Library of the University of California at Berkeley. Some clippings are undated and some sources unidentifiable.

McLain evidently applied for relief, and was given a job on a city unemployment bond issue project. When the project was about to close, McLain, now a subforeman, organized a group of workmen. The Los Angeles *Record* reports that he borrowed $400 from his wife, money that had been saved to last them through the winter, and formed the Los Angeles Unemployed Voters' Association, Inc. (LAUVA), chartered on September 25, 1931. Dues were $1 per year, $10 for life, with voting power vested only in life members. McLain was president, and throughout the organization's history his name dominated whatever news reports there were; a district leader and the leader of a Glendale branch are mentioned once. In November, 1931, LAUVA claimed 1,000 members; in 1932, 50,000; and in 1933, 105,000. It also claimed a circulation of over 200,000 for its four-page newspaper, "Los Angeles Voter," of which at least three issues were published.

The aims of the association were broad and exalted. According to the third issue of the "Los Angeles Voter," it was

. . . for the organization and development of a social, recreational and educational association; to foster and promote employment for its members; to secure the interest of others in promoting projects providing employment for the unemployed persons; to stimulate industry so as to provide employment for the unemployed persons; to urge a program of public improvements to provide employment for the unemployed; the promotion of benevolence among its members.

It is difficult to assess the degree of influence and success achieved by the organization. There was talk of setting up employment centers throughout the city for its members, but nothing seemed to come of it. LAUVA endorsed such schemes as "Tradex," whereby member businesses were to accept, in exchange for goods, coupons issued for labor performed in their behalf, but it does not appear to have been active in implementing them. In November, 1932, it held a demonstration at city hall which made the front page in several newspapers. The size of the turnout is variously reported. The *Herald Express* estimated it as 500. The *Daily News* followed LAUVA's own count of 1,500, adding, with tongue in cheek: "Leaders said they had sent out 20,000 invitations to members, but agreed it was unlikely that 18,500 of them had gone to work suddenly, so their opinion was that the rest didn't have carfare."

LAUVA sponsored or co-sponsored political meetings at which speeches were made by local candidates and dues were collected. Each of the few issues of the "Los Angeles Voter" available for inspection carried a couple of pages of endorsements of candidates.

From the perspective of McLain's future career, the most important aspect of LAUVA was its president's lobbying activities. He sent resolutions to the governor, presented recommendations to the President, and appeared before the city council and the board of supervisors with requests and proposals. For some of these at least he got publicity. On February 16, 1932, under the heading, "Big Power Bond Issue May Go On Ballot," the Los Angeles *Herald Express* said the following:

> In response to an appeal of the Los Angeles Unemployed Voters' Association, the city council today virtually pledged itself to submit a power bond issue at the May third presidential primary. . . . Acting President A. E. Henning complimented McLain and members of the association upon their suggestion and the communication was ordered referred to the council's water and power committee for study and reports.

The bond issue did not, however, appear on the ballot. The *News* was less impressed, giving McLain one line in a short article: "The request was made by George H. McLain, head of a so-called 'unemployed voters' association.'"

According to the third issue of the "Los Angeles Voter," five days after the organization received its charter McLain appeared before the city council and proposed a luxury tax as an "emergency measure for the relief of our unemployed." A copy was sent to President Hoover. "Locally this plan died 'in committee' from minority, but well-organized, opposition. Today, however, the federal government has incorporated a measure strangely similar to our luxury tax in their sales tax." The paper went on to list other successes of the organization. Ten days later McLain sent a petition to the governor urging action to halt further immigration into the state. Immigration was severely restricted. Two months later he recommended that the construction of a dam, temporarily halted, be continued. Within two days it was. LAUVA had, of course, merely been one of many organizations clamoring for action on these matters.

McLain favored a thirty-hour week and, along with most of the articulate community, fought to curtail private power interests. He urged that resident citizens be given priority on public improvement projects over nonresident labor, and that local and state products be bought. He opposed cancellation of war debts and "secret agreements aimed at bringing about such cancellation," standing "squarely for the policies of W. R. Hearst on those issues." LAUVA also joined the movement to recall the mayor because of his inactivity on the unemployment issue and his favoring of private power interests. The recall movement was defeated in the subsequent election.

Throughout its history, LAUVA was at pains to deny radical influence, being "founded on 100 per cent American principles." It had no connection with other unemployed groups such as the Unemployed Council, the Unemployed League, and the Workers' Alliance.

Explorations.—In 1933 McLain entered the Democratic mayoralty primary. His slogan was "Clean House," and his program centered on unemployment relief, lower taxes with a more equitable distribution of the tax burden, and protection of the municipal water and power departments. He cautioned voters

. . . against becoming alarmed over the attempts by certain interests in Los Angeles to make political capital of the fact that I am the only candidate for the office of Mayor still under the age of forty. [He was thirty-two.] Such propaganda is nothing more than the hysterical outburstings of frightened senility. To say that a man must needs have one foot in the grave by reason of advanced age before he is qualified to occupy public office is sublime insanity and I urge the voters of this city to please remember that public servants of extreme age are desired chiefly because they more readily bow to the dictates of the before-mentioned organized interests and minorities.

In 1952 he was to run for Congress as the head of an interest group 95 per cent of whose members were sixty-five years of age or older. The "Los Angeles Voter" of May 2, 1933, carried the headline "Special Interests Doomed! Avalanche of Support Rallies to McLain for Mayor." McLain ran ninth in a field of ten candidates, receiving 2,354 votes at a time when his organization claimed 105,-

000 members. In the general election McLain supported the same mayor whom the year before he had campaigned to have recalled. After the election LAUVA seems to have gone out of existence.

In 1933, or possibly earlier, McLain formed the California Citizens' Loyalty League with the motto, "Vigilance Is the Eternal Watchword to Success. Join Now, 'Be Prepared.'" It is far from clear what the members were to prepare for or in what success was to consist. The organization incorporated the diffuse aims of the former LAUVA, but was open to all, unemployed or not, in order "to be of greater service to all citizens of the State of California." It urged more strongly than LAUVA the purchase of California products and, failing that, of American ones. It also supported the Roosevelt administration's "admirable effort to rid the country of the slavery of low wages, too cheap prices, and no work." The yearly membership fee, $2.50, included a subscription to "Your Newspaper," no issue of which has been discovered. Nor is there evidence of any activities of the organization.

In 1934 we find McLain on the fringes of EPIC, a depression-inspired, quasi-socialist California party. The End Poverty in California organization, which was running Upton Sinclair for governor, favored taking over idle plants and employing state resources for "production for use." Its program included old-age pensions, but neither their amount nor the method of financing was stipulated.

During the EPIC campaign, McLain attached himself to the movement, and received a nominal salary for making speeches and taking up collections. He remained in EPIC only a short time, leaving before it was absorbed into the Democratic party in 1935.

McLain went back to running for office, this time for the board of education. He ran twenty-second in a field of thirty-one candidates.

In 1936 McLain returned to organizational promotion, this time setting up "Natives of California, Inc." Its purpose, as set forth in the articles of incorporation, was to "restore the Government of California to the natives of the State, and keep it there." McLain, already a member of the Native Sons of the Golden West, may have used this organization's mailing list of 60,000; some of its local "parlors" supported his new organization. According to a legislative committee report, "the movement does not appear to have gotten past the mass meeting stage." [4]

In his next try for public office, McLain did better than usual. Running for city council in the tenth congressional district, he polled 5,306 votes; the only other candidate received 8,065. Mc-Lain tried again the next year, running for state assemblyman from the fifty-eighth district. He received 3,474 votes out of a total Democratic vote of 10,288, the vote for all parties being 20,914. It was probably at this time that he first served as chairman of the Democratic district committee in the fifty-eighth district, it being customary for the candidate to do so.

At the end of 1938, after his electoral defeat, McLain joined another burgeoning cure-all, the Ham and Eggs movement. The venture was to have special significance for McLain's future career. As a volunteer organizer he persuaded the Ham and Eggs leadership to let him try out his ideas, and was in turn impressed by the political resources of the California pension movement. The Ham and Eggs leadership was now ready to tap the abundant fountain of pension discontent for political ends.

As manager for Los Angeles County, McLain set up local groups on the basis of Assembly districts, with a captain, lieutenants, and subsidiary officers in charge of house calls, mass meetings, distribution of literature, and radio advertising. McLain's ideas worked, and he set up the entire state organization along similar lines. Many of McLain's present organizational techniques he learned in the Ham and Eggs movement. According to a former leader and founder of Ham and Eggs, McLain was extremely effective and "a hell of a hard worker."

McLain probably joined Ham and Eggs soon after the November, 1938, election, when that organization's initiative constitutional amendment lost by only 255,329 votes out of a total of more than 2,500,000. At this juncture the final success of Ham and Eggs might have seemed to many merely a matter of time. But in 1939, Ham and Eggs lost by 1,000,000 votes, and McLain left the organization soon afterward. His departure was not amicable and Mc-

---

[4] Report of the Senate Interim Committee on Social Welfare, Fred Weybret, chairman, California Legislature, 1949 Regular Session, Part One, p. 68. Hereafter cited as Weybret Report.

Lain took with him about twenty-five of the more active members. This splinter group, which called itself the "Militant Body," attempted to hold meetings competing with Ham and Eggs, but lasted only a few months.

After this foray into the pension field, McLain tried partisan politics once more. In 1940 he ran for assemblyman from the fifty-eighth district. There were four candidates; McLain polled 3,370 votes out of a total of 21,968. After doing campaign work for the successful Democratic candidate for district attorney of Los Angeles, McLain obtained a job in 1941 as an investigator on the vice squad. Four months later he left, apparently to work with the American Citizens' Pension Association. Later in the year he organized the Old Age Payments Campaign Committee, which subsequently became the Citizens' Committee for Old Age Pensions and is now the California Institute of Social Welfare.

It is worthy of note that McLain's early efforts to find a political base were restricted largely to marginal, relatively unorganized publics. These were rather amorphous groups that could be approached by a combination of vague moralizing and specific appeals to self-interest. Such groups have little internal structure of their own and are therefore wanting in the kind of indigenous leadership that would resist encroachments from outside. By the same token they have few bonds, apart from a narrow common interest, and tend to take on the characteristics of a loosely bound audience rather than of a well-integrated community. McLain's sense of direction was not in error, for in time he was successful with just such a constituency.

Origins of the CISW.—The origins of the American Citizens' Pension Association, which McLain joined in the spring of 1941, are obscure; even McLain does not seem to remember how it was formed. According to the Weybret Report it was incorporated in November, 1940, as a nonprofit organization. The directors were Fred J. Smith, Charles Ohlson, H. J. Loch, A. E. Taylor, and F. J. Talbott. It sought an annuity or pension for all United States citizens over the age of fifty-five to be paid by the federal government.

McLain came into the organization, or took over its name, soon after he left his job with the district attorney. Of the association nothing is known prior to McLain's leadership, and Ohlson was the only leading member who stayed on to work for McLain.

The beginnings of the Pension Association were humble. Meetings were held twice a month with a "small but determined" membership. Offices were in a rooming house at first, "a couple of rooms on the main floor; later we moved to a one-room office on the fourth floor." The radio program, broadcast twice weekly at first, expanded during the next year to five times a week, though it was still carried by only one or two stations. Dues were one cent a day. In a broadcast on August 18, 1941, the following three-point program was enunciated by McLain:

> The establishment of Pension study clubs in each of the eighty assembly districts in the State of California, a Pension Counsel in each community to advise members how to secure the present Pensions and intercede for speedy action. Representation for Citizens receiving State Aid to the Aged, and to conduct Dinners, Dances, Socials and meetings of interest.
>
> Number Two: Intensive Drive Nationally to petition Congress to lower the age to Sixty and to increase the amount of payments to the States.
>
> Number Three: Campaign for signature to place on the Nineteen Forty Two Ballot, our Constitutional Amendment now being titled by Attorney General.

In the broadcast the constitutional amendment was described as "the foundation of our movement." Eight years later McLain characterized the initial emphasis differently. At hearings before the Unemployment Insurance Appeals Board he argued that the organizations he had headed since 1941 had not attempted to influence legislation and therefore were not subject to the California Unemployment Insurance Act. In retrospect he described the primary function of the Pension Association as that of providing advice and service to pensioners. McLain says of his early activities:

> For a long time we didn't have any money, and I did practically all of the work myself, interviewing the cases, handling the cases, going before the County Welfare officials, appearing before the State Social Welfare Department. I did practically all of the work myself, and only when we started on the radio did we start receiving money, and add more girls to handle the necessary functions of the organization.[5]

---

[5] Unemployment Insurance Appeals Board, Hearing, February 9, 1949, Sacramento.

The service aspect of the organization may have been important in attracting an initial following. Its propaganda, however, emphasized political action aims and called for $60 a month at 60.

In September, 1941, the Old Age Payments Campaign Committee supplanted the American Citizens' Pension Association. The articles of incorporation stated its purposes as social, recreational, and educational. But even here the main emphasis was on the $60 at 60 issue, and most of the articles are taken up with explaining in detail the amendment that the Campaign Committee would seek to qualify; nothing is said about handling welfare cases.

The initial target of the Campaign Committee was the state legislature, which was "making life more miserable" for the citizens receiving old-age assistance. A repeated argument took advantage of isolationist sentiment: "We Americans are a strange and great people; we always stand ready with our checkbooks to answer the plea of foreign countries for aid and then shout that giving aid to our own needy American citizens would be contrary to American principles of rugged individualism" (broadcast, August 22, 1941).

In August, 1942, McLain ran for state senator in a hasty write-in campaign, and was again defeated. He had entered the race only a few weeks before the election, and called upon all members of his organization and all pensioners to vote for him. By October of that year a petition drive was under way to place the organization's constitutional amendment on the ballot. Now called the Citizens' Committee for Old Age Pensions, the organization claimed an average income of $100 a day. The drive to qualify the petition for the constitutional amendment failed, and no similar attempt was made until 1948.

During 1943 the principal activity of the Citizens' Committee was McLain's lobbying in the state capital. McLain was appointed to Governor Warren's Old Age Pension Committee for the 1943 legislative session. This position, testifying to McLain's industry and growing prominence, was used by him for many years thereafter as proof of his legitimacy. Together with several others, McLain submitted a minority report advocating an increase in payments to $60, the lowering of the age limit from sixty-five to sixty, and the elimination of the relatives' responsibility clause. The legislature voted to increase old-age assistance from $40 to $50 beginning July, 1943.

That year saw the addition of larger headquarters for the Citizens' Committee, and of a newspaper, the *California Pension Advocate,* which began publication in February. During 1943 the *Advocate* displayed a favorable attitude toward the new governor, Earl Warren, and favored his appointee, Charles M. Wollenberg, state director of social welfare. The propaganda targets were usually the county welfare workers, the lobbies at Sacramento, and the members of the state legislature. As time went on, McLain was to shift his attack from state legislators to those "private interests" whose "creatures" the legislators were.

In August, 1943, the *Advocate* claimed 8,000 members. Membership drives were almost always under way. In September it was reported that more than 200 billboards had been put up from Sacramento to San Diego urging pensioners to join the Citizens' Committee.

In 1944 three issues occupied the organization: the blind, the elections, and a Townsend-sponsored proposition on the ballot. Judging from broadcasts and newspaper space, concern for the blind was by far the most important issue. Every month the *Advocate* carried some items on the blind, and often these items accounted for most of the space.

The Citizens' Committee supported several legislative bills to increase payments to the needy blind to $60 a month. When major bills pertaining to the aged and the blind were not acted upon, it demanded that these be included in the next special session of the legislature. According to the February, 1944, issue of the *Advocate,* members were to collect 300,000 signatures on a petition asking the governor to include the bills; nevertheless they were not put on the agenda of the first nor of a subsequent special session. This was the first occasion on which Governor Warren came under concentrated attack; he was charged with indifference to the plight of the aged and especially of the blind.

The year 1944 saw the first general state-wide endorsement of candidates on the basis of their pension records; a long list of approved candidates, both state and national, was published. When the organization polled some of its members on their choice for president, and a slight majority favored Thomas E. Dewey, he was officially endorsed, though not with enthusiasm.

Just prior to the November, 1944, elections, a great deal of space in the *Advocate* was given over to attacking the Townsend proposition. The Townsend plan, like Ham and Eggs, provided for a pension fund to be financed by taxes on money. The government was to make the initial outlay of pension payments, but was to be reimbursed, and a pension fund created, by a 2 per cent transaction tax on every dollar that changed hands. If a dollar passed through ten hands in one month, the government would receive twenty cents in taxes to be placed in its revolving pension fund. The Citizens' Committee warned not only that the plan was financially unsound but that recipients, who would be required to file two affidavits each month, would be spied upon by government officials. The plan was decisively defeated not only in California but in other western states where it was voted upon. This was the first serious attack on a rival pension organization. McLain had once interviewed Dr. Townsend on his radio program, and during an illness of the aging leader had called upon all members to pray for him. Since 1944, however, McLain has criticized the Townsend organization freely.

At the end of 1944 McLain began preparing for his most ambitious lobbying program thus far. The December issue of the *Advocate* called for a "march of five-dollar bills" to send a powerful lobby to Sacramento and McLain to Washington, D.C. The Sacramento activities dominated the news items in the paper for the next six months. It is evident from reports in the *Advocate* that McLain had now become the target of much criticism in Sacramento. When it was proposed in the legislature to raise pension payments to $60, some assemblymen, according to the February, 1945, *Advocate*, reacted with hostile comments. A bill was introduced to investigate all organizations lobbying for pension bills, another to forbid membership in such organizations.

In 1945, McLain, Myrtle Williams, and Arthur Damon took out a charter for a new organization, the California Institute of Social Welfare (CISW). Its purposes were stated as follows:

The purposes for which it is formed are to preserve and collect corneas of the human eye to be used for the restoration of sight to the human blind and to scientifically investigate into the causes of old age and to endeavor to obtain an antidote for longevity [*sic*] and to make a scientific study into the human ear and deafness and to formulate social plans for the development of child welfare and to survey housing for needy persons and to do generally all acts necessary to carry out the general purposes herein enumerated without limit and without specifically limiting the purposes allowed to this corporation under the laws of the State of California, and that it is a corporation which does not contemplate pecuniary gain or profit to the members thereof.

The new organization was inactive until 1950, when it took over the assets of the Citizens' Committee for Old Age Pensions. Until then, McLain's activities were carried on in the name of the Citizens' Committee. They reached a climax in an unexpected victory in the 1948 elections. For a brief time McLain's program for the aged became the law of California; one section of the referendum provided that Myrtle Williams, secretary-treasurer of the Citizens' Committee, an associate of McLain since 1941, become state director of social welfare. (See chap. vi.)

The Chairman

Since 1943 the offices of the California Institute of Social Welfare have been housed in a rambling two-storied building in downtown Los Angeles. A former mortuary, the house was purchased for $26,000. Its most remarkable feature is the elaborate and expensive equipment it contains: a bank of automatic typewriters; two modern electric bookkeeping machines; automatic addressing machines and complex filing equipment; a large print shop, with offset printing presses and folding, stuffing, inserting, and mailing machines; and a radio broadcasting booth. Aside from this machinery, the office equipment is neither new nor expensive. Indeed, an air of poverty and shabbiness pervades the headquarters.

The Los Angeles office is the main, and almost the only, center of the fund-raising drive which McLain conducts among the recipients of old-age assistance. For this drive he uses a daily radio program carried on 28 stations, a monthly twelve-page newspaper, 125 fund-raising meetings monthly throughout the state, and a network of perhaps as many as 125 "social welfare clubs." In 1954 a weekly television program broadcast on three channels was added for the duration of that year's campaign. The income of the organization has been as high as $750,000 in a single year, most of it contributed by members whose monthly income is well under $100 a month.

Legal control is in the hands of a board of trustees whose members hold the sole voting power in the corporation, elect new members to the board, and set their own terms of office. Though not required to be so, board members have always been employees of the organization, a fact which reflects the political reality within the board. The chairman of the board is also the chief executive officer of the corporation and, according to the by-laws, "shall have general control and management of its business and affairs, subject to the control of the Board of Trustees." This position has always been held by George McLain. As chairman he has the power to hire and fire employees; he thus may dismiss members of the board and has in fact done so.

The chairman has direct control over the ten departments of the organization, all of which are located in the Los Angeles headquarters. These are (1) the welfare service, which assists members with individual problems; (2) the mail and finance department, which handles the large incoming "money mail" of letters containing contributions; (3) the newspaper *National Welfare Advocate;* (4) the print shop, which produces most of the fundraising literature; (5) the membership department, which keeps the files up to date; (6) the club department, which organizes local social welfare clubs for members; (7) the public relations department, which issues news releases and related materials; (8) the meeting department, which schedules fund-raising meetings, held independently of the clubs throughout the state; (9) the personnel department; and (10) the radio department, which handles details of the daily broadcast. The headquarters staff varies from twenty-five to sixty persons, the larger number when campaigns are in progress. In addition, there is a small and fluctuating group of area managers in San Francisco, Oakland, San Diego, Fresno, and San Luis Obispo. These offices close down rather frequently, however, and are not always manned by paid employees.

McLain dominates the organization completely. The *way* he dominates may be analyzed as follows. (1) McLain has the *formal authority,* unquestioned within the organization, to make policy and control all activities. (2) His domination is *personal,* based on direct loyalty, dependence, and influence rather than on the legal or impersonal prerogatives of an official position. This marks Mc-Lain's relations to his employees as well as to his aged followers. (3) He is *indispensable.* The members know McLain as their only leader, the man with the contacts, the know-how, the will and the way to protect them. The staff recognizes him as the indispensable fund-raiser and action-mobilizer, the one with whom the CISW is inescapably identified and without whom there could be no organization. (4) His leadership is *exclusive.* McLain's indispensability, real enough on other grounds, is reinforced by conscious efforts to forestall the development of strong secondary leaders who might stand between him and the members. He does not permit the emergence of groups able to initiate their own actions and policies on the strength of an organized following. However, it is doubtful whether many such groups would arise even if they were encouraged. The relation of the members to McLain is direct and unmediated, not filtered through and modified by loyalties to intermediate groups and leaders.

Formal authority.—Complete control was asserted by McLain from the very beginning of the organization. At its first meeting in September, 1941, the board of trustees of the Old Age Payments Campaign Committee gave McLain the authority to "manage, operate and conduct the business of this corporation and to do any and all acts necessary or required therefor, under the supervision of the board of trustees."

The "supervision" of the board has amounted to approval of all the actions or intended actions of McLain. An examination of the minutes of the board of trustees revealed only one financial report rendered between 1941 and 1952. Meetings that discussed finances simply approved McLain's plans without detailed inquiry. The following quotations show the pattern:

December, 1941: Resolved: that all sums of money received by, for and on behalf of this corporation in any way whatsoever and such sums of money that have been expended for and in behalf of this corporation has been expended for the benefit of this corporation.

May, 1942: Resolved: upon motion duly made, seconded and carried the expenditures of money received by this corporation were approved and each and all items expended heretofore at any time for the benefit and advancement of the general purpose for which this corporation was incorporated, and that all sums of money, if any, borrowed or to be borrowed by the chairman for and on behalf of this corporation, be and the same are hereby approved.

July, 1942: Upon motion duly made and seconded and carried, was resolved that all activities of this corporation carried on by George H. McLain as chairman for and on behalf of this corporation and the same are hereby approved. And that all sums of money received and expended by, for and on behalf of this corporation be and the same are hereby approved.

The minutes reiterate votes of confidence in McLain. There is no recorded instance of any expenditure being disapproved or even questioned by the board, except when an open break with McLain occurred and a board member on his way out of the organization registered his protests. Originally, board meetings were to be held monthly, but they have become infrequent and perfunctory. Special meetings have been held occasionally when McLain wishes some explicit authority, for instance to buy a car with organization funds.

McLain's complete control over decision-making is factual as well as formal. The production of campaign materials and fund-raising letters, the purchase of office equipment and supplies, even the choice of songs to be sung at meetings—all are subject to McLain's personal supervision. Since he finds it difficult to delegate responsibility, even trivial tasks are under his direction.

Two CISW departments have maintained some autonomy: the print shop and the welfare service. The former, a purely technical operation about which McLain knows very little, is supervised by McLain's son, who is an employee of the organization. McLain shows scant interest in the day-to-day operation of the welfare service, probably because this activity is not directly related to the main publicity and propaganda functions of the organization. The work tends to be routine and requires considerable patience. The head of the welfare service is blind, yet more independent as a person than are other members of McLain's staff.

McLain has continually exercised detailed administrative authority within the organization. He is in no sense a figurehead leader behind whom operates a strong, relatively independent machine. His jealously guarded control lends the Institute something of the character of a personalized private enterprise. His attitude is similar to that of the successful entrepreneur of a past generation who would watch carefully all phases of the business he had founded and to which he had given his creative energy. McLain is being precise when he says, repeatedly, "This is *my* organization." And indeed, from his point of view, he is only guarding what he personally brought into being and shaped in his own image.

Personal domination.—McLain runs the organization in a highly personal way. His likes and dislikes dominate the scene at headquarters, where the staff is dependent on his personal favor. As a result, no strong professional group has developed around McLain that might be able to exercise a restraining influence over him.

This personal control is reflected in the way staff members are recruited. McLain does not draw upon people with experience in the established organizations of local politics and community life. Yet, because there is no internal hierarchy to train employees or members and move them into top positions, he must recruit his staff from outside his own organization. McLain does not maintain contact with other nonprofit "cause" organizations, and thus does not participate in the informal training and circulation of personnel that goes on among these groups. He places little emphasis upon professional background or experience. These recruiting practices reflect the Institute's marginality with respect to conventional community life. This type of recruitment has made it relatively easy for persons of mixed motives and backgrounds to attach themselves to the organization.

In such a milieu, only the most hardened, the least employable, or the most deeply committed person can survive. The natural result is a high turnover, especially among the professional employees. More important, there seems to be a strong tendency for McLain's former employees to turn against him after they leave. At the 1949 investigation of the CISW by a State Senate committee, eleven former employees appeared to testify against McLain. These included two of his early associates in the organization, a former welfare consultant, two bookkeepers, an editor, a lawyer, and four public relations or campaign workers.

Indispensability.—McLain's unique value to the organization is apparent in many ways. His voice on the radio raises most of the money. When he appears at a meeting, attendance triples and the collection rises sharply. On the radio McLain asks that contributions be sent to the CISW, but most of the "money mail" is addressed to him personally. It is to his personal exhortations that the members respond, and when the staff appeals for money or action it does so in the name of McLain. Members are urged to "Show George," "Let Uncle George know how you feel about him," "Don't let George down." The opposition recognizes this central importance of the leader, and criticisms of the organization do not usually mention its name or the names of other leaders. The attack is concentrated on George McLain the "pension promoter."

The indispensability of McLain is a continuing guaranty of one-man control. To challenge McLain's authority would be to attack the organization and to threaten its existence. It is common enough for leaders to interpret criticisms of themselves or their regimes as attacks on the institution itself. In the case of the CISW such an interpretation is quite realistic. The staff members sense that McLain is indeed the focal point of loyalty, the organization's main source of cohesion and strength.

Political responsibility is best enforced when a man is dependent upon others who can do without him if need be. McLain's indispensability to the organization necessarily weakens that source of social control, and the members are correspondingly dependent upon his sincerity and good will. The staff members, especially, are at a disadvantage because McLain can point to his special worth and unique contribution as the ultimate justification for whatever he chooses to do.

Exclusive leadership.—Responsible leadership is usually collective leadership. Even when formal authority is in the hands of one man, others may be strong enough to restrain arbitrary action and insist on a share in decision-making. This independent strength can have many sources. Some individuals may have ties to the organization's allies or to other groups on which it is dependent. Special skills and professionalism can stiffen the spines of staff members. And in political associations the independent followings of secondary leaders will often create positions of strength which must be taken into account.

None of these conditions is significantly present in the CISW. The organization is isolated even from the welfare-oriented community. Hence informal representatives of the labor movement, the Democratic party, or other groups are not found among the headquarters personnel, who tend rather to be marginal and dependent. Nor does the social structure of the organization and its constituency lend itself to the formation of independent followings. These are most likely to arise when a political party, trade union, or other association is organized on a territorial basis. Strong local groups, having distinctive interests and capabilities, can then produce their own leaders and win a measure of autonomy.

In the CISW, however, territorial organization plays only a small role. Membership participation is primarily (though not solely) a matter of giving financial support to a public relations and lobbying headquarters. These contributions can be and are made by individuals whose relation to the central organization is direct, without intervening memberships in neighborhood, community, or county organizations. Since McLain himself is the chief organizer and reaches the members directly on the radio, local groups are likely to be weak and dispensable.

There have been a few abortive challenges to McLain's leadership. A San Francisco area manager, who seemed to be influential among the members there, was recalled to Los Angeles. He soon resigned from the organization, charging McLain with exercising dictatorial powers. In 1953 the head of a small pension group in Oregon, nominally affiliated with the CISW, came to California. He joined with the area manager in northern California in an attempt to bring the members into a new organization. They leveled serious charges against McLain at a mass meeting in Oakland, and called for a responsible democratic organization independent of the CISW.

On another occasion, in an apparent maneuver to capture the organization, two staff members attempted to have the board of trustees expanded to include themselves and some pensioners who had acted as ushers at the weekly meetings. Other disaffected staff members have sought an accounting of funds through court action. These revolts have not originated among the elderly constituents themselves; but at least one local club did repudiate the policies of headquarters and attempted to set up an independent organization. None of these efforts gave McLain any real trouble. No other leader or group has been strong enough to threaten his exclusive control. This success is due only in part to McLain's deliberate action. It must be attributed also to the limited aims of the organization and the basic willingness of the members to support their leader so long as he promotes their interests in the legislature and at the polls.

The "Promoter"

The public image of McLain, as reflected in the leading newspapers of California, has been decidedly negative. He has been pictured as a "pension promoter," a self-seeking, arrogant exploiter of his aged constituents. The attacks upon him reached their height during the 1949 campaign to repeal the constitutional amendment that had put an officer of the CISW at the head of the State Department of Social Welfare.

During this campaign, no large daily paper in California gave McLain its support. The attack in the press was highly personal, directed not to the virtues of the repeal amendment but to the purported evils of George McLain. He was depicted not only as a financial racketeer but as a potential dictator seeking political power through the Department of Social Welfare.

The anti-McLain arguments were most fully stated in a report of the California Senate Interim Committee on Social Welfare based on hearings held in the summer of 1949. The public hearings and the subsequent report were part of the anti-McLain repeal campaign. The Committee sought to prove that McLain was enriching himself at the expense of the old-age assistance recipients and that his attitude toward them was one of cynical contempt.

Testimony taken from former CISW employees emphasized the unceasing fund drives carried on by McLain. Much was made of the variety of devices or "gimmicks" used to solicit money from the members. On the other hand, this testimony supports the view that the chief purpose of the money drives was the maintenance of the organization and its political activities. While McLain's fund-raising tactics sometimes went beyond the bounds of good taste, especially considering the poverty of his constituents, they would not be unknown to men experienced in the maintenance of "cause" organizations through the small voluntary contributions of many members.

The Committee investigated McLain's personal finances in detail, although the evidence collected was incomplete and often unclear. Much of the difficulty in estimating McLain's actual income stemmed from the fact that McLain did not always draw his full salary but permitted part of it to remain on the books as a debt to him. There was also some evidence that McLain's expense checks considerably exceeded his salary checks.

Another complicating factor in calculating McLain's income is the Williams Advertising Agency, which, according to some of the testimony, was at first partly owned, and later solely owned, by McLain. This agency has handled all advertising contracts for the CISW and its predecessor, the Citizens' Committee for Old Age Pensions, including contracts with radio stations carrying McLain's program. Following a pattern established by the Ham and Eggs organization, this agency collects the usual 15 per cent discount allowed by advertising outlets to advertising agencies.

The evidence indicates that McLain's total income is substantial enough to permit him a standard of living well above that of his members. Until a few years ago, as the Senate Committee noted, McLain and his wife lived "rent free" in an apartment in the Institute building, and his wife worked as a beauty operator in a large Los Angeles department store. His new home, evidently financed by McLain personally, cost an estimated $35,000, including swimming pool.

To his opposition, McLain's relative affluence is an obvious sign of his exploitation of the aged and his lack of sincerity. That McLain is himself somewhat uneasy in the situation is evidenced by the lengths to which he has gone in minimizing his official income and in depreciating his new home as a "four-room bungalow." But there is no evidence that his followers concur in the opposition's moral judgment or even share McLain's uneasiness. And there is little reason to assume that a deprived rank and file wishes its leaders to be similarly deprived.

McLain exposes himself to charges of insincerity by his attempts to create an impression of modesty and asceticism. Thus, in a broadcast from Sacramento on March 23, 1950, McLain spoke of his salary as follows:

> Let me say this, if there is any doubt in your minds. I am donating my services. Yes, I am donating my services, I am not receiving a salary for my appearances up here. Last year I received only $650 for the whole year from the old folks' organization. This year I am only receiving enough money while I am up here for food, lodging, and transportation. If I am willing to do this, you should be willing to send in a little money to help carry on this work. The address is . . .[6]

The following day, discussing his registration statement as a lobbyist in the state capital, he added:

> The next question was compensation. In other words, how much money do I get from the old folks for my work? One hundred thousand a year? No. Well, what did I put down for my compensation for all the abuse and kicking around I got during the campaign last year? $650—yes, that's what I said—only $650 was paid to me by the old folks' organization last year. That's all for the full twelve months of 1949.[7]

There is no evidence that McLain is forced to make such statements in order to retain the allegiance of his followers. On the contrary, members of the CISW have emphasized, in interviews, that McLain is worth even more to them than the large sums which, according to adverse propaganda, he draws from the Institute.

The charge of cynicism raises more complicated problems. To many of the citizens of California, some elements of McLain's "political style" have doubtless carried overtones of manipulation and opportunism. McLain's talents as a kind of high-pressure salesman have helped to create this image. Moreover, he has learned that it is possible to become an organizational entrepreneur, that one man can "own" an organization much as another may own a business. His single-minded interest in the CISW can-

---

[6] *Ibid.*, p. 124.
[7] *Ibid.*

not be seen as merely the devotion of an idealistically dedicated man. McLain is no "do-gooder," nor is he driven by ideological passion. His obsession with his organization is not unlike another's obsession with a business. It is an interest, a source of livelihood, prestige, and status, to be protected and fought for in a lively and competitive market. Like many another entrepreneur in a marginal area, McLain has adopted methods which have led to the accusation, on the part of those who dislike him, that he violates the accepted rules of organizational behavior.

Nevertheless, there is little doubt that McLain takes his obligations as a leader seriously. He does work hard for the organization and tries to maximize its political impact. Indeed, his life is almost completely an organizational one. He has few outside interests, and most of his time is devoted to the CISW. Within the limits imposed by his own abilities and the nature of his constituency, he works diligently for the attainment of the organization's goals.

McLain is no ideologue and shows no interest in the elaboration of political doctrine. Yet a vague political imagery does play an important role in his propaganda. He does not appear to have any deep political attachments, and in some ways he has been inconsistent. McLain regards himself as a liberal Democrat, but the nativistic slogans which he used in at least one of his earlier ventures are difficult to reconcile with this position. Yet he shows no signs of racial or religious prejudice and has frequently voiced his opposition to intolerance, insisting that minority members are welcome in his organization. He has appealed to isolationist sentiment by arguing that aid to our own citizens should take precedence over foreign aid. This mixture of welfare-oriented and faintly xenophobic attitudes is somewhat reminiscent of the ideology of populism and similar American movements.

In accordance with his own predispositions, and with the needs and capabilities of his constituency, McLain has built an organization based on one-way communication. For his type of audience he does an effective job on the radio, and he can generate much enthusiasm among his followers when he speaks at Institute meetings. His appeals have often been criticized because he uses publicity devices rather than serious arguments. Indeed, McLain himself has likened his activities to those of a publicity man.

The welfare community.—McLain's reputation among the general public is common knowledge and need not be labored. But it is important to consider his role in a more limited community. How does McLain fare among groups and agencies that are especially interested in the furtherance of social welfare programs? What is the image of him among his potential allies?

Groups with common interests and shared perspectives form a rudimentary community. Cohesion among such groups is enhanced when they realize their mutual dependence. They must then consider the consequences of their own conduct for other members of the community; failure to do so brings censure and withdrawal of coöperation. To be a member of a community is to become subject to its social control, to accept its restrictions as to aims that may be pursued and means that may be used. Community membership defines responsibility. Granted that the wider community of California organizations does not accept McLain and his Institute, it yet might be that a more narrowly defined community does accept him and is able to impose restraints upon him.

The more restricted community which might be expected to exhibit less antagonistic feelings toward McLain consists of the organizations whose orientation toward public welfare programs is similar to McLain's. Among these are labor unions, organizations of minority groups, social work agencies, and some church organizations.

In order to gauge the attitudes of such community organizations, the opinions of thirty-six staff members and directors of groups affiliated with the Los Angeles County Conference on Community Relations were sought. This is a coördinating agency that brings together organizations interested in improving relations among ethnic and racial groups and supporting social welfare programs. Among these organizations are the YWCA, Urban League, Congregational Social Action Department, United Church Women, AFL Central Labor Council, American Jewish Committee, and Japanese-American Citizens' League. In addition to a number of interviews, standard questionnaires were filled out at two meetings of the County Conference. The responses to eight of the questions show a clear pattern.

1. Do you think older people ought to have an organization of their own?

Yes	23	Qualified	3
No	9	No answer	1

2. Do you think such organizations are potentially successful?

Yes	23	Qualified	1
No	7	No answer	5

3. Did you vote for or against Proposition 10 [a McLain-sponsored proposition barring use of public funds for chambers of commerce]?

For	20	No answer	2
Against	14		

4. Did you vote for or against Proposition 11 [McLain's 1952 pension proposal]?

For	18	No answer	1
Against	17		

5. What do you think are the main activities of the McLain organization?

Negative answers (political manipulation of the aged)	16	Mixed	4
		Don't know	4
Positive answers (legitimate interest group)	8	No answer	2

6. Do you know McLain personally, and if so under what circumstances?

No	30	No answer	1
Yes	5		

7. What is your opinion of McLain?

Negative	25	Mixed	6
Positive	2	No answer	3

8. Would you consider organizational coöperation with McLain and under what circumstances?

Unqualified no	18	Other	12
Unqualified yes	1	No answer	5

It is evident that this group was by no means opposed to the general idea of organizations for "senior citizens," nor were they unsympathetic to some of the aims put forward by McLain. A number of those who responded negatively to McLain's 1952 propositions did so because they were suspicious of McLain, but might have voted otherwise if the measures had had other backing. Some evidently were so strongly in favor of the measures that they voted for them despite McLain's sponsorship.

Most of these community leaders thought of the CISW as McLain's personal instrument, and would coöperate with it reluctantly and only within well-defined limits. They felt, however, that there was no real question of coöperation because of McLain's lack of interest in anything outside the pension issue.

Only five of those questioned knew McLain personally or had ever had dealings with him. The people active in the social welfare area do not receive an image of McLain from personal knowledge but depend upon the reports of others. Consequently, the influence of an antagonistic press is, even within this circle, greater than it might otherwise be.

Although a negative attitude toward McLain is the dominant pattern, there is an interesting variation among community organizations, particularly those representing special publics. Rejection of McLain is strongest among firmly established organizations, which have highly professionalized staffs and do not depend on protest devices, emotionally charged movements, or mass leaders. Such groups are much concerned about their reputations in the community, and jealously guard their good relations with the press and with influential citizens and organizations. They are therefore reluctant to be associated with McLain or anyone else who might upset a carefully developed public relations program. The Jewish community organizations represent this orientation most fully. They are sympathetic to McLain's professed aims, but are highly suspicious of his personal aspirations and methods.

Although labor unions also have developed a concern for good community relations, they tend to be less consistently opposed to McLain and his proposals. Neither the CIO nor the AFL officially endorsed McLain's 1948 initiative; but both supported his proposals in the 1949, 1952, and 1954 elections. In the 1949 campaign the California CIO Council, the California State Federation of Labor, and the California lodges of the Brotherhood of Railway Trainmen all announced their opposition to Proposition 2, the repeal amendment directed against McLain. In urging a "no" vote, the Los Angeles AFL weekly warned its readers that "big business interests are attempting to foist Proposition 2 on the little taxpayers of California" and "are trying to create the same hysteria which resulted in passage of the Taft-Hartley Act." On October 20, 1949, another AFL paper, the *Redwood Empire Labor Journal*, published in Eureka, released a picture of McLain and William Green with the caption, "McLain discussed problems of the aged and blind in California with President Green during a recent meeting in Coronado." The *Journal* pointed out that Proposition 2 was opposed by the California CIO locals as well as the AFL, and declared that the 1948 pension initiative "had been passed through the efforts of organized labor, backed by the thinking people of our state."

Unions are not only less directly dependent than other organizations on the good will of influential and respectable persons or institutions but also less likely to receive it. Two other factors have undoubtedly played a role. In the first place, McLain's proposals have become somewhat more responsible and less power-oriented. Second, McLain's organized opposition has gradually crystallized under the leadership of business groups, especially the Chamber of Commerce.

The situation of minority organizations is similar to that of labor unions; they would like to gain acceptance but know that certain community elements are unwilling to accord them full equality. Part of the California Negro press gave its support to McLain. The Los Angeles *Sentinel* said that McLain's opposition was "the same motley crew [that] had led campaigns against social security, the whole range of New Deal and Fair Deal reforms, and has choked off every effort to enact either municipal or state FEPC legislation in this state" (October 13, 1949).

Interviews with Negro and Mexican-American leaders indicate some positive attitudes toward McLain in organizations representing the most depressed groups. There is a sense of identification with McLain as another minority person rejected by the "respectable" and self-righteous elements of the community. As one Negro publisher and attorney expressed it, "There's no more public opprobrium attached to McLain than there is to me, as a minority person. We're both in the same position." He felt that since both lacked respectability in ordinary middle-class circles, coöperation with McLain was by no means out of the question.

For such people, McLain's "bad press" is not an influential factor. "When the Los Angeles *Times* takes him on," one Mexican-American labor organizer remarked, "it's the same as when they take on the unions or some minority groups. He's in the same position as a labor leader, always under attack." McLain's bad press merely strengthens the lelief that "his enemies are our enemies too."

For a large part of the Negro and the Mexican-American communities the struggle is not so much for respectability as for bare equality, a decent standard of living, political representation, and other immediate and concrete gains. Results are more closely examined than motives. For the Negro publisher, McLain is "a source of positive good in the community because he presses the claims of the aged. Most of the time his program is good even if he's bad." A Mexican-American member of the Community Service Organization strongly expressed his immediate practical orientation: "If McLain could do us any good, I wouldn't hesitate a minute to ask him to join up."

Despite some willingness to coöperate with McLain and to support his proposals, leaders of minority groups share the community's suspicions of McLain. Since McLain is not affiliated with any of the organizations and committees that bring together the many different groups and agencies interested in community problems, they have little opportunity to revise this general attitude through personal contact with him.

Although McLain harbors no ethnic prejudices and has expressed no anti-Negro or anti-Semitic attitudes in his prepared political propaganda, or even in unguarded moments, he has failed to press or support the claims of minority groups. A Mexican-American leader once sought without success to interest McLain in the problem of pensions for noncitizens. He now feels that McLain's indifference has greatly reduced any chances for coöperation.

It is clear that McLain is a marginal figure in the liberal, welfare-oriented community. Marginality characterizes his role in party politics also. McLain has intermittently held official positions within the Democratic party. James Roosevelt, son of Franklin D. Roosevelt and candidate for governor, publicly supported the McLain side in 1949, as did former United States Senator Sheridan Downey. On occasion, McLain has sought to influence the choice of Democratic candidates. But, although he regards himself as a Democrat, his association with the party has never been intimate or lasting. He is not guided in his pension activities by consultation with party officials, nor does he identify his proposals as Democratic ones.

Democratic leaders tend to criticize McLain on the ground that he fails to observe the rules of the political game. His search for direct and immediate political advantage offends the regular party organization. During the election campaign of 1948 he managed, without permission, to board the train carrying President Harry S. Truman and appear next to the President on the platform when the train arrived at Los Angeles. A similar occurrence took place in 1952. Such incidents would be avoided by a man more interested in getting along with other politicians. In 1952, running against the Democratic congressional incumbent who was the clear-cut choice of "regular" Democrats, McLain attempted to bypass political channels by exploiting his resources outside the party, primarily the funds and machinery of the CISW. This campaign also revealed McLain's poor relations with the labor movement.

McLain's marginal position in the organizational and political life of California has two effects: (1) his potential influence is limited because he cannot form stable alliances and thus move from leadership in a special sphere to a more general political strength; and (2) he is relatively free of the responsibilities and restraints that go with membership in an integrated community.

Chapter III | *The "Old Folks"*

In 1952 approximately 68,000 names appeared on the membership roster of the California Institute of Social Welfare. Of these, all but 5,000 were Old Age Security recipients. Almost one out of every four pensioners in the state had some connection with the Institute; but there was wide variation in degree of participation in and depth of commitment to the organization. Institute headquarters sends the monthly newspaper to anyone who contributes the equivalent of a year's subscription, and a membership card to anyone who contributes the equivalent of a year's dues. Many of the purported "members" are in fact merely occasional contributors to a cause; they resemble citizens who, in return for a contribution to the local community hospital, receive the hospital's house organ for a year or so. The membership includes pensioners so devoted to McLain that not only have they made the considerable payment for a life membership but also they have continued to contribute heavily and participate consistently in the activities of the organization. The 5,000 members who were not OAS recipients were, with few exceptions, close to or past their sixty-fifth birthday; most of them had responded to McLain's appeal because they expected that some day they might qualify for OAS grants.

What is there about pensioners as a group that makes McLain's organization attractive to them? What distinguishes McLain's followers from pensioners in general? In order to arrive at the similarities and dissimilarities of members and nonmembers two samples were studied. A questionnaire was sent to 4,969 members of the CISW, 2,224 of whom responded. A similar questionnaire was sent to 3,430 nonmembers drawn randomly from those on the California Old Age Assistance program, of whom 915 replied.[1]

In addition, interviews were conducted throughout this study with both members and nonmembers of the CISW. Frequent conversations on a variety of topics were held with members of Mc-Lain's headquarters and at meetings; some were visited in their homes. One of the authors accompanied a case worker on his visits to the homes of recipients so as to gain insight into the living conditions and attitudes of pensioners in general.

The content of the questionnaires was developed by means of a series of informal and often lengthy interviews. Finally, a more formal intensive interview was conducted with forty-two CISW members who had participated in a drive to collect signatures on a petition qualifying an Old Age Security initiative. The insights gained from these interviews were of great value in interpreting the questionnaire replies.

The data thus accumulated often show great similarities between the backgrounds and attitudes of members and nonmembers of the Institute. However, the problems which are common to all pensioners often come into sharper focus and are more keenly felt among Institute members. A number of marked differences between the two groups do emerge (see chap. v), but the present chapter deals primarily with the *similarities* between members and nonmembers and with the extent to which the Institute membership displays, in a more extreme form, the social and political characteristics of the total pensioner population.

Who Are the Pensioners?

Age and health.—The average age of the pensioners in our samples is 74.1 years for Institute members and 74.6 years for nonmembers.[2] Our respondents are slightly younger than pensioners

---

[1] For details of the sample see Appendix III.

[2] See table 7 for age distributions. (All numbered tables appear in Appendix I.) The members' average age reported in the text is based only upon that portion of the sample aged sixty-five years or older. It will be recalled that a small number of Institute members have not reached retirement age.

at large. The State Department of Social Welfare reported an average age of 75.6 years for its 2 per cent sample of all pensioners. (See chap. i.) These differences in average age[3] are almost certainly a result of the self-selection of questionnaire respondents. With increasing age there is a greater likelihood that people are incapacitated and incapable of answering a questionnaire.

The respondents were asked to rate their health as excellent, good, fair, poor, or very poor. The proportions in each category are almost identical in the two samples. In both samples the number who regard their health as excellent or good is 21 per cent; 46 per cent of the members and 42 per cent of the nonmembers think of their health as fair; approximately one-third in each group think of themselves as in poor health. Likewise, our inquiry whether the respondents find it easy or hard to get around yields almost identical results in the two samples, with about half of each saying that it is "sometimes easy, sometimes hard." One-quarter of both groups say they find it easy to get around. Our interviewers, in rating the health of the signature collectors whom they visited, were probably more impressed with the respondents' physical disabilities than were the old people themselves; they regarded 22 of the 42 cases as being in poor or very poor health. Only 25 of the 42 had no visible handicap; of the remaining 17, 8 suffered from some motor impairment such as paralysis or severe tremors. Yet some of the rather severely handicapped had collected up to a thousand signatures on the most recent initiative petition.

The questionnaire data and the observations of our interviewers do not support the view that the Institute members are physically better off than nonmember pensioners. Physically, the two groups appear to be equally capable of participating in social or community activities.

Background.—Most of the pensioners are of rural origin; their early experience was gained on farms or in small agricultural centers. At the time they attended school, 50 per cent were living on farms or in country towns; only 20 per cent were raised in cities.

---

[3] In this and subsequent statements concerning sample differences it may be assumed that the difference is statistically significant at the 5 per cent or a higher level of confidence. Statements that "there is no difference" mean that such small differences as may appear in the tables are not statistically significant and may have arisen by chance.

Only 32 per cent had spent *most* of their adult lives in a large city; 28 per cent moved from the country to the city during adult life.

Of the pensioners, 49 per cent grew up in the midwestern region of the United States, 6 per cent in the mountain states, and only 7 per cent near the Pacific coast; 13 per cent are of foreign origin.[4] On the average, migration to the west coast took place about thirty years ago. In spite of their long residence in the more urbanized environment of the West, many of the pensioners interviewed made significant references to the Midwest, where they still had friends and close relatives.

As a result of patterns of migration into and within California, the aged population has become one of the most urbanized in the United States. According to a group of investigators at Pomona College, only 7 per cent of persons sixty-five years of age and older live on farms; 70 per cent live in cities of 10,000 and larger; the remainder live in small towns and in nonfarm rural environments.[5] Nor are there strong cultural pressures upon California families in urban environments to maintain traditions of filial care for the aged. Few California families identify with ethnic groups. Only a small proportion of the migrants to California came from abroad; those who moved from eastern and midwestern cities to California for the most part did not maintain in the West the patterns of ethnic segregation which characterize much of eastern city life.

The very fact that a large proportion of California's population is made up of migrants tends to loosen family bonds. Ordinarily, families do not migrate to California as units. Most of the persons sixty-five years of age and older gave their desire to be near relatives as the most important reason for coming to California.[6] Such solidarity as may have existed previously is thus broken when part of a family goes westward; yet it is doubtful that traditional forms of family behavior can be resumed after the older members reach California. Moreover, during all waves of migration into

---

[4] Data on regional origins and former affiliations of pensioners could not be broken down by membership status. For details see table 1. See also Appendix II on questionnaire forms.

[5] Floyd A. Bond, Ray E. Barber, John A. Vieg, Louis B. Perry, Alvin H. Scaff, and Luther J. Lee, Jr., *Our Needy Aged: A California Study of a National Problem* (New York: Henry Holt, 1954), p. 11. Cited hereafter as Pomona study.

[6] Pomona study, pp. 16–17.

California, most of the newcomers have settled in urban centers. Migration thus accentuates the process of urbanization.

Urbanization has two important results for the life of the older generation: occupational careers end earlier and more abruptly than in rural societies; and family ties become looser. In an urban, industrial society the incapacities of old age do not permit a gradual shift in activities; rather, they result in the loss of a job after which securing a new job often proves very difficult or impossible. The aged person who has lost his function in the economic sphere is not likely to find substitute activities and responsibilities in the family. Once the family is removed from the rural environment it ceases to be an economic unit of co-producers and co-consumers, and the feeling of family obligation is thereby attenuated.

Family responsibilities are likely to endure, however, where there are strong community pressures to maintain them. Such pressures at times develop in religious and ethnic groups in which the maintenance of family unity is seen as a way of defending the integrity of a subculture or of enhancing individual security in a hostile world. But as the ethnic and religious groupings are gradually dissolved in modern city life, community pressures toward maintenance of the extended family tend to subside.

There is some evidence that city life entails increasing geographical isolation of older people. In our big cities, particularly in the West, the proportion of older people is steadily increasing in certain neighborhoods, while the newer neighborhoods tend to become inhabited by younger people.

The extent to which older people have become concentrated in certain neighborhoods can be ascertained by the use of an index number based on census tracts. We have computed indices of geographical isolation for six metropolitan areas, three in the West and three in the Midwest and East. These numbers reflect the degree to which the aged in a given metropolitan area are unevenly distributed over neighborhoods.[7] If all neighborhoods had the same proportion of old people, the index number would be 0; if all old people in the city were compressed into neighborhoods composed of old people only, the index number would be 1.0. Comparisons between such index numbers show that ecologi-

---

[7] For a description of the procedures and the detailed data, see Appendix IV.

cal isolation of the aged is greater in western than in eastern and midwestern cities. In 1950 the index for metropolitan Los Angeles was .314, while it was only .198 for St. Louis. Furthermore, the rate of increase of the index between two decennial censuses, 1940 and 1950, is greater for Los Angeles than for St. Louis: the index increased from .262 to .314 in Los Angeles and from .180 to .198 in St. Louis. The rates of increase were 20 per cent for Los Angeles and 10 per cent for St. Louis. For the San Francisco metropolitan area, the rate of increase was 45 per cent, the index numbers for 1940 and 1950 being .194 and .282.

Thus older people tend increasingly to live in neighborhoods that have high proportions of older people. Moreover, we found in the Los Angeles area a high correlation (.81) between the proportions of people above sixty-five years of age and those between fifty and sixty-five years of age. This development somewhat removes the aged from the total community and may inhibit their adjustment to newer styles of living.

The present status of the pensioners is largely a function of their past. One vestige of this past is found in the character of the voluntary organizations to which they belong. Most of their memberships, usually acquired before retirement, suggest the small town rather than the big city.[8] A very small proportion (1–2 per cent) belong to organizations that can be regarded as political, including veterans' groups or associations sponsoring special causes. Only 2 per cent belong to unions. They did not attend union meetings before retirement, and very few went to meetings of their political organizations. Most of the pensioners who have affiliations belong to fraternal and social groups—lower-middle-class lodges and their auxiliaries; 26 per cent say they participate in church service organizations, and 5 per cent list other types of religious organizations.

In their religious preferences the recipients run the gamut of the denominations and sects common in America.[9] Among the members of the Institute we find a fairly strong fundamentalist influence: 17 per cent belong to fundamentalist and evangelical sects (e.g., Holiness, Four-Square Gospel, Church of the Naza-

---

[8] See table 2.
[9] See table 3.

rene, Pentecostal Church). This is appreciably higher than the corresponding proportion for nonmembers (8 per cent). Moreover, fundamentalist participation is greater among those more deeply involved in the organization, reaching its peak among members who are making payments toward life memberships, 23 per cent of whom belong to evangelical sects. These statistical findings, however, do not adequately reflect the strength of fundamentalist influences among pensioners and particularly among McLain's followers. In conversations, many of the members of the more conventional denominations express religious beliefs similar to those of the fundamentalists.

Former occupation.—The best clue to a pensioner's social status is his former occupation. Nearly one-third of the respondents were uncommunicative on this point; so we cannot report with assurance on the occupational composition of the groups studied. A respondent may refuse to answer questions concerning his former occupation either because he feels it will throw an unfavorable light upon his social background or because he does not wish to be reminded of the fact that he has fallen from respectability to the status of assistance recipient. Since, however, the number of nonresponses is approximately the same among members and among nonmembers, it is possible to make comparisons between the two groups.

In spite of their predominantly rural background, only 14 per cent of members and 11 per cent of nonmembers mention agricultural occupations.[10] This compares with 31 per cent of the men sixty-five years of age or older in a national sample.[11] Particularly striking is the very small number of farm owners and managers (including tenant farmers) among the pensioners—3 per cent as compared to 27 per cent in the national sample. The extremely low proportion of farmers in our samples must be ascribed to the fact that so large a proportion of the pensioners migrated to California from elsewhere; when they left the Midwest and other farming areas they abandoned agricultural life. California, with its predominantly urban population, counted only 4 per cent of farm owners and operators in its 1950 labor force.

---

[10] See table 4.

[11] Peter O. Steiner and Robert Dorfman, *The Economic Status of the Aged* (Berkeley and Los Angeles: University of California Press, 1957), p. 42.

For pensioners who do not belong to the Institute, the three largest occupational groups are the professional, technical, and managerial occupations, the clerical and sales occupations, and the service occupations, each of which accounts for slightly more than 20 per cent of the total. Skilled manual occupations make up 13 per cent of the total.

Among McLain's followers, only 11 per cent come from professional and managerial occupations; only 15 per cent from clerical and sales occupations. They are more likely than other pensioners to have service occupations in their background or to have been skilled craftsmen. Each of these occupational groups claims about one-quarter of the membership.

Compared with the national cross section of aged persons and with the California labor force distribution of 1950, the nonmember pensioner population is overrepresented in the clerical, sales, and service occupations, while McLain's followers are still more concentrated in service occupations. Industrial workers are underrepresented both among nonmember pensioners and in the Institute.[12]

As these figures show, the pensioners tend to come from occupations having relatively low job security. This is certainly true of service occupations, and it applies also to many clerical and sales jobs. It would seem that Institute members were even less secure in their jobs than pensioners in general: they count among their number a particularly high proportion of persons not only from the service occupations but from skilled blue-collar work as well. The latter group in our sample consists chiefly of individuals with obsolescent skills (e.g., blacksmiths) or journeymen in small establishments not covered by social security.

Changes occurring toward the end of the occupational career had the effect of increasing job insecurity still more. A drift into service occupations accounts, among members, for one-third of all last jobs held.[13] This increase took place chiefly at the expense of professional-managerial and clerical-sales occupations. It seems that for some pensioners the downward drift in occupational and

---

[12] The U.S. Census describes as "service occupations" all domestic service jobs as well as relatively unskilled occupations in nonindustrial or nonagricultural establishments (e.g., gas-station attendant, janitor, shoeshine-parlor attendant).

[13] See table 5.

status hierarchy began before retirement; to job and financial insecurity was added the realization that they were gradually losing the position in society they had earlier attained.

Retirement.—Retirement doubtless has profound and often disturbing effects upon today's aged. In modern society the job constitutes one of the most important links between the individual and his social world. Moreover, before reaching retirement, California's older generation was perhaps less firmly bound to a familiar social scene than are older people elsewhere. Their western migration may have severed old ties; for many the depression disrupted the normal course of occupational life, removing some from the labor market and transforming others into occasional and casual workers; the occupations with which many of these people finally concluded their working years often represented, both in earnings and in human contacts, a break with the past.

For most of the recipients, occupational life is a thing of the past. Only 8 per cent of the recipients indicate that they do occasional work. (Among Institute members, 12 per cent make this claim, and an additional 3 per cent say they are working full time.) Even the figure of 8 per cent is an exaggeration. Less than 1 per cent of the pensioners report any income from earnings; and social workers are familiar with the recipient who insists that he is doing odd jobs but who, upon closer examination, turns out to have had his last work experience (such as sharpening tools or mowing a lawn) several months or even years ago. There is a tendency to maintain the fiction that one is still, somehow, in the labor market—a symptom of the anxieties which accompany the loss of occupational status.

Most recipients feel that the end of their occupational career was an event of great significance in their lives: 58 per cent remember that they "felt bad" about giving up their last job; only 15 per cent now think they were "glad" about being able to stop working. It is remarkable that long after the event so many people still remember retirement as painful. In interviewing recipients, we often noticed their reluctance to talk about previous occupations. On the printed questionnaire, the number of people refusing or neglecting to answer questions dealing with previous occupations is unusually large: 22 per cent did not answer the question concerning their feelings at the end of their occupational career; 18–25 per cent did not indicate their last occupation; and nearly 30 per cent did not indicate their main line of work before the age of fifty.

One of the circumstances making retirement a painful experience was that, for most, the event came unexpectedly: 45 per cent of members and 54 per cent of nonmembers were forced to give up work because of ill health; 9–11 per cent were "laid off" and were unable to find another job; 2 per cent gave up working in order to care for an invalid or sick spouse. After having given up or lost the jobs which turned out to be their last ones, nearly one-quarter of the recipients looked for work but could not find suitable employment. Only 8–9 per cent were discharged at an official retirement age; only 6–7 per cent withdrew from the labor force of their own free will. Again, close to 20 per cent gave no information about the circumstances of their withdrawal.

The psychological significance of a job transcends the economic or skill aspects of working. For many people, work provides the most important opportunities for social intercourse. Many of those interviewed, when asked what they liked about their jobs, stressed the fact that they were meeting people. One of the signature collectors, a lifelong cripple with a sporadic employment history, had enjoyed most a three-year job as elevator operator because he was "meeting people all day long. Everyone that worked in the building knew me and they always had a good word for me." A woman who had been a salesclerk in a dry-goods store felt that the most enjoyable part of her job was meeting the customers. A woman who had had a magazine agency liked the job because she "had lots of telephone friends." A newsstand employee said, "The one thing I liked most was greeting people that came into the store, and the work was fascinating." A man who, after a leg injury, did yard work for sixteen years found that "it kept my mind active. It kept me physically active. It kept my health up. I always got to meet people. It was good for me."

Direct expressions of having enjoyed a job because of social contacts came chiefly from recipients whose work entailed meeting the public. Others said they liked the physical activity or the exercise of their skills. For these people the loss of employment meant they were deprived of the experience of being useful to themselves and to others—an experience for which there could be no substitute. Only four of the forty-two petition circulators mentioned earnings as a primary satisfaction. In retrospect, the social and activity aspects of working appeared more important to them than the economic ones.

Participation in voluntary associations.—Since people without regular work have more free time, we might expect them to increase their participation in voluntary associations, such as church groups, social clubs, or organizations sponsoring programs of social action. If this is true, it does not apply to the aged poor: 36 per cent of both samples indicate that they belonged to some organization before retirement, but only 26 per cent state that they belong to any organization now (church and Institute membership being excluded for the purpose of this comparison). Aside from belonging to McLain's organization, there is no difference in this respect between members and nonmembers. In both samples, only 8–9 per cent had ever belonged to more than one organization.

Most of the signature collectors and other Institute members interviewed say they do not go to meetings as frequently as they did in the past, nor do they take on as many organizational tasks or offices as they did before retirement. Their health does not permit as much activity as in the past; with more restricted financial resources they are less able to do their share; younger members "take over" and do not like to see the older people have too much of a hand in the affairs of their organizations. The latter seems particularly true of the fraternal-social organizations (e.g., Moose, Rebeccas), which command the largest following among our respondents.

The most common form of voluntary participation is attendance at church services. Even in this activity, only about half of the pensioners are able or willing to participate; 44 per cent say they never attend church. On the average, the recipients attend church 2.5 times per month; 35 per cent attend church every Sunday or more often; 26 per cent take part in special church activities such as missionary societies, service groups, and the like.

It may well be that people become more interested in religion as they grow older, but participation in formal services or in organized church activities appears to decrease rather than increase. It was a frequent complaint among the pensioners we interviewed that they were not able to go to church or participate in church events as much as they had in the past. Physical disability was cited as the reason, but in view of the respondents' participation in a petition campaign this explanation is not altogether convincing.

Voluntary associations appear to be no retirement substitute for the social contacts people ordinarily find in their jobs. Instead, retirement is accompanied by retrenchment in the amount of participation in voluntary associations.

Informal participation.—It is difficult to assess the effect of retirement upon the informal contacts of the pensioners. Their recollection of past social contacts with friends and relatives is often dim, or colored by more recent experiences. At present such contacts do not appear to be frequent. More than half of the pensioners state that they never visit their relatives or receive visits from them; only 11 per cent see relatives more than once a week; the average number of family visits is slightly over two a month. About 45 per cent of the pensioners never visit friends; the average number of visits is 2.3 per month. For Institute members this average is slightly higher—3.0 visits per month.

Signature collectors were questioned about the number of people with whom they maintained contact rather than about the number of visits in a given period of time. For three-quarters of them, active relationships with others suffered no substantial reduction after retirement. In only thirteen of the forty-two cases was there clear evidence that retirement was accompanied by a severe loss in the number of friends and acquaintances. Only eight respondents had been able to maintain virtually all their previous informal contacts; fourteen signature collectors had experienced important qualitative changes in social contacts: old friendships had had to be dropped, some ties were severed by death, and new relationships had been established. The interviewers gained the impression that the new contacts were superficial. None of the individuals interviewed used their free time after retirement to expand and enrich their social life.

Most of the pensioners, though aware that retirement has meant a profound change in their lives, complain less about the absence of social contacts than about other difficulties. Only 16 per cent state that they are not quite satisfied or are actively dissatisfied with the number of visits from members of their families; and only 8 per cent feel that they do not enjoy a sufficient number of visits with friends.[14] However, interviewers frequently noted signs of emotional strain when the pensioner's children were discussed. The pensioners often displayed a defensive attitude in regard to the letter-writing habits of their children.

Status-Anxiety

The pensioners give little evidence of concern about the paucity and precariousness of their personal contacts. The major preoccupation of members and nonmembers alike is their social status as pensioners. They appear to feel less a desire to "belong" to a community of friends and kin than a need to be "respected" by society at large.

With the attenuation of kinship relations in our society, the pensioner no longer feels he has a just claim upon his children. His basic concern is not with personal relations but with his relation to society. He is moved and motivated in large measure by status-anxiety.

What is an old-age assistance grant? Is it a handout, a sign of an improvident and unsuccessful life? Or is it a just reward? And what is a pensioner? Is he a "has-been," a failure? Or is he one whose old age and past productivity entitle him to respect and gratitude? Is he a ward of the state? Or does he have rights, moral as well as legal, to a decent pension? Is he a highly respected member of the community or a burden grudgingly borne?

The dubious attitude with which society regards the pensioner is duplicated in the ambiguities of his own self-image. In our society the emphasis is on *achieved* status, recognition being given for what a man does rather than for what he is. Though respect for old age as an *ascribed* status persists, it is little more than a

---

[14] See table 16.

remnant; given the emphasis on achievement, this respect is apt to be grudging, uncertain, and even tinged with mockery. The pensioner, too, believes in achieved status. Robbed by old age of the possibility of achievement, he feels simultaneously robbed of status; he loses self-esteem and self-respect.

There gnaws at him also the guilt which his own stereotypes induce. At bottom he is apt to believe that he ought to have been successful enough to have saved for his old age. Anxieties concerning his past life often manifest themselves in the twin attitudes of defensiveness and aggressiveness as he seeks to justify himself and fix the blame on others. However exemplary his past life, however high his former status, the pensioner fears to be identified with the careless, the immoral, the lazy, and he fears it all the more because of the nagging suspicion that he himself is responsible for his present situation.

For nearly all the responding recipients, "being on the pension" is at best a mixed blessing. Only 29 per cent of the members and 38 per cent of the nonmembers are able to say without qualification that they are glad they are receiving the pension; 30 per cent of the members and 19 per cent of the nonmembers state that they "feel entitled to it" or "feel glad and entitled to it." Pensioners who insist on their moral or legal title to the grant are often ambivalent about their role and position as pensioners. An additional 13 per cent of the members and 17 per cent of the nonmembers admit that they "feel embarrassed" about taking the pension. The remaining 28 per cent of the members and 24 per cent of the nonmembers express mixed or negative feelings.[15]

Only a small proportion of the recipients appear to believe that they have changed in their attitude toward the pension. The proportion who say that they were embarrassed at the time of their application but who do not feel embarrassed now is about 10 per cent. The proportion who think they have changed from negative feelings to being glad or entitled is not quite so large, since there is also a slight increase in mixed feelings.

Recipients may feel that there is something inherently shameful in being "on the pension." A former housewife, discussing the pension law, said: "They tell you it's just a hand-out and that

---

[15] See table 9.

you're not entitled to a real pension. I don't want no hand-out and I wish the Lord would give me the strength so's I could work and tell 'em to keep it. That's why George is out after the national. . . ." (In the members' jargon, "the national" means a federal old-age pension system.)

A former railroad worker, one of McLain's signature collectors, when asked how a $20 increase in the grants would affect the pensioners, stated:

"It would give them more to live on. Why not? When you're suffering from starvation you're degraded. You're diseased. You have to live in a filthy place. If those pensioners who were single would double up it would make it easier on them. They won't help one another, though." ["Would $20 more make a difference to you?"] "It'll give me a chance to get out of this hole. Also give me enough to get another hole. I'm out to buy a burial lot now."

Similar feelings are displayed, though less aggressively, by recipients who do not belong to the Institute: "I wish I didn't have to take the pension. I'd rather work if I could."

Members often complain of being treated disrespectfully by social workers. "They talk terrible to old people. It's not their fault, don't you see. It's because they are told to, they have to. . . . I don't like this state system at all. One thing—I won't be dictated to. If they bother me too much I'll just tell them to leave me alone."

Most threatening to the self-respect of the old people is what they regard as the social worker's propensity to "snoop."

Shame!? I'm proud that I'm old enough to get my pension!! But these social workers, these girls that they send around. They come and ask you everything and they want to know every little thing about you. Three people have committed suicide around here because of them.

We thought McLain was doing the right thing. He tries to get a little more money for the older people. Now take these damn little bitches they are sending around. I hear the less they give to the old people the more money they get. And they're paying them $100 a month. For what? For torturing the old people. I think it's a dirty shame. Take it away from the old people and they give it to them girls. Like I said to my son the other day, what we need is to do away with them. He's the sweetest kid. . . .

Self-justification.—Pensioners often make a special point of the fact that they have been hard-working, thrifty, and reliable. Many of the questionnaires returned to us were accompanied by elaborate accounts of the pensioner's former life and the indignities he is now made to suffer.

Dear Madam,

I feel I should explain a small part of my history. . . .

At the age of 20 I entered the State Normal University. . . . Teacher at the age of 22 began teaching in Mo. Taught 5 yr. in county schools then went into City School . . . worked for 6 yr. I enjoyed the work better than anything I ever did, but my health began failing so I did not apply for the next term; but took a position with large Mercantile Co. for three years. Then resign and came to Calif. with family of wife and four children. I clerk with some good business firms in Los Angeles for eight years.

I was 40 then and no jobs for old men.

Then I went to work for myself. First Road and St. building for Realty Company's under County supervision, and County inspection. . . .

I had no idea that I would ever have to apply for a pension. It was very humiliating to me. It wasn't any fault of us that we went broke. It was national conditions that broke us and many others too. . . .

As former teacher, long time businessman, and a student in business economy; please permit me to express my personal opinion.

On account of the advanced technological age in which we now live, and the longevity of life; it has become imperative that some form of retirement annuity be extended to those no longer needed in industry. . . .

Respectively submitted.

Another pensioner writes:

To whom it may concern:

. . . Could write a Book of my life, very interestingly: Im only 4 F. 10 inh high, but what Work this little Body has done: — Came from Europa (Germany) well educated, in 1913, no Reason to leave, just: Wanderlust, ha, have I paid for it, am still paying!! Had to get out after 3 Days of Rest after arrival, worked 24 Years almost steady: . . .

Anyhow, being on the Pension is *no* Yoke!! Hubby dos not receive Social Security, neither would I, as his & my work never included Social Security: So what good dos that do?!

O jes, Hubby arrived from France in Ferndale, there he pressed the Garments of Teddy Roosevelt, and President Taft, quite interesting. . . .

. . . The good Book, the Bible, Gods Word tells us, may the time come soon, that this World System will be for All People, not for a few!!. . . .

The following letter from a CISW member is an extreme example of self-justification:

Reference to question 8a

I would have had plenty of money to carry me and a wife through life without a pension. Except for the following partly explained reasons.

First. False professing women who invigilate a man into marriage or matrimony when they have no intention of carrying out the obligations they assume.

Second. The racketering lawyers and other clicks that grow fat on the miserable broken homes and rob the victims and force little children to suffer the abomination.

I was the victim 3 times and lost a Boy the pride of my life in the result.

Boose & cigarettes are another demoralizing and hellish Curse. I wish they could all be nocked out of existance.

Thank you for letting me answer your questions.

Hopeful

The letters of nonmembers closely resemble those of members.

Comment

My husband and I came to Los Angeles with plenty of money—enough to take care of us for the rest of our life.

We have *never left* Los Angeles, but *spent every nickel right here* in this city and had ample until the "CRASH," which took *all*.

We sold our better belongings, moved into cheaper apartments, did all we could; till we felt we *had* to ask for the "pension" . . .

And I don't feel I am receiving *1 cent charity*, as we spent *all* (and it was plenty) right in Los Angeles, so now I am only receiving back what is due me. Am thankful for it however, though do wish it could be a *speck* more.

Yours truly,

A pensioner—

Statement

Some of the foregoing questions do not fit in very well with my history. I feel that I am entitled to a pension as I worked hard most of my life with *no remuneration*. As a young woman was a physician's office assistant. Also a book-keeper. Then trained for church and welfare work in Mo. "Bible Schools." Worked for "Brethren," Methodist and Presbyterian Churches . . . No relatives left and death has taken most of my friends.

My greatest *practical* problem is the *high rent*. Have my own furniture and want to have a *home* as long as I can . . .

Neglected to state that all my work for church, family and friends furnished me only a place to stay and something to eat—no salary . . .

I find that the principle cause for bitterness of spirit among pensioners is the spending of public money in an unfair and unjust way. "Top bracket" political jobs afford a pension out of proportion with amount paid in and in no relation whatever to need. Private utility companies are allowed to give their executives enormous pensions and spend great sums of money to publish political propaganda and count *that* as necessary expense and hand the bill to the poor who can scarcely obtain the necessities of life. The victims are not being deceived . . .

I am not a Communist or Socialist.

My Fore fathers was in the Revolutionary War.

But I do think the county supervisors and many state official make it very hard on old people.

If we can send millions abroad all the time to help them a forin people better give a little more for a respectful living for old pioneers that made this country what it is to day.

And you young people better help. You will be old someday.

The following letter by a nonmember reflects the general mood of many letters in a style made more dramatic by the apparent onset of mental illness.

This questionnaire coming from an educational institutional is the most disgraceful, heartrending, hope killing thing I have contacted in 80 years.

I insist that you forward this whole thing to the united states chamber of commerce (which is also the insurance companys) and let them know how efficiently they have blackmailed this helpless decent, respectable American citizens out of their constitution right, and forced them into concentration camps from which they will never escape.

I will spend the rest of my life begging God to teach me to pray that America may somehow be saved from the drasticall organized fifth columns.

This was written on the back of a mimeographed statement which the pensioner appears to have prepared as an explanation of and protest against his condition:

TO WHOM IT MAY CONCERN:

Why I am a Pauper and an Indigent. In the first place the only thing I know is work, and you will remember that one of the first things they did after the world war for recovery (about 1919) was to blackmail every man off from the job by an irresistible power, when they were 45 because they were 45, for no other reason.

THE REASON WHY

Press dispatches show that about all of the wrecking, burglary, holdups and thefts, are done by men under 45 years of age, so they sacrificed me to the youngsters they are afraid of. So to mask the cause of their crimes against me they instructed the dear intelligent people that I am indolent and won't work.

So this is why the Chamber of Commerce and the Supervisors have branded me a Pauper and an Indigent.

Another technique for supporting respectability is to point to the high status of one's children. Our respondents tend to emphasize the fact that their children have good jobs and adhere to standards of Christian morality. A typical statement reads: "I sure got reason to be proud of my kids. The oldest is with . . . , that big car outfit downtown. [Shows son's business card, with photo and slogan: If it's a *car* you need, Call for Cal.] The girl is married in Oregon, and they have the nicest house . . ."

The respectability of their children is often discussed not merely in terms of achievement but against the background of hypothetical depravity: "The kids I brought up sure ain't no jailbirds. They're all nice saintly children." Another form of self-justification is found in frequent protestations that they are decent citizens with high standards of morality. "I never drank and I never smoked and I never did no running around. I used to stay home and take care of my house and family. I guess I'm kinda making up for it now . . ." (Interviewer's note: It is to be presumed not that she has begun drinking and smoking, but only that she goes out occasionally.)

Statements of this kind occur frequently in the interviews, though the phrase "I guess I'm kinda making up for it now . . ." is unusual. However, the remark of this respondent hints at one of the factors which may motivate the many references to respectability by pensioners. With the disappearance of family and occupational responsibilities, many older people may feel tempted to relax their former standards. One of the presumably rewarding features of old age is the possibility of being more self-indulgent. But in the lower-middle-class culture of our respondents, rigid standards are regarded as a sure sign of respectability, and the relaxing of old standards may be perceived as a threat to status.

Need for respect.—The preoccupation with status and respect is supported by the results of our questionnaire. The respondents were asked to express their views on the social worker and the pension law by checking appropriate adjectives on a list submitted to them.[16] The list, consisting of pairs of antonyms, was designed to probe the respondents' thinking about "the welfare." For instance, the words "respectful" and "humiliating" refer to the com-

---

[16] See Appendix II.

mon theme of respect, the words "generous" and "stingy" to the theme of generosity. Both members and nonmembers most frequently chose the terms "respectful" and "humiliating" to describe the social worker; approximately two-thirds of the respondents checked one of these adjectives.[17] When applied to the pension law, the two terms are second in frequency; about one-half of the respondents in each group select either of them. This is all the more remarkable since the adjective "respectful" is not ordinarily used to refer to law. The theme of respect thus serves most often as the frame of reference within which the social worker and the pension law are evaluated.

A second criterion by which the recipients very frequently judge "the welfare" is considerateness; more than half of the recipients judge the social worker in these terms, while two-thirds of the members and one-half of the nonmembers apply this frame of reference to the pension law. The relevant adjectives are "efficient" and "full of red tape." When used by a client of the welfare administration, these terms do not, of course, imply a judgment of administrative efficiency as seen from the perspective of the government official or the student of administration. The client, when describing the law or the worker as "efficient" or "full of red tape," refers to his feelings of comfort or discomfort in dealing with the administration. Is he made to wait for long hours before his case worker will see him or can he get prompt attention? Are there long delays between his requests and the social worker's answer? Does he have to complete many difficult forms or does his worker help him over such obstacles? Is it a rather simple matter to obtain the grant or does the procedure appear to be fraught with danger? Broadly speaking, is he being treated in a considerate manner or is he subject to bureaucratic chicanery? "Considerateness" comes closest to describing the significance which the terms "efficient" and "full of red tape" have in the pensioner's mind.

The importance to pensioners of respectful and considerate treatment can be gauged by comparing these two values with that of generosity. It is striking that the proportion of people in either group who think of their social worker as generous or as

---

[17] See table 8.

stingy is one-quarter or less. Responses to the pension law show that generosity is more important to nonmembers than it is to members; more than half the nonmembers couch their judgments in terms of generosity, while only slightly more than one-third of the members do so. In nonmembers' appraisals of the pension law, generosity is equal (if not greater) in importance to respect and considerateness. Thus, while respect and considerateness are important to all, they are apparently more important to members.

When the adjectives in the check list are not grouped into pairs of antonyms, but responses to each adjective are tabulated separately, large disparities between members and nonmembers appear. Not only are members more concerned with respect; they also tend to see it violated more often. (See chap. v.) This difference between responses of members and nonmembers is typical of many similar differences to be discussed in subsequent pages. Such variations reveal a disparity in attitudes but not in experience and concern. At present we are concerned only with the latter. Both members and nonmembers tend to see their relations to "the welfare" and especially to the social worker in a frame of reference of respect. If members differ from nonmembers it is in being even more likely not only to define their situation in terms of respect but also to feel disrespected. If status-anxiety characterizes pensioners in general, then members are "exaggerated" pensioners. McLain's followers appear to be like other pensioners, only more so.

The fact that McLain's followers suffer from status-anxiety more frequently and more acutely than do other pensioners may have at least two explanations. It will subsequently be shown that the social situation of Institute members differs to some extent from that of nonmembers, and differs in ways that probably make the former even more susceptible to status-anxiety than the latter. Membership in the organization may also serve to stimulate and facilitate a status orientation toward the world. These two explanations are not mutually exclusive; in fact, they may work to reinforce each other. Nevertheless, it will become increasingly clear that McLain's followers tend to differ from the general pensioner population in degree rather than in kind.

Dependence.—The fact that the aged poor are dependent upon others for sustenance and support is as evident as it is hurtful to their pride. Although the pensioners would prefer to be self-supporting, the only choices open to them (so far as there are any) are to rely on their children or on public agencies. In view of these alternatives, pensioners are inevitably caught up in the conflict between the proponents of the welfare state and of rugged individualism.

Superficially, pensioners cling to the traditional values of home and family; but the logic of their situation in a more and more atomistic society drives them to prefer public to family support. In the world of today, primary group relations have lost much of their importance, while the matter-of-fact relations among strangers embrace an ever larger part of each individual's existence. The extended family has almost ceased to function as a social unit for joint enterprise and mutual support; in its place, social institutions have been created to provide individuals with jobs and security. Children do not feel the obligations toward their aged parents which they assumed in former generations. Nor do parents wish to be dependent on their children. The pensioners are aware of these changes. They explain the lack of support from their children as a consequence of economic necessity. And they fail to understand why some segments of the population insist upon the maintenance of the economic family unit when, in fact, it has ceased to exist.

The continuing fight over the matter of relatives' responsibility is a fitting illustration of the peculiar ideological conflict which arises as a result of the discrepancy between social fact and social belief. In terms of actual savings to the state or of expenses to the responsible relatives of recipients, the stakes are small. Contributions from relatives amount to only 3.4 per cent of the total outlay for OAS grants.[18] It has frequently been argued that the expense of administering the relatives' responsibility clause is greater than the amount saved through these contributions.[19] Although some writers seem to think that the removal of the relatives' responsibil-

---

[18] Computed from unpublished statistics (tables 5 and 7 A) of the State Department of Social Welfare, Bureau of Research and Statistics, April, 1952.

[19] Bond and his associates report this as the opinion of two-thirds of the county directors of social welfare. See Pomona study, p. 316.

ity clause would result in a considerable increase in the case load, the experience of 1949 does not bear this out.[20]

The financial burden which the clause imposes upon relatives —mostly children—is rather small. For 56 per cent of the relatives, monthly contributions do not exceed $20. Since the economic stakes are not large, it is fair to say that the issue of relatives' responsibility is ideological for the most part.

Interestingly, both sides build their case on the need for family cohesion. Those who support the concept of relatives' responsibility argue from the sacred duty of children to support their aged parents or from the beneficial effects of family solidarity. The other side maintains that relatives' responsibility disrupts family relations by injecting elements of official pressure and constraint.

Our respondents' discussion of relatives' responsibility is often couched in purely altruistic terms. They say the children have a primary responsibility toward their own families and that it is unfair to ask them for contributions for their aged parents. The following quotations are typical:

"I'd do away with the relative's responsibility clause. Because it just isn't right. It costs more to enforce it than if they paid everyone. I'm not making that off the top of my head. Like they say, that's official. And, too, that business, the relative's responsibility, causes trouble between families. Like my son. I know."

". . . they should do away with that relative's responsibility clause once and for all. It's almost like putting a body in jail just 'cause they got a mother. It's terrible. They haven't got more than they need. It's a crime. They shouldn't be asked to take care of parents. They even try to bring in daughters [i.e., make married daughters responsible], have both of them responsible."

"Those that are against the pension can't see through our minds. They can't administrate this relative responsibility clause with any fairness today. That's the worst thing about the whole pension today. . . . If my daughter should get sick tomorrow she hasn't anything socked away for tomorrow because she has to help pay my doctor bills. And next year she'll lose her daughter as a dependent and have to give more to my support."

"I think, it [the pension] takes a load off their [the children's] shoulders. But I don't think they should be responsible for their parent's support. When

---

[20] The increase in the number on OAS in 1949 was due primarily to the lowering of the eligibility age, not to the dropping of the clause on relatives' responsibility.

a young man marries, he marries his wife and not his in-laws. He shouldn't have to take care of them. I'm against that relatives' responsibility clause. I guess old people feel about the same as young people about it."

These statements reflect attitudes which appear to be widespread among the aged. The Pomona group reports that only 36 per cent of all persons sixty-five years of age and older and 29 per cent of all OAS recipients are in favor of relatives' responsibility.[21]

It is tempting to suppose that these arguments are chiefly superficial rationalizations designed to hide a real disappointment over the lack of support received from children. On this view, ideas concerning the lot of the aged in retirement were formed by pensioners in their younger years, and they now expect to be treated in the same way as their grandparents or as they themselves treated their parents. We found no evidence for this theory, however; if pensioners have such expectations, these are so deeply buried as to be inaccessible to ordinary methods of interviewing.

During pretests and in the early stages of interviewing, the respondents were asked to recall their younger years and to compare the way older people lived then with the present condition of the aged. We asked the pensioners to give concrete descriptions of the life of older people in former days, in the belief that disappointment with the treatment they are receiving from their families would manifest itself in nostalgic remarks about "the good old days." Since our queries consistently failed to elicit such comments, this line of questioning was later abandoned. Some of the answers to these questions are worth quoting:

"They had a pretty good life—lives o. k." [Interviewer: "Were they happier?"] "Well, we kind of think they were happy enough." [Respondent's wife breaks in.] "But they depended upon relatives then, though, the old people. They were not so happy. They had to go from relative to relative, living in one place awhile, then another, just rotating, a burden on children." [Respondent seems to agree with this. Interviewer: "Well, don't many people do this now?" Respondent's wife:] "If you can get the pension and stay together it's better. Now you can get the pension, and get a little place to live in and not be a burden on the children. They have their own life to live."

"I came from Germany. I lost my mother early in life, and I had a stepmother. She was always kind to me. But when I was thirty or so, she was

---

[21] Pomona study, p. 299.

an old woman—all finished, nothing left for her to live for. Here older people have a good life. Even with the pension, they can do a few things. They
can go a few places, buy a few things. 'Course there are those with no home
who don't have enough."

"When father died I was only thirteen and my sister Emily, she was two
years ahead of me. Mother took in wash for a couple of years or so, but it
was pretty hard on her. Her health wasn't much good and she had the house
to take care of and the two boys [younger brothers]. So Emily took a job
in a soap factory and I went and got a job in a store. Mother used to say it
was a great comfort to her and we took care of her for many, many
years." [Interviewer: "Were old people better off in those days, or now?"]
"Well, Mother didn't get a pension and it sure would have helped in those
days. Young people have their own life to take care of. We took care of
Mother and we were sure glad we could do it, but people are better off with
the pension."

Since the topic of dependence was bound to be emotionally
loaded, the questionnaire approached it indirectly. The respondents were asked to say to whom a fictitious pensioner should turn
when in distress. The most important fact about this question is
that, in spite of its cautious wording, about two-thirds of all respondents, members and nonmembers alike, refused or neglected
to answer it. Only 5 per cent of the members and 10 per cent of
the nonmembers said that the pensioner should turn to his children for help; 18 per cent of the members, though only 8 per cent
of the nonmembers, suggested that he consult his social worker.
However, 24 per cent of the members and 22 per cent of the nonmembers selected the doctor or the social worker (or both); only
8 per cent of the members and 12 per cent of the nonmembers suggested turning to children or friends.[22]

It appears, from the lack of response to this question, that both
members and nonmembers have great difficulty in coping with
the problems of dependence. Of those who are able to face this
problem only a small proportion wish to depend on children or
personal friends. Nonmembers are somewhat more likely than
members to turn to their children, while McLain followers are
more likely to turn to the social worker.

Emotional difficulties concerning dependence may have two

---

[22] The percentages given in this paragraph add to more than one-third of the
total sample because some respondents gave more than one answer.

sources. First, the respondents may be unable to acknowledge the dependence which stems from their incapacities; dependence may arouse feelings of shame or guilt. Second, they may be unable to decide upon whom they can make a legitimate claim. Relatives' responsibility is in practice a thing of the past, yet public responsibility is only grudgingly admitted. Nevertheless, it is telling that those who are able to make a choice prefer dependence upon outside agencies rather than upon kin or friends. Reliance on impersonal or official sources of help may be a way of maintaining a modicum of independence. But also it probably reflects the historic trend away from primary group responsibility for the individual.

Activities of recipients.—Dependent and socially handicapped people often feel a need to prove themselves by increased activity. In order to maintain their self-respect, they will take on more and more varied tasks. But frequently their accomplishments do not measure up to their aspirations.

Figure 1 shows the kinds and frequency of activities in which recipients engage. The list is composed of activities mentioned in pretest interviews, except those which are unavoidable in normal everyday living, such as cooking and cleaning. The recipients do very little beyond daily chores, but most of them claim that they are keeping themselves busy: 24 per cent of both members and nonmembers assert that they have "more things to do than they find time for," 45 per cent say that they are "mostly busy," and only 21 per cent of the members and 24 per cent of the nonmembers feel that they "often have time on their hands." Members appear to be a little more active than nonmembers. An activity score was calculated for each pensioner; this is simply the number of different activities in which he engages. Members have a higher activity score (4.4 activities) than nonmembers (3.9 activities).[23]

The respondents were asked to mark also the activities in which a hypothetical pensioner, Loren Winter, should engage in order to "lead a happy, contented life." The question specifies that Loren Winter is "in pretty good health" and has "some income."

---

[23] See table 10.

Our question was designed to elicit activity aspirations rather than realistic desires.

The number of people proposing any given activity for the

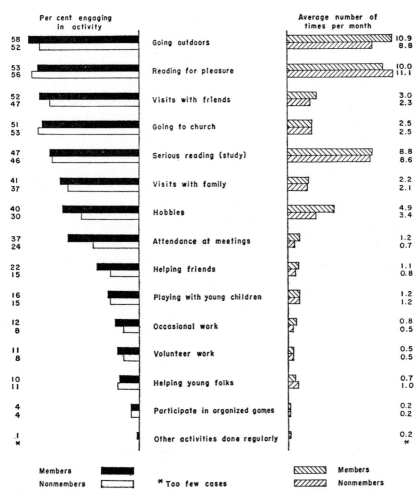

Fig. 1. Recipients' activities.

health and happiness of the mythical pensioner is consistently larger than the number of those engaging in it themselves.[24] The differences between the proportions of people engaging in and

---

[24] See table 11.

recommending a given activity are often sizable—frequently around 20 per cent, and as high as 47 per cent in one instance. Whether this constitutes a large excess of aspirations over actual accomplishments cannot be decided in the absence of comparable data from other age groups or from nonpensioners.

It is, at any rate, more fruitful to consider the qualitative aspects of these aspirations. Do pensioners suggest an increase in the activities in which they are already involved? Or do they wish that they might be able to engage in different types of activities? Three types of activities are no more or less frequently desired than engaged in: light reading, serious reading, and outdoor activity. The number of recipients suggesting friendly visits as a source of happiness is not much larger than the number who actually visit their friends. These four activities are among those most commonly engaged in, but the recipients seem already to "have their fill" of them.

On the other side of the picture, we find that some activities in which very few people engage are in heavy demand. Only 11 per cent of the members and 9 per cent of the nonmembers do "volunteer work for some good cause"; but 58 per cent of the members and 51 per cent of the nonmembers consider it a desirable type of activity. Similarly, although only 12 per cent of the members and 8 per cent of the nonmembers do part-time work, 38 per cent of the former and 41 per cent of the latter feel that this would be desirable for the mythical pensioner of the question. Hobbies are desired by 53 per cent of the nonmembers, although only 30 per cent engage in hobbies; among members, however, the difference between those engaging in hobbies and those desiring them is only 16 per cent, the average for all items.

The most striking difference is between those who say volunteer work is desirable and those who actually engage in it. The excess of people valuing volunteer work over those involved in it is even larger than the corresponding excess for full or part-time work. Both items show a larger increase than the item of hobbies.

Similar discrepancies might well be found among other groups in American society that place a high value both upon work in general and upon "doing good," at least in an impersonal philanthropic sense. Nevertheless, the gaps between actuality and desire point to the fact that pensioners, despite their advanced age, continue to make demands upon themselves which they cannot satisfy. The discrepancies probably point to areas in which their most poignant anxieties come into play. Pensioners often declare that they would rather work than accept old-age assistance; they share the American view that work, including a hobby, is in itself salutary and self-justifying. Their heavy emphasis on the desirability of doing something for a good cause may well reflect their conviction that they are no longer useful to society. They feel a loss not only of sheer status but of a meaningful role. Their high valuation of volunteer work probably reflects the American middle-class tendency to identify usefulness with participation in formal "cause" organizations.

Conversations with the aged reveal that volunteer work means knitting; making slippers and other articles for servicemen or for charity, to be sold at raffles and other benefits; doing light maintenance work in buildings of charitable, church, and similar institutions; making sandwiches, packing lunch baskets, and the like for organization picnics; addressing envelopes; watching children while parents attend official functions. Volunteer work should, at least in principle, appeal to pensioners who are of uncertain health and advanced age, for it combines work activity with sociability, and, unlike part-time employment, does not endanger the old-age assistance grant. Earnings from part-time work are likely to be less than the grant, and, if their amount is at all significant, are deductible from the monthly check.

Again, CISW members show the characteristics of the pensioners in a more extreme fashion. The gap between average amount of activity and average aspiration is consistently larger among members than among nonmembers. Moreover, the proportion of members desiring any given activity is almost always larger than the proportion of nonmembers. The activities for which the difference is smallest are of two kinds: either they belong to the group of activities of which the pensioners already "have their fill" (such as reading) or else they attract only a small proportion of pensioners. Finally, the differences between members and nonmembers also show up between the more involved and the less involved members. The more involved a group is in the work of the

CISW, the more likely it is to contain a higher proportion of people advocating an activity which is generally favored by pensioners.[25] We reach a similar conclusion when we compare the average aspiration scores for members and nonmembers as well as for the various groupings among members.[26]

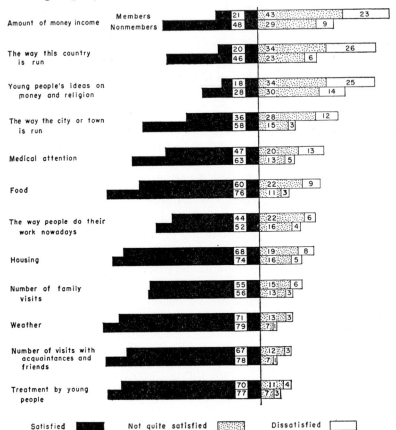

Fig. 2. Degrees of satisfaction with various experiences.

Demands on society.—A check list of items garnered from informal interviews was included in the questionnaire to ascertain how many of the recipients found certain areas of experience unsatisfactory. Figure 2 shows that the items eliciting dissatisfaction most frequently refer to material circumstances or are abstract

[25] See table 14.
[26] See table 15.

and ideological in content.[27] Moreover, except for money, the items relating to the material circumstances of life tend to elicit less dissatisfaction than do those relating to abstractions. Fewer members complain about deficiencies in medical attention than about "the way the country is run," "the way the city is run," and "young people's ideas about morals and religion." This occurs in spite of the fact that medical facilities in California (as elsewhere) are overloaded and that it is difficult to obtain adequate medical care for the aged, especially in chronic cases. Dissatisfaction thus has a vaguely political or moralistic content; the concrete interpersonal relations of the aged are at the bottom of the list.

Pensioners tend to perceive problems in ideological terms, although this is somewhat more true of members than of nonmembers. It is probable that McLain recruits his followers particularly among pensioners who are especially given to formulating their problems abstractly. This can be seen more clearly when average amounts of dissatisfaction are considered.[28] It then turns out that the members who are most deeply involved in the Institute express dissatisfactions of an ideological nature more frequently and more strongly than the less involved members and the nonmembers. There is also a positive relationship between dissatisfaction with material conditions and strength of involvement in the organization; but this relationship is not so pronounced as that pertaining to ideological dissatisfaction. Finally, dissatisfaction with interpersonal experiences is uniformly low and unrelated to involvement in the organization.

Figure 3 shows the responses to a question dealing with the treatment which, in the respondents' opinion, should be accorded the aged.[29] In many respects figure 3 has the same properties as figure 2. The proportion of members endorsing any one demand is consistently higher than the corresponding proportion of nonmembers. Again, McLain's followers emerge as the more extreme representatives of the pensioners' common preoccupations. Also, the average number of demands endorsed by the recipients becomes

---

[27] See table 16.
[28] See table 17.
[29] See table 18.

larger as knowledge of, and involvement in, McLain's organization increases.[30]

Most of the demands included in this check list are not very realistic; they were designed to test whether recipients can be made to take unpopular positions. The demand for an honor roll, for example, would almost certainly be regarded as extravagant by

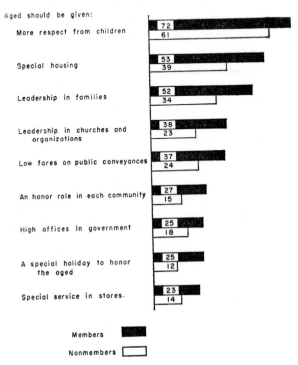

Aged should be given:

More respect from children — 72 / 61

Special housing — 53 / 39

Leadership in families — 52 / 34

Leadership in churches and organizations — 38 / 23

Low fares on public conveyances — 37 / 24

An honor role in each community — 27 / 15

High offices in government — 25 / 18

A special holiday to honor the aged — 25 / 12

Special service in stores. — 23 / 14

Members

Nonmembers

Fig. 3. Demands for improved treatment.

large segments of the community. Nevertheless, though only 15 per cent of the nonmembers regard it favorably, 27 per cent of the members think of it as desirable.

Figures 2 and 3 yield some apparent discrepancies. Dissatisfaction with housing is relatively low in the order of complaints, but is second in importance as a demand. Treatment by young people and number of family visits are both relatively low on the scale of complaints, yet a desire for more respect from children is first in

[30] See table 19.

the order of demands. However, some dissatisfaction with young people's ideas on money and religion is expressed by 59 per cent of the members and 44 per cent of the nonmembers. The aged seem to be concerned primarily with the more abstract aspects of their relations to the young, expressing dissatisfaction with the ideas of the younger generation and implicitly with the not unrelated lack of respect accorded age. They are relatively satisfied with the number of family visits but not with their status as old people.

Group identification.—It is extremely rare for our respondents to refer to pensioners or the aged in the first person plural: they speak about "the old people," "the oldsters," "the pensioners," "the elderly," or, more honorifically, "elderly citizens" and "senior citizens." One of our respondents told us that she had written to "George" suggesting "retired citizens" as the only acceptable term. Anxiety concerning their status both as aged and as pensioners manifests itself in several ways: the pensioners hesitate to identify themselves with other aged persons; they are reluctant to identify themselves as aged; they prefer to be called "citizens" rather than "old" and "pensioners." The interviews with the forty-two signature collectors were rated for manifestations of identification with the aged. Criteria for this rating were the use of the pronoun "we" as well as other expressions of we-feeling. In only seven cases could such manifestations be detected, and even in these they occur only occasionally.

In spite of this lack of group feeling among the aged, there is a fairly high demand for "special groups or organizations that look out for the needs or rights" of older people: 89 per cent of the members and 69 per cent of the nonmembers believe that such organizations are desirable.[31] Only 7 per cent of the members and 16 per cent of the nonmembers explicitly reject the idea of special

---

[31] According to the Pomona study (p. 101), "only 16 per cent of California's aged seem to believe it is necessary for them to join groups, such as the California Institute of Social Welfare or a Townsend Club, in order to get a square deal in American society." Unfortunately, the authors neither give the wording of the relevant question nor reprint their questionnaire. If the phrase quoted above reflects, in any way, the question used in their interview, this would explain why our results differ so sharply from theirs. The answers to the Pomona questionnaire may register responses to such terms as "pressure groups," "square deal," and "join," while our question concerns merely feelings about organizations.

groups. Of those rejecting special groups, only 15 per cent state that special groups are unnecessary because the aged are not a special class of people; most of the rest indicate that they are satisfied with the present situation; only 10 per cent declare that nothing can be done to improve their lot or that special organizations only cause trouble for the aged.

When asked why they considered special organizations desirable, slightly over one-third of the respondents explain that the aged need help or protection because they are old and cannot help themselves;[32] 30 per cent believe that the aged must organize in order to be able to do things for themselves. Only 12 per cent think that the aged need to defend themselves against a hostile world. The pensioners' desire for old-age organizations seems to grow out of their perplexity over the problem of dependence. In their view, organizations will either do for them what they cannot do for themselves or enable them to manage their own affairs more actively. It is not identification with older people, or a general desire for political action, that impels participation in organizations.

As to the purposes of old-age organizations, most of the pensioners are rather vague. About one-quarter of them are unable to specify any particular needs which might be served; another quarter suggest that some sort of activity might be provided; 31 per cent think of organization meetings as social events which it might be interesting to attend; and 21 per cent mention economic problems which old-age organizations might help them to solve.

The pensioners regard such organizations as groups *useful to* the aged, not as groups *of* the aged. When asked whether the organizations should be made up of old people only or of all ages, 73 per cent of the Institute members and 52 per cent of the nonmembers express a preference for mixed groups. Only 18 per cent of the members and 19 per cent of the nonmembers are in favor of groups composed of old people only. The preference for mixed groups is significantly greater among members than among nonmembers.

Those who join McLain's Institute do not belong to a special type of pensioner. It might be supposed that followers of a pension movement are lonely people who join for the sake of companion-

[32] See table 20.

ship. According to our data, this is not so: Institute members are no lonelier than other pensioners who are still vigorous enough to be capable of social intercourse. If there is any difference at all, McLain's followers have a somewhat fuller social life. Nor can we detect any strong need for social contacts among those who respond to McLain's appeal. It was shown also that there is scarcely any difference in the cultural background of members and of nonmembers; before reaching the retirement age, members are no more prepared for pressure-group participation than others. Nor does any tradition of political participation exist among them. A very few followers of McLain have belonged to such movements as the Townsend clubs or Ham and Eggs, but their number is so insignificant as to rule out any explanation of membership in the Institute as a result of previous experience in organizations. Union membership is particularly rare in the past experience of the pensioners.

We have concluded that status-anxiety is the most significant attribute of pensioners in general and that it makes them susceptible to the appeals of a McLain. Those who respond seem to be characterized by an even greater degree of status-anxiety than nonmember pensioners. This heightened concern seems to have its source in the existence of a "slightly privileged" group among pensioners.

The Slightly Privileged

Within a narrow range the economic situations of Old Age Assistance recipients vary to a degree which is perhaps as significant to them as differences in income are to corporation executives. While the law puts a ceiling on the property and (generally) the money income of pensioners, it does not establish economic equality. Indeed, the law as now written has the curious and largely unanticipated effect of enhancing or establishing economic distinctions among pensioners. "Slight privilege" is therefore to some extent a product of the law.

The slightly privileged are the pensioners who have acquired some modest property in the past and have been able to hold on to it, or whose spouses are still living and who therefore benefit from combining two grants. For these fortunate individuals, income may exceed a minimum subsistence level. Because of their slight advantage they identify with other recipients even less than do those whose grants are grossly inadequate. At the same time they realize that the aged who do not need the grant and the pensioners who have some independent income are more solidly middle class than they. The aspirations as well as resentments with which the slightly privileged respond to their situation make them the natural targets of a pension advocate.

Comparative advantages.—It is interesting to observe how the law achieves this unexpected result. The law provides that the applicant's needs shall, if possible, be met, but that the total grant cannot exceed $80. The social worker first establishes for each applicant a "budget of needs" reflecting (with some ceilings) his monthly expenses. From this figure are deducted his monthly resources, which may include Social Security benefits, railroad and other pensions, income from rental property, and contributions from relatives. The resulting figure is the size of the grant, provided it does not exceed the maximum of $80. An applicant's resources may be relatively great, but if his budget of needs is also great, with some exceptions he is entitled to the total amount of the difference if it does not exceed $80. Another applicant with no resources at all may have a budget of needs as large or even larger, yet he can receive no more than the maximum of $80. In practice the law often operates to *increase* the income of those already relatively well off, and to broaden the gap between those with an adequate and those with a mere subsistence income.

Perhaps the most effective way to get along on the $80 is to own one's own home. The law states that a person is eligible for Old Age Security if his real property is assessed [33] at no more than $3,500. Home ownership is considered a resource of the recipient for purposes of his budget, and an amount thought to reflect the value of occupancy is deducted from the grant. The basis for the deduction is the assessed value of the property; $5 is deducted for the first $500 and $1 for each additional $500 of assessed value. For a property assessed at $2,000 (probably an average) the de-

---

[33] In California, assessed property valuations amount to 20–25 per cent of the market value.

duction amounts to $8; the lucky pensioner who owns a home assessed for as much as $3,500 has to sacrifice no more than the legal maximum of $9 for the advantage of living in more spacious and comfortable quarters. The living conditions of the home-owning recipient are thus far superior to those of the pensioner who must rent a shabbily furnished room for, say, $25 a month. Moreover, under the law, the allowance for shelter in the basic budget of $85 is only $15. A recipient whose actual rent amounts to, say, $25 is considered to have an "excess need" for housing of $10. His total budget of needs is therefore $95 (assuming he has no other excess need). If this recipient has no income, he can pay for his shelter only by reducing correspondingly his expenditures for other essentials, such as food and clothing.

But if the recipient has some slight income, $10 of this can be applied to his excess need for housing. Only that portion of his income which is not used to meet excess needs is deducted from his total budget of needs.

A third advantage accrues to those who share their household expenses with one or more other recipients. Usually this applies to married couples where both partners are eligible for aid. The law considers each applicant as an individual case; if recipients live together, this circumstance does not affect their budgets of needs. No doubt it is easier for a couple to manage on $160 a month than it is for a single person to get along on half that amount. The law thus has the curious effect of giving a special award to the pensioner who is fortunate enough to have his spouse still living.

The law maintains, and perhaps even accentuates, social distinctions. The slightly privileged—so labeled because, in absolute terms of money income, their advantage over others is really small —may appear as greatly privileged in the eyes of the average recipient of old-age assistance. For people who live very near the bare subsistence level, and sometimes below it, the advantages of home ownership and lower-middle-class comforts may seem enormous. Nor can there be any doubt that the slightly privileged are aware of their favorable situation and contemplate with dread the possibility that their lot might become similar to that of pensioners who own nothing and have no families.

Owning one's home, having a spouse living, and enjoying some income other than a state grant all represent slight economic advantage. In all these ways McLain's followers tend to be more privileged than nonmembers. These social advantages probably make some pensioners more "organizable" than others and, together with the fact that members are slightly less urbanized than nonmembers, facilitate social participation.

Home ownership.—Among Institute members, 47 per cent live in their own homes; among nonmembers, only 26 per cent enjoy this advantage.[34] Besides its distinct economic advantage, home ownership affects a person's life in other ways: it makes him property-conscious; it links him to community affairs by making him a taxpayer; it increases the number of decisions he must make (concerning building maintenance, the yard, etc.); and often it enhances his opportunities for receiving guests and visitors. Home ownership, then, tends to increase social awareness and involvement.

Since almost half of the Social Welfare Club meetings are held in private homes, most frequently in the home of the president, home ownership in a sense predestines a person for this role. Club presidents are particularly likely to be homeowners, the proportion being 67 per cent.[35] The opportunities arising from home ownership may also account for the fact that Institute members have, on the average, more frequent social contacts; the average number of visits with friends is 3.0 for members and 2.3 for nonmembers.

Among the signature collectors, also, the ratio of homeowners was relatively high. Of these forty-two respondents in Oakland-Berkeley and Los Angeles, nineteen lived in single-family dwellings and six in duplexes; the remainder were found in small apartments, rooms, boardinghouses, and tenements.[36] Typically, the houses visited by our interviewers (whether owned or rented) were found to be in good or medium repair; less than a quarter of them were rated to be in bad condition. Of the buildings in bad

---

[34] See table 21.

[35] See table 21.

[36] Our figures may overestimate the proportion of homeowners among the petition circulators, partly because of our selection of sample areas and partly because the ratio of "noninterviews" (addresses in the sample where no interview could be obtained) was highest in the downtown sections.

repair, all but one gave adequate shelter.[37] The furniture in more than half of the households was rated in good condition, that is, it showed signs of consistent care; in only five of the forty-two households did the interviewers find dilapidated furniture. Likewise, in only seven dwellings were the interiors rated as disorderly. Most of the homes were regarded as neat or slightly disorganized (i.e., in a condition such that a slight "picking up" would restore order). Interviewers rated thirty-four out of forty-two neighborhoods in which petition circulators lived as lower middle class.

The sampling areas selected for the purpose of interviewing petition circulators were those in which the largest number of petition circulators lived. Members of the Institute, particularly the core group, tend to live in lower-middle-class neighborhoods, to show some concern for both the exterior and the interior of their dwellings, and to maintain the standards of neatness and cleanliness that go with respectability in our society.

Areas of residence.—Home ownership also has geographical corollaries which affect the pensioner's style of living. Privately owned homes are usually found not in the centers of large urban communities but rather in the outskirts and in smaller towns. Accordingly, McLain's followers tend to live in the less urbanized places.[38] Only 47 per cent of the members live in communities of 100,000 or larger, whereas 60 per cent of the control group live in such communities. The bulk of the membership is clearly concentrated in towns of medium size. This is particularly true of the more involved members. The proportion of members in communities of more than 100,000 population decreases as we move from regular members to life members to club presidents. Among the club presidents, only 16 per cent live in the larger cities, as compared with an average of 47 per cent in the Institute sample.

Of the unorganized pensioners, the residents in the larger communities are less likely to know about McLain than are those in smaller places. It would be erroneous, however, to conclude that the membership is rural. Los Angeles County, with its large urban

---

[37] The rating was made for the purposes of assessing social rank, not sanitary conditions. Accordingly, interviewers were instructed to note primarily the pensioner's visible efforts to maintain building and yard in a condition of "respectability" rather than the adequacy of the dwelling in terms of the occupant's comfort.

[38] See table 22.

center, accounts for nearly two-thirds of our cases.[39] This means that McLain members in Los Angeles tend to live in the smaller urbanized communities adjoining Los Angeles rather than in the large incorporated communities of Los Angeles, Pasadena, Long Beach, and Glendale. They are not rural, but are less likely than other pensioners to live in typical big-city environments.

Since suburban areas tend to have younger populations than the downtown sections, members are not so heavily concentrated in areas with high average age as are other pensioners. Evidence for this statement was gained through an examination of the census tracts in the Los Angeles area. This analysis has the advantage of being unaffected by any bias due to nonresponse; we were able to obtain addresses from the rolls of the Institute of Social Welfare and the Los Angeles Department of Charities (Bureau of Public Assistance), and not merely those of people returning their questionnaires. The census tracts in Los Angeles County were classified according to the proportion of people sixty-five years of age and older and the proportion of Old Age Assistance recipients; the proportion of Institute members living within each category of census tracts was then computed.

This analysis shows that the median census tract for all people sixty-five years of age or older contains 11.3 per cent of people in the same age group; for recipients of Old Age Assistance we arrive at practically the same figure—their median census tract contains 11.4 per cent of people aged sixty-five and older; but the median census tract for Institute members contains only 9.8 per cent of individuals in their own age groups.[40] Thus, within rather narrow limits, there tend to be fewer old people in neighborhoods inhabited by McLain's followers than in neighborhoods inhabited by old people in general. A lower proportion of people above the age of sixty-five in a given census tract usually means a lower proportion of people above the age of fifty, the correlation between these proportions being .81. This residential pattern of Institute

---

[39] Since the control group was drawn from seven counties, only Institute members who live in these same seven counties were included in table 22.

[40] A χ^2 test was used to test the hypothesis that the sample of Institute members, as distributed over the census tracts, was drawn from a population identical with that of all people aged 65 years and above. For 9 *df*, χ^2 is 62.5 and $P < .001$. The Institute sample is therefore independent of the old-age population.

members living in "younger" neighborhoods is probably associated with the members' greater optimism about and desire for maintaining contacts with the community. Their wish to belong to organizations in which old and young may mix bears witness to this attitude.

Income.—While it is relatively easy to assess the economic and social advantages of home ownership, differences in the recipients' incomes are not readily calculated. We therefore confined ourselves to ascertaining how many respondents had resources other than the OAS grant.

If we consider only those Institute members who receive OAS (it will be remembered that a small proportion of members are not pensioners), the proportion of McLain followers who must subsist on their state grants alone is 61 per cent. This compares with 67 per cent among nonmembers. That is, 39 per cent of the members had outside income, as compared with 33 per cent of nonmembers.

If we include members who do not receive state aid at all (13 per cent of the total sample), the over-all proportion of members depending on the pension exclusively drops to 53 per cent. Nearly all the CISW members who do not receive the pension are more than sixty years of age, and exactly three-quarters of them are sixty-five years or older. Only 8 per cent of the whole group have their own earnings or those of a spouse to live on; 33 per cent receive financial support from relatives; 69 per cent receive Social Security benefits (OASI); and 7 per cent have other sources of income. Several of these sources of income may be combined.

Although the income received by these Institute members has not been ascertained, most of them appear to be close to the status of assistance recipients. Social Security benefits received by persons in this age group are generally small; a slight increase in state pensions might make many of them eligible for additional aid. Those below the age of sixty-five who are not working are likely to be in such circumstances that they look forward to the day when they will become eligible for the state pension. There is little psychological difference between the person who has some outside income in addition to his pension and the nonpensioner whose income is barely large enough to keep him ineligible. For these reasons we have included in our sample the Institute members who do not receive OAS.

Marital status and living conditions.—More members than nonmembers enjoy the advantage, both economic and psychological, of having a spouse still living; 47 per cent of the members as against 30 per cent of the control group are married.[41] Pensioners who are more deeply involved in Institute activities contain a higher proportion of married people than those less involved; among the least involved members only 35 per cent are married, whereas of those who make the largest contributions to the Institute 49 per cent are married. The highest proportion of married people is found among the club presidents (71 per cent).

Among nonmembers there is a relation between marital status and information about the Institute. Those who have heard of McLain are more likely to be married people (32 per cent) than those who have not heard of him (19 per cent). Recipients with spouses still living are probably reached by more information from the community than widowed pensioners, who are more likely to be both socially isolated and apathetic.

The pensioners' living arrangements reflect their marital status. Fewer Institute members (36 per cent) than nonmembers (42 per cent) live by themselves;[42] moreover, the proportion of people living alone decreases fairly steadily as we go from nonmembers who have not heard of McLain (51 per cent) to the most involved members (life members, 34 per cent; presidents, 26 per cent). A similar observation can be made about the extent to which members and nonmembers participate in households consisting of more than one person: the greater the involvement of a given group, the larger the proportion of people who share their living expenses.

In view of the small cash budgets of the recipients, the sharing of expenses for housing and other necessities represents a considerable economic advantage. Those who are married are therefore in a more favorable financial position, provided both husband and wife are eligible for assistance.

---

[41] If only the OAS recipients in the CISW membership are considered, the proportion of married people is reduced to 45 per cent. See table 24.

[42] See table 26.

Cumulated advantages.—The same pensioner may enjoy several advantages at the same time. The effect of this cumulation is shown in figure 4. The degree to which pensioners cumulate advantages is unrelated to either the knowledge which nonmembers have of McLain's organization or the depth of involvement of Institute members. "Slight privilege," if understood as a cumulation of advantages, may predispose individuals to membership, but it does not affect the amount of energy and interest which they

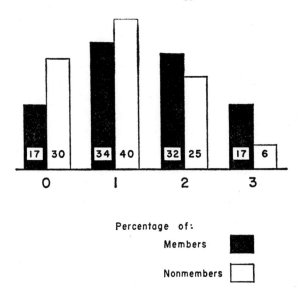

Percentage of:

Members ■

Nonmembers □

Fig. 4. Number of advantages held by members and by nonmembers. Note.—Percentages for CISW members who receive OAS (i.e., excluding nonpensioners) areas follows: number of advantages, 0: *22* per cent; 1: *29* per cent; 2: *33* per cent; 3: *16* per cent.

put into the organization. The same is true of home ownership: with the exception of the club presidents, the most involved groups of members do not include a larger proportion of homeowners than the least involved groups. The other two advantages, married status and additional income, are weakly related to involvement, but in different ways: the more involved groups contain a larger proportion of married people but a smaller proportion of people with income other than their OAS grants.

These findings lend additional support to the hypothesis that "slight privilege" predisposes people for participation in the Institute but does not determine the extent to which they are willing to commit themselves. Once they have joined the organization, those who have only their pension to depend on may become more deeply convinced of the importance of the Institute to their welfare. However, those who have additional incomes may perceive a possibility of leaving the ranks of the recipients altogether, and this would weaken their allegiance. The married state, however, appears to make for involvement in the CISW. Those who are still married may become more faithful followers of McLain because they reinforce each other in their attitudes and because elderly couples tend to take more interest in social events and community affairs than do widowed persons.

The slightly privileged pensioner may therefore be regarded as the prototype of the Institute member: he is most easily mobilized and he may, by his presence and his respectable demeanor, act as a model for other pensioners. This does not mean, however, that he necessarily belongs to the core group most deeply committed to the Institute.

Slight privilege and its consequences.—"Slight privilege" is a largely unanticipated consequence of the welfare law and its administration. The justice of the present arrangements, or the desirability of maintaining a modicum of social status for those who have once achieved it, cannot be discussed here. Few would maintain that the aged should be allowed to sink to a level of complete indigency (by selling their homes and consuming the proceeds) before becoming eligible for assistance. Fewer yet would suggest that the law should raise all to a common level of relative prosperity. It is, of course, possible to show that many of the social distinctions which arise or are maintained through the agency of the Welfare and Institutions Code are fortuitous or arbitrary. Yet, apart from radical solutions, any such legislation, however carefully designed, will tend to perpetuate differences in class or status as well as create new differences.

The problem of abstract justice aside, these distinctions among pensioners have great political and psychological significance for those who participate in the daily drama of welfare administration: the social workers and the clients. The recipient who is a property owner is likely to equate justice with his personal rights of ownership. The harder it was for him to acquire property, the more true will this be. As a result, he is likely to act the part of a defensive, hurt, suspicious, and often uncoöperative "crank."

This conclusion is supported by some of the questionnaire data. A comparison was made between pensioners who have no slight privilege and those who have one or more of the three economic advantages. The only responses in which the slightly privileged differed from pensioners without privileges were those relating to the welfare law and institutions and to distrust. According to our findings, slight privilege does not seem to raise the general level of dissatisfaction or of demands upon the community; no differences between privileged and nonprivileged groups showed up in responses to questions dealing with these two attitudes. There does exist, however, a relation between the attitude toward the pension and the number of the recipient's economic advantages: the greater the number of advantages, the less likely is the pensioner to say he is glad he is receiving the pension.[43] But the pensioner who has a greater number of advantages tends to feel entitled to his pension. The greater a pensioner's need, the more likely he is to accept the state grant without having to justify its acceptance by pointing to his rights.

The slightly privileged are more distrustful of other individuals and groups.[44] They tend to apply more unfavorable epithets to the pension law and the social worker than do those in less desirable circumstances. Our results show that distrust of others and unfavorable appraisal of the law and the social worker reflect the presence or absence of advantages, although not of the number of advantages held. Distrust, according to these data, can be activated whenever a person attempts to hold on to a possession which he regards as precarious, and the amount of possession has no effect upon the depth of his distrust.

The suspiciousness of the slightly privileged is expressed in their attitudes toward the welfare agencies. According to the stories that circulate among this group, amounting to an incipient folklore, government agencies have no greater ambition than to de-

---

[43] See table 27.
[44] See table 28.

prive the aged of their last belongings. One Institute member told the interviewer that the house of a deceased pensioner on her street had been "locked up and sealed" by the county so that her children could not get it (this may have been part of a legal procedure to establish legitimate succession to ownership.) Another pensioner had bought and was making payments on a television set; she was keeping this set hidden under a blanket in the belief that the amount of her monthly payments would be deducted from her pension check if the social worker learned of this acquisition. One woman thought she was "getting away with something" by concealing a gold chain with a cross, a pair of pearl earrings, and a few other trinkets of little value; she feared that "the welfare" would make her sell these if they were discovered.

A somewhat bizarre example of the extent to which some pensioners perceive the welfare adminstration as a conspiracy against them was given by a female respondent. She believed that the State Welfare Department was in alliance with her separated husband, whom she accused of all manner of malfeasance. Among other things she stated:

> Now I figure the verse in the Bible where it says a husband should take care of his wife, and darn right he should. I said to them [the public welfare agency] that it's the law that a man has to support his wife, and they said they have a different law here. [R. believed that she had a right to her separated husband's assistance check and had asked the agency to send this check to her.] You're darn right they have different laws! They make them up! The laws of California are disregarded all the time.

The social worker's sense of justice is likely to differ from that of the slightly privileged client. Conversations with public assistance workers reveal that they often feel "put out" by the insistent demands for special consideration which come from the slightly privileged group, and are annoyed by the unwillingness of such clients to accept the rules governing Old Age Security. Public assistance workers who must refuse adequate amounts of aid to many applicants who have no outside resources are often offended by the demands of those who are already living in relative comfort. Tensions arising from these differences in perspective and standards of justice disturb the relation between clients and social workers or between clients and social service departments. As a result, the treatment which is accorded the slightly privileged by the social workers tends to be somewhat inconsistent.

In general, social workers try to give the client the benefit of anything to which he is entitled under the law. Where there is room for administrative discretion, social workers and their supervisors frequently interpret the law in a manner most favorable to the client. Social workers often find it necessary to defend themselves, however, against the insistent demands and the hostility of the slightly privileged client. Many develop some prejudice against these clients, and are therefore less patient with them than they are with others. Thus the privileged clients tend to receive unusual treatment—either special regard or special harshness. They are therefore singled out from the common run of recipients not merely by virtue of their social and economic situation but also by the ambivalence which characterizes their relations with welfare workers.

The tensions between slightly privileged clients and the public service agencies have their roots in the ambiguous social status of these clients. The slightly privileged are bona fide members of neither the middle class nor the disinherited and dispossessed, but they cling desperately to middle-class standards despite their dependence. To the social worker they are not typical clients needing and wanting to be cared for; yet they are clients in the administrative sense.

The persistence of middle-class standards among people who, according to the stereotypes of the surrounding culture, should not be counted as part of the middle class, accounts for much of the confusion and uncertainty in regard to the status of the slightly privileged. The attitudes of this presumably underprivileged group are identical with the middle-class attitudes which are shared by social workers and large segments of the public: insistence on private property rights, a propensity to fight and bargain for personal advantage, resistance to manipulation by government agencies, and a strong belief in respectability. But the economic dependence of the clients of welfare agencies makes such middle-class attitudes seem inappropriate. The social worker is tempted to sympathize with the slightly privileged client at the same time that he is repelled by demands that are often unreasonable. Likewise, the welfare legislation, with its ambivalent treatment of pensioners, does nothing more than reflect the perplexity of middle-class legislators and the middle-class publics whom they represent.

Legislative "intent."—California's Old Age Security legislation reflects the complex and shifting motivations of those who make the laws. The "legislator" reflects the cultural beliefs pervading the community, the special interests and attitudes of pressure groups, and the outlook of the adiministrative official and his colleagues in the legislature. Faced with the problem of an increasing population of aged people without resources, and subjected to a variety of forces and pressures, the legislator seems to pursue the following often contradictory objectives:

1. He wishes to be philanthropic and to provide for those who have no income and cannot help themselves. In order to insure that the grants do not exceed what the state can afford to give to its "less fortunate" citizens, the legislator sets a limit on the amount of the grant by fixing the maximum amount that can be paid to any one recipient. If Old Age Security is viewed as a philanthropic program, the grant certainly cannot be regarded as something to which the recipient has a right. Hence the aid is not to be regarded as a pension.

2. At the same time, the legislator wishes to apply principles of social case work by virtue of which the amount of the grant is controlled by the actual needs of the recipient. To the extent that the legislator acts upon this principle, he must provide an appeals procedure enabling the client to show that his needs have not been met. Such a procedure implies that the recipient has a right to an adequate grant.

3. Although, according to the preceding two points, aid should be reserved to those in immediate need, the legislator wishes also to protect the self-respect of the recipient. Hence he infringes upon the principle of need by specifying that the receipt of a grant shall carry no implication of indigency or pauperism, and by permitting the recipient to retain a certain amount of personal and real property.

The law embodies and attempts to reconcile three often antithetical principles: philanthropy, social case work, and social security. It limits the amount of the grant that may be paid out of the state treasury, but also tries to meet the needs of the recipient if this can be done without exceeding the maximum. It states that grants are to be made only where actual need exists, but it shies away from requiring that before becoming eligible a recipient turn into cash, in order to convert into food, the house in which he may have lived most of his life or expend a last $1,200 presumably earmarked for emergency and burial expenses.

Slight privilege, status-anxiety, and conservatism.—By its ambiguity, the law exacerbates the anxieties of a clientele which, by virtue of its position in society, is already predisposed to anxiety. The law also creates within the pensioner population a group of slightly privileged who, because of their precarious situation, are inclined to be distrustful and even hostile. It would seem that a pension "promoter" need do no more than exploit the apprehensions generated by the law in order to gain the pensioners' support for his movement.

The slightly privileged are a conservative group. Their conservatism is not very different from that of the average small businessman: they believe in the rights of private property; they believe in privacy and in freedom from interference by the government in their financial and personal affairs. The slightly privileged have more reason than any other pensioner group to support McLain's fight for higher property exemptions and against the introduction of lien provisions into the welfare law—a program which has relevance only for those who own property. Moreover, the elimination of relatives' responsibility is of special importance to those who have children able to contribute to their support.

At first glance the demand for a pension may appear quite radical. But this overlooks the fact that the subsidizing of deserving groups is a well-established American practice. Veterans' benefits and farm subsidies are familiar examples. The notion of a subsidy is hardly revolutionary; the only thing new is the demand that this practice be extended to a new sector of the population. McLain couches the demand for pensions in terms quite consonant with middle-class ideals. First, the old people deserve the pensions because they are "the builders of a nation." This argument closely resembles those advanced in favor of veterans' benefits. Second, the intrusion of the social worker into the private affairs of the recipients represents an attack upon their dignity. This argument has particular appeal for those who, rightly or not, feel they have something to conceal—recipients with small amounts of property, extra income, and comparatively well-situated relatives. Thus the pension program, as presented by McLain, should prove more attractive to the slightly privileged than to the rest of the recipients.

McLain directs his appeal to the more conservative elements among the pensioners. His method of gaining support differs markedly from that used in other pension movements. Townsend attempted to appeal to *all* the people by proposing a grand plan which would solve the problems of many social groups and which, in its ideology, could attract people from many walks of life. So long as a sense of crisis prevailed as an aftermath of the Depression, Townsend's appeal met with a certain amount of success. His movement disintegrated when the atmosphere of crisis disappeared. But today's slightly privileged, living in a period of general economic stability, are less concerned about how society at large should be organized. They want their personal place in society defined for them. They are much more interested in knowing that "George is working for us in Sacramento" than they are in broad social plans.

This practical attitude explains the support for McLain, even though he has never really pushed his only far-reaching proposal, the pension plan itself. None of the initiatives sponsored by the Institute involved the establishment of a pension which people would receive "as a right." In comparing McLain with Townsend, the slightly privileged member will say:

Townsend was asking for too much. I hear he's in Washington now asking Congress for $200 a month. He won't get nothing, he's always asking for too much.

Now when Townsend came up with his plan he said the Government should give the elderly $200 and the people were all for him. But he didn't do nothing, he was just talking and talking all the time. I don't say he wasn't straight. I think he was, but it was nothing but big ideas and big talk and nothing accomplished.

Townsend's demands are sometimes regarded not only as unrealistic but also as excessive on moral grounds. One woman stated in response to a question concerning McLain's popularity in her neighborhood:

> I never talked much about it to people around here, but from what I've heard they think he [McLain] has done wonderful work. I don't think Townsend has been as good. He's asking for $150 now, I understand. But I guess if we get the $100 that would be enough for awhile. I don't believe in being greedy.

The conservative attitudes of those most easily attracted to the Institute help give the organization its special character. The problems of the slightly privileged are in the forefront. McLain's program is their program. What is more, the slightly privileged personify the membership to other followers. The readers of the *Welfare Advocate* see their pictures in the paper. The radio listeners hear McLain talk about them on his program. Implicitly, McLain seems to ask: "Are you not like these nice people in their neat flower-print dresses and their dark blue suits with conservative ties? People who believe in God? People who have raised their children to be upstanding Christians and who can be proud of them?" There emerges a group of people whom McLain can present as typical members of his organization. Some in the larger audience will identify with that group and will join the movement because they feel that they are or should be like them. If strongly motivated—for a moderate amount of status-ambiguity will breed a large amount of status-anxiety—they may become part of the organization's core of devoted followers.

In our view, status-anxiety is a common characteristic of all the pensioners potentially interested in McLain's Institute of Social Welfare. It reaches far beyond the confines of the organization. Slight privilege is a common characteristic of those pensioners who can be most easily activated. For this reason the slightly privileged determine the style and social attitudes of the Institute of Social Welfare.

Chapter IV | *Organizing the "Old Folks"*

In the face of determined opposition, McLain succeeded in organizing and holding together up to 75,000 followers, many of whom have given lavishly of time, money, effort, and devotion. He has created a substantial continuing enterprise, with a large headquarters, a sizable budget and staff, and extensive operations. In person and by mail, thousands of aged citizens have come to the organization's state headquarters in Los Angeles, above whose entrance is a sign: "Through these portals pass the builders of a Nation." There they have received help and expressed their solidarity with the leader. In their eyes, McLain is the only active worker for the aged, the guardian of their interests.

This success, however, has its own peculiar features. McLain's members are like customers who are devoted to a product and will buy it faithfully but have no independent role. They are akin to radio fans and similar publics held together by a public relations program that is carried on by an outside source for its own reasons. Moreover, by dint of hard work and salesmanship McLain has created a valuable "property," and his members do not question his right to assert complete "ownership" of the organization.

McLain has learned from experience that his most effective appeals are those which play upon the status-anxieties of the pensioners. In his own way he helps them to locate themselves on the map of society. And among his strategies for building the indispensable core of devoted members, the most successful is the singling out of certain members for commendation or reward. These tools McLain uses skillfully to insure a steady flow of cash into the treasury.

The main task of the CISW is to maintain a permanent headquarters capable of organizing the constituency and acting for it. Fund-raising, the major day-to-day activity of the leader and his staff, means a constant preoccupation with members and supporters, for in this organization there is only one significant source of money—the voluntary contributions of the pensioners themselves.

To finance its activities the organization carries on a continuous drive for money by means of a daily radio program on 28 stations, a monthly twelve-page newspaper, 125 fund-raising meetings monthly throughout the state, and a network of about 125 social welfare clubs. In 1954 a weekly television program carried on three channels was added for the duration of that year's campaign. The income of the organization has been as high as $750,000 in a single year, most of it contributed by members whose monthly income is well under $100 a month.

The external political action of the headquarters is intermittent, carried on mainly when the state legislature is in session and during election campaigns. But the task of holding the members together, increasing their numbers, and maintaining a permanent staff requires a steady propaganda effort. Members and supporters are inevitably the prime targets of fund-raising appeals.

Whatever other obstacles there may be to raising funds and conducting successful propaganda, the lack of physical facilities is not one of them. The equipment is new, elaborate, and efficient. Incoming mail—as many as 1,500 letters a day—is systematically handled with the help of consecutive numbering devices: letters are opened by a central group of clerks who extract the donations and route the accompanying messages to appropriate departments; and a bank of automatic typewriters handles routine replies.

The membership control department has speedomat plates for all members, with separate files for delinquents and life members. The status of the member and the number of times he has made donations are recorded. Within a few hours McLain can send out a summons to a meeting or an appeal for funds addressed to all the members, to all life members, or to members living in a particular area.

There was also an extensive political file which at one time listed 2,500,000 registered voters in alphabetical order as well as according to party and precinct. It was the only such list in California and represented a huge investment. For some time it was kept up to date by a crew of girls whose only work was to type the plates and file them.

A print shop managed by George McLain, Jr., handles all the printing for the organization except the newspaper and large campaign posters. The elaborate equipment is kept busy preparing material which is sent out to members in a continuous stream: propaganda, fund appeals, membership cards, receipts, notifications of special meetings, and technical information on the old-age assistance laws. During political campaigns, the presses and the stuffing, folding, and tying equipment are used also by other organizations.

The daily radio programs are usually recorded on tape at headquarters or at McLain's house. The program originates in a broadcasting booth at headquarters and is carried by telephone wire to the various stations.

Between 1948, the year of the CISW's ephemeral victory, and 1954, income never dropped below $28,000 in any given month. The best years were 1951 and 1952, with incomes of $655,000 and $661,000, respectively. The monthly income of the organization has averaged about $50,000 during the period 1949–1954. The income peaks occur in months of intense political campaigning. The highest month was October, 1952, during the referendum campaign of that year, when the Institute collected a total of nearly $130,000. Since that time, average monthly and yearly income has been declining (see fig. 5).

Some of this money is earned by making available the mailing facilities to other organizations and to political candidates for a fee; and vitamins and mineral tablets are sold to readers of the *Welfare Advocate*, following a pattern begun by the Townsend movement. But the bulk of the money comes from membership dues and contributions.

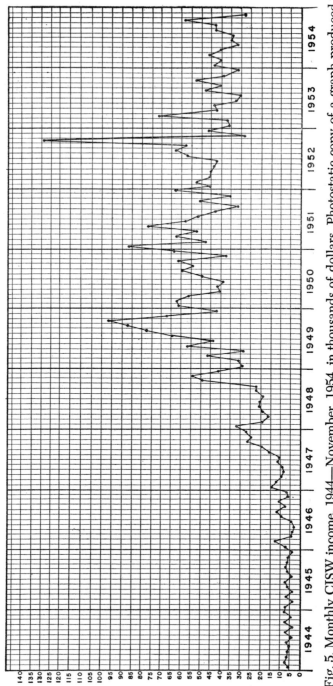

Fig. 5. Monthly CISW income, 1944—November, 1954, in thousands of dollars. Photostatic copy of a graph produced by McLain's office for the internal purposes of his organization.

Members and Dollars

Slightly over half of the money raised by the CISW appears to be collected in the form of dues, and the remainder comes from voluntary contributions solicited over the air and by various other devices. A complete breakdown of income is difficult because the CISW does not maintain separate accounts which would make it possible to distinguish the sources of income.[1] Our estimate is based on the number of members and subscribers carried in the files of the organization, allowing for the probable number of obsolete addresses.

McLain offers his followers two kinds of memberships: regular and life memberships. Until 1954 the yearly dues of a regular member amounted to $5; they have since been raised to $10. Life membership, which formerly cost $75, was increased to $100 in 1954. Most of the aspiring life members are unable to raise the required amount at once, and the usual arrangement is to pay in monthly installments of $5 until the whole sum is paid. Since the only record of such payments consists in notching the address plates, it would be exceedingly difficult to find out how many would-be life members fall by the wayside and never complete their payments. Judging by the "money mail" which we have been able to examine, delays and interruptions in such installments are not infrequent. It might be added that, in view of the average member's life expectancy, the purchase of a life membership does not appear to be a very wise investment.

Those who do not wish or are unable to contribute the full amount of a regular membership can enter into a somewhat looser connection with the organization by subscribing to the *Welfare Advocate* for $2 per year. In 1957 McLain added an associate membership which can be acquired for $5 per year. Thus, there are now five possible financial relationships between a follower and the Institute: subscription, associate membership, regular membership, candidacy for life membership, and life membership.

All subscribers and members receive the monthly *Welfare Ad-*

---

[1] An accounting system that attempted to distinguish between membership dues and voluntary contributions would probably break down because the members themselves frequently fail to specify their reason for sending a given sum of money.

vocate. None has voting rights. Subscribers and associate members are not entitled to the welfare service, which offers advice on pension matters, but this restriction is, in the vast majority of cases, purely academic. Any pensioner can have a consultation if he pays for his membership at the time of seeking advice. There are no other short-term practical advantages to the pensioner in being a member.

The significance of this graduated system of membership is chiefly psychological. The members derive satisfaction from their own feelings of loyalty and accomplishment. Many of them treasure letters of thanks (almost always disguised form letters) from McLain or "certificates of merit" attesting to special efforts they have made for the organization. Life members receive more lasting proof of their leader's affection. They are allowed to wear a golden button bearing McLain's profile in relief. At Institute meetings they are often called upon to stand up and receive the homilies of the speaker and the applause of their fellow members. At times they are allowed to sit on the platform behind the speaker. Annual banquets for life members are held throughout the state.

McLain has invented special devices to convert the life members' devotion into cash while increasing their pride. During the referendum campaign of 1954, life members were given the exclusive "right" of sponsoring a television program which McLain initiated at that time; in exchange for $5 per month they received a gilt-edged certificate naming them as sponsors of the show. Somewhat earlier in the same year, McLain found he was able to channel the enthusiasm of the life members in another direction. In the month of August the Institute organized its first "national" conference in Sacramento. McLain made all life members "delegates" to this conference—provided they could pay their own way. As a special inducement they were assured that no attempt would be made to raise money during the conference. While in Sacramento, the members voted unanimously for all resolutions which were laid before them, and McLain took them on a tour of the state capitol.

The life members themselves are ever conscious of their position. In conversations with outsiders they volunteer the information that they are life members and thus document their devotion to the organization. Regular members, when questioned on this point, will admit that life members are "better" members because they have made a greater sacrifice, or will point out that they themselves have made heavy contributions. Status in the organization is achieved almost exclusively through money gifts. Hence there exists among members an undercurrent of competition to be decided by the magnitude of financial sacrifice.

Status in the organization and cash payment are in some sense equivalent. Our data indicate that the members clearly perceive this equivalence, and that monetary contributions are a way of overcoming status-anxiety. Should they ever be in danger of forgetting this important connection between status and contributions, the Institute's propaganda will serve as a reminder.

"Your Radio Defense"

A daily fifteen-minute radio broadcast has been a feature of the organization since its inception in 1941. This program brings in most of the money and is the major vehicle for sustaining morale and communicating with the members. McLain's followers are devoted listeners.[2] For many, the radio program is a high point of the day. It offers an opportunity for ritual reaffirmation of loyalty to "George," and provides a renewed sense of belonging to something, being cared for, and being in some way a power to be taken into account.

For the first few years, the radio scripts were cautious and uncertain; McLain was apparently searching for a clear-cut propaganda posture. Moreover, he lacked competent help in planning and writing the program. By 1944, however, and especially after 1946, a more self-confident note appeared. The broadcasts quickened in tempo and were shriller in tone. The fund-raising goal became more prominent and the propaganda themes more clearly defined. As the organization grew, and McLain sensed his strength, he undoubtedly felt that he could engage in more urgent appeals for money, and voice complaints about the apathy and ingratitude of his elderly audience.

The appeal for funds is never-ending and insistent. Sometimes contributions are justified as a wise investment: "I could show you

---

[2] See table 42.

in cold cash how your five dollars to the California Institute is the most productive investment in financial return that you could ever make" (March 11, 1952).[3] More often a rhetorical question is posed: "Would you spend five dollars to get back from $60 to $300 a year increase in your pension checks? . . . Now don't tell me that amount isn't worth a five-dollar bill, because YOU know it is and so do I. So do our members who can't understand why you don't join up" (May 9, 1952).

Requests for money are made in connection with special campaign projects also. In the following, the rhetorical question is again posed: "How much is it worth to you—to be assured of a $75 a month old-age pension check?" McLain goes on to explain that the $75 provided for by Proposition 11 would be a minimum based on the value of the dollar in 1948 and would rise with living costs. *"Ain't that something?* Ain't that something worth while putting out a few dollars a month from now on until the November election, to get?" (April 9, 1952).

The need for funds is usually represented as critical: "We hardly have enough money to see our organization through the week" (April 9, 1952). Sometimes the very life of the organization is at stake; at other times, merely the continuation of the broadcasts.

. . . today—it is my sad duty to inform you that unless we can raise some money very quickly—our radio programs will cease—because we cannot meet the bill that is entailed by my broadcasting on this state-wide network of radio stations daily. This situation is not a new experience. It has happened to us before. Every time the folks don't send in their pledges and contributions—we find ourselves in this position . . . if these radio programs stop—we would be forced to close up. [May 28, 1952]

McLain is undoubtedly right. If the membership is to be motivated to contribute money or secure signatures to petitions, they must be reached directly, personally, and emotionally. The goals and needs of the CISW are not mediated and supported by other institutions in the community. Direct communication from the leadership to the rank and file is essential if the membership is to be mobilized for action.

The unmediated and unsupported relation between McLain and

---

[3] All quotations of CISW broadcasts are from the scripts for the dates shown in parentheses.

his membership accounts for the strikingly informal and emotional tone of the broadcasts. The listeners are "the old folks." McLain is "Uncle George." "Uncle George" cajoles and berates; he "exposes" plots and "unmasks" enemies, in language that is sometimes conversational, sometimes haranguing, and almost always ungrammatical.

Lacking institutional support for the implementation of policy, the broadcasts "shock" the membership into activity: "And if this broadcast—and what I am going to tell you—doesn't shock you into activity—then nothing will" (January 9, 1952). Appeals for money are usually crisis-ridden, but so are the requests for signatures to qualify pension propositions for the ballot: ". . . unless we get busy . . . the cause of the aged will be lost. This will not happen—if you people listening to me right now—will stir your stumps—and in more ways than one. Every effort and sacrifice upon your part—is not too great to ask in this all-out campaign" (February 8, 1952).

Not all the broadcasts, to be sure, are so importunate. Occasionally McLain opens the program with a cheery remark about the weather, and may even express satisfaction with listener response: "I am happy to see in the last few weeks—some of you folks— taking out your life memberships and paying the full $75 at one time. . . . It is also encouraging to note the pledges that many of you made—are being kept" (March 10, 1952). Sometimes McLain's request for money is casual: "Would you like to send in some money?" but this is exceptional.

Most of the following analysis of the form and content of the broadcasts, which became more or less stable after 1946, is based on scripts written since that time, especially on a sample of about four scripts a month from January to September, 1952.

The pattern of the broadcasts.—McLain's broadcasts tend to follow a uniform pattern. The introduction, McLain's standard greeting, "Howdy, folks, are you with me?" is followed by a description of the organization: its recent accomplishments, why one should join, and how to join. A plea is made for money and for subscriptions to the *Welfare Advocate*. The address of headquarters is usually repeated two or three times.

The main theme of the broadcast varies with the time of year.

From September until November, in election years, attention is centered on the current political campaign. The broadcasts consist of propaganda for the initiative and efforts to activate the members to collect signatures. When McLain is running for office, the broadcasts are used to support his campaign. In defense of this practice, McLain asserts that he runs for office for one reason only: to make certain that the aged have a spokesman in some legislative body.

After the November election the holiday season provides a convenient occasion for human interest stories and testimonials. Members are interviewed on "what the organization has done for me." The organization's accomplishments are extolled and appeals are made for solidarity.

McLain uses this more relaxed time of the year to make informal comments on the state of the world. One broadcast was devoted to a discussion of "three types" of capitalism and to an elucidation and defense of what McLain calls "People's Capitalism" (August 14, 1944); another discussed the nature of "law" (September 17, 1947). At another time McLain commented, in a philosophic vein, "To me, our movement appears like a precious sweet flower mid a vale of tears and sorrow, and the world's misery with its hate and starvation should make all of us that much more determined to do our bit to uplift mankind while we remain on the earth plane" (November 29, 1945).

During this off season between elections and the opening of the legislative session, someone may substitute for McLain, who is usually described as "busy at his desk," lobbying in Washington, D.C., off on a speaking tour of the state, or testifying at hearings.

From the opening of the legislative session in January until its close, McLain broadcasts from the state capital at Sacramento. On the basis of his "inside knowledge" he testifies to the power and wickedness of the enemies of pension legislation, to his own valiant and successful fight in the committee rooms, and to the constant need for financial support.

The end of each broadcast repeats the introductory exhortation to join and to send money. After an announcement of local meetings, McLain usually closes with a prayer and the familiar, "How about it, folks, are you with me?"

Propaganda themes.—Social movements desiring to mobilize people for unfamiliar and unconventional behavior must tap non-routine, extraordinary, and strong motivations. One way to do this is to arouse basic emotions; anxiety, fear, rage, hostility, aggression. An enemy is depicted whose evil is absolute and intentional and against whom it is morally right to fight because it is a matter of life and death. However, negative feelings are usually insufficient to provide a justification for action. There must also be a sense that positive virtues are expressed, that absolute good is to be reclaimed by a struggle against the enemy.

Out of the broadcasts an ideology emerges. Far from being a rigorous set of intellectual beliefs, it is rather a loose collection of typical American stereotypes; the propaganda is designed not so much to reshape attitudes as to touch off preëxisting prejudices. Negative attitudes toward "special interests," toward the big and the powerful, are stimulated and elaborated, while the welfare movement is equated with the positive virtues of rural life, self-reliance, Christianity. The connections among these are not logically established; the broadcasts merely throw an aura of virtue over the organization by the juxtaposition of ideas, by metaphor, by summoning sacred symbols.

In addition to belaboring the enemy, which arouses negative attitudes, and justifying the cause, which arouses positive attitudes, there is a third propaganda theme: the leader as martyr. Whether intentional or not, the broadcasts tend to augment and elaborate the personalized relation between McLain and the members: McLain gives his all, but is *rejected;* the membership is *ungrateful;* he threatens *abandonment.* The concept of the self-sacrificing parent is never far off.[4]

Enemies.—It is, McLain has said, the "big and powerful special interests who . . . are determined to wreck our social welfare system and make poverty a crime in the State of California" (March 11, 1952). This picture of the enemy began to emerge around 1946, as the radio broadcasts shifted from decrying the bad treatment of the aged by social workers to an attack upon elements in

---

[4] Much of the discussion of CISW broadcasting follows patterns of analysis used by Leo Lowenthal and Norbert Guterman in *Prophets of Deceit* (New York: Harper, 1949), especially chap. iv, "Self-Portrait of the Agitator."

the community that were opposing liberal welfare programs. The enemy is pictured as powerful and well organized. The chambers of commerce and the California County Supervisors Association are presented as having great resources of money and influence at their command. In 1952, when an amendment attached by Senator Jenner to a federal tax bill authorized states to publish, without loss of federal grants-in-aid, a "shame" list of those on the assistance rolls, one broadcast explained the amendment's origin in this way: "This new 'hymn of hate' against the needy—was started slowly—some months ago—by the County Supervisors Association, and by the Chambers of Commerce here in California" (January 9, 1952).

The enemy is portrayed as venal; they are "evil men, with evil ideas and intentions" (January 3, 1952). Opposition to liberal welfare programs is "unmasked" and "exposed" as a deliberate plot.

THIS is George McLain, the Voice of Freedom, speaking *out* and saying—yesterday—if you were listening—I am sure that I dropped a bombshell—when I opened your eyes to the latest maneuver of the "behind-the-scenes" string-pullers of the big chambers of commerce.

Remember—I only got wind of this over the week-end. So on yesterday's broadcast—I exposed the plot and explained to the listeners what we must do if we are to beat these rascals at their own game. [February 26, 1952]

Nor is it the aged alone who are the victims of this plot. The "big chambers of commerce" are the enemies of all the "little people." McLain calls upon his listeners to tell their children and other working people about his "exposures."

Of course, the chambers of commerce are the bitterest foes of ALL of the little people, by which I mean the average wage earner, homeowner, small farmer, veteran, laborer and county taxpayer. [January 3, 1952]

The plot against the aged and the needy is nationwide. Make no mistake about it—what is happening in Washington—and what has happened in Indiana, Arizona and the rest of the country—is a deliberate and planned action by the United States Chamber of Commerce, followed by the various state chambers—to starve needy Americans. And the sooner you people—who are listening to me—make up your minds to join with us—by giving us your moral and financial support—the very same thing will happen here—should we not have the money to put over our pension program. [February 22, 1952]

The financial resources of the enemy are not merely private but public; the enemy is in a position to divert public funds to propaganda against the aged. Here is McLain's accusation woven into his traditional apening:

> Howdy, folks—are you with me?
>
> This is George McLain, the Voice of Freedom, transcribing and speaking out against the enemies of the needy and the enemies of the state and county taxpayer. Today, I shall expose to you how the California State Chamber of Commerce, your big local chambers of commerce, your County Supervisors Association, your real estate lobby, and "phony" taxpayer lobbies, have this year COST you, the people of California, "many" MILLIONS of dollars. [January 18, 1952]

He goes on to argue that chambers of commerce in California receive something like $3,000,000 a year from county and city officials through a special tax levied against real property. This money, according to McLain, quoting statements of lobbying expenses as evidence, is used to fight pensions for the aged and welfare measures for all the "little people" of the state. "Can't you see—how every decent right-thinking person must come in with us—because UNTIL we stop public funds from going into the pockets of the enemies of the people—the enemies of humanity itself—they will keep on forever in their diabolical plot to entirely destroy the dignity of man" (January 14, 1952). One of McLain's favorite terms is "merchants of misery," and he calls for help in his effort to "put a stop to these misery merchants from doing their evil work with public funds" (February 22, 1952).

The late Senator Fred Weybret, chairman of the California Senate Interim Committee on Social Welfare, was a constant target for McLain. The following attack on Senator Weybret shows McLain in one of his more genial and folksy moods as he "exposes" another misuse of public funds.

> Seems like Fred Weybret and his anti-pension Senate Committee has been doing a lot of investigating into the statements made to the county welfare authorities by the children of old age and blind pensioners. Plenty HEAVY investigating—and "frantic Fred" found—that a son—whose mother was receiving the old-age pension—had filed what *Frantic Freddy* claimed was a "false report."
>
> Even tho' the son had no less than FIVE dependents—Weybret said—"he should have contributed $30 a month to his mother." I can just see Senator

Weybret's jowls "quivering" and his chest "heaving" in righteous indignation—against the sons and daughters of old-age and blind pensioners who are unable—for one reason or another—to contribute to the support of their parents.—Now let's take a second look at this. If you will remember—in the last regular session of the state legislature—the Senate put thru an appropriation of $40,000 of our tax money—for the use of Senator Weybret and the rest of the pension "hatchetmen." To date—under this appropriation—Freddy has spent $10,000. TEN THOUSAND DOLLARS TO DO WHAT? To find a "son" who—FREDDY SAYS—should be contributing to his mother—$30 a month!

Now I ask you—ladies and gentlemen—isn't that a "heck of a way" to spend the people's money? Here we need money for schools and for veterans' administration—for hospitals—for relief of the physically handicapped—and men in public office like Weybret—get $40,000 no less to "squander away." [March 10, 1952]

An occasional target is the press, which is bound to be antiwelfare, the argument runs, because it is controlled by the money and political interests of the state. In McLain's political guidebook the chambers of commerce and the county supervisors are controlled by big business; the pension foes in the legislature are in turn influenced by the chambers of commerce and the supervisors; at the bottom of the hierarchy stand the newspapers. A substitute made the following statement in a broadcast when McLain was ill:

The propaganda supporting publication of "shame lists" is enough to make any decent person sick at their stomach. The Los Angeles *Daily Mirror*—some weeks ago—published a cartoon entitled: "Don't Invade My Privacy." It had a spotlight titled: "Publicity for Relief Cases"—and the spotlight was on a rat stealing a piece of cheese which was entitled: "Taxpayer's Money"—and the rat was called: "A Welfare Chiseler." [January 9, 1952]

Occasionally about a third of the broadcasting time is spent in telling some story about "persecution by the enemy," and the *Advocate* prints additional accounts. One anecdote concerned an Oakland man who was "arrested, handcuffed; brought all the way down to San Bernardino; finger-printed and photographed—and thrown in the County Jail like any felon, or a murderer." The man was considered legally responsible for the support of his mother, who was receiving old-age assistance in San Bernardino. The authorities charged him with failing to fill out a "responsible relative's" form, which, according to a recent law, was a felony. When the Institute investigated the case, they discovered that the man had an income of only $160 a month to support himself and his wife, and therefore was not legally responsible for contributing to his mother's support. It seems that he had filled out and sent in the proper form, that it had been misplaced, and was found after the imprisonment. McLain's broadcast, commenting in the case, maintained that the county supervisors had no authority to ask for a bench warrant for the man's arrest and had violated a law in having him picked up and taken from Oakland to San Bernardino. McLain added that, in fear of reprisals, the man was not bringing suit against the supervisors. "In telling you this, I do so to let you know that the same thing might happen to your son or daughter if you are on the old-age pension" (April 15, 1952).

One broadcast was a defense of McLain's portrayal of the enemy. McLain reported that "an elderly lady" had told him that the chief administrative officer of Los Angeles County could not be as bad as McLain had pictured. "You are just saying that to get people to join your organization." McLain recounted to his radio audience that in reply he had shown her a clipping from the May 8, 1952, edition of the Whittier *Star-Reporter*. He then went on to read and comment on the clipping.

"RELIEF TOO LIBERAL—SAYS NEW COUNTY ADMINISTRATOR"

That was the heading. The story then went on to quote Mr. Wills' remarks before the Whittier District Realty Board and I'll quote a few of them to you. This is Wills speaking: "It isn't charity—any more, it's a payroll," Wills told his audience. "We hardly ever see these people. We just grind out checks. It's a grand deal for everyone except the county taxpayers," he said.

McLain added: "These are enemy statements, folks. These are the things your enemy thinks and says" (May 28, 1952).

Justifying the cause.—Whatever the degree of truth in representing the enemy as evil, powerful, wealthy, and organized, the conclusion is driven home that the power of the enemy is achieved through organization and money. The answer is counter-organization with ample financial resources.

The California Institute of Social Welfare—does not mean George Mc-Lain. Nor does it mean pensions. The California Institute means a great group of people who are fed up with being pushed around—they are fed up with having to fight and struggle to stay alive—they are fed up with politicians who promise them everything and once elected—give nothing. They are fed up—"period." They want to do something about it—but to do something costs money. So they pooled their resources and by membership dues—they build and still maintain the California Institute of Social Welfare. The results they have produced—the changes they have wrought— have almost been miracles. Theirs is a public service record that [they] can be justly proud of. As their chairman—I invite you to join with them. [March 24, 1952]

The anxiety-creating effect of the image of the enemy drawn by the broadcasts is sometimes acknowleged and defended: "You know—lots of times—I have received letters from you listeners —accusing me of trying to scare the old folks—that the things I said could never happen—and that I was making mountains out of molehills" (February 20, 1952).

It is highly probable that McLain's listeners do express such sentiments, if for no other reason than that organized action against the pillars of the community must appear to many as unconventional and unprecedented. One device to spur such organized action is to emphasize the venality of the apparently respectable opposition; another is to convince his listeners that organization on their part is merely a new variation of a traditional and accepted virtue—the American virtue of self-reliance.

In one of his least strident and most reflective broadcasts, Mc-Lain spoke of the "words and the views of some of our American leaders on the social welfare state of the nation." He quoted several statements including the famous: "If all Americans want is security, they can go to prison," and then went on to say:

The future—the future of social welfare and human dignity will reveal for all to see just what our leaders think in their own hearts about the needs all over the land. And the people will be waiting to find out. That is, all the people except those in California. Here in California, we have an organization called the CISW, that has taught and preached continuously to the people to get out and think for themselves and to "DO FOR THEMSELVES." [January 23, 1952]

Implicit in many statements is the effort to create and augment distrust of politics and politicians. This is countered by assurances that the CISW is a practical, service-minded enterprise; it is distinguished from utopian ventures and dissociated from politics.

Old-age pensions were a political football—and a "come-on" put forth by individuals and organizations, for years and years before we came into the picture. Nothing was ever done for the old people or the blind—who were considered as nothing but objects of charity—who had to be paupers before they could even get a pittance of aid. And their need was played upon by the politicians and the promoters. We came into the picture from a service angle. To help in the daily welfare problems of the individual—and it was in this way that we learned the inequities of present laws, and the need for a good down-to-earth, practical humanitarian program. To take the place of the glittering soapbubbles blown up to attract the old—as a drowning man would grasp at a straw.

Today—the maximum amount of the old-age pension payments per month is $75. The maximum amount paid to the blind is $85. We did it. [June 16, 1952]

The CISW is under repeated attack from an articulate section of the community; some of these attacks question the motives of its leaders, and especially of McLain. The broadcasts, recognizing and relaying these attacks, reassure listeners that the organization is respectable and trustworthy.

This ten-year record of achievement and labor is proof in itself of the public confidence, faith and trust enjoyed by us and should be proof to even the most skeptical, that ours is an effort worth contributing to. [January 23, 1952]

The very fact—as I have pointed out in the past—the very fact that we have been making consistent progress for eleven years—proves that we have the trust and confidence of the people of this state. [April 15, 1952]

Such remarks are defensive, reflecting the weakness of the CISW rather than its strength.

It is somewhat startling, in view of the age of his constituency, to hear McLain calling himself "Uncle George." When Charlie Bender substitutes for McLain on the broadcasts he speaks of himself as "Cousin Charlie." The CISW is often described as a "family": "You know, as Uncle to the thousands that go to make up our great family of members in the California Institute . . ." (April 15, 1952).

One function of propaganda is to surround the new and doubtful with an aura of the tried and true. The image of the CISW as a "great California family" evokes a sacred stereotype. The broadcasts sometimes link the CISW to the virtues of rural and small-town life—a propaganda device that tends to trigger uncritical positive responses. McLain once described decision-making at headquarters in this way: "All of us folks down here in your state headquarters—kind of got together yesterday morning—around the pot-bellied stove—to form a 'spit and argue club'" (March 18, 1952).

Another function of propaganda is to relate parochial interests to the general good. "We are proving beyond the question of a doubt, that not only do we stand for livable pensions, but that we stand for everything that is good for the community" (January 3, 1952).

Although the propaganda of the broadcasts plays upon a number of typically American themes, the distrust of politicians, of money, of the city slicker, it does not exploit racial and ethnic feelings.

> Our organization, the CISW, spends its time and effort working in behalf of the people—people like the old and the blind, physically handicapped, poor little children and even for the homeowners, the farmers, the county taxpayers, and organized labor. . . . It's composed of folks from all walks of life, of every race, color and creed and of horizons, and what is so important to a true citizen—a new happiness founded in the knowledge that they are helping to improve their community, help their fellow man, and defend and protect the rights we hold so dear. [January 23, 1952]

The appeal to religious or semireligious attitudes is the most prominent device used to justify the CISW. References to "God's work," the Christlike mission of the organization, and the piety of its members and its leader run through the vast majority of the broadcasts, each of which ends with a prayer. Some begin with one also; sometimes a word like "faith" or "charity" is taken as the keynote of the broadcast.

> This is George McLain, the Voice of Freedom, transcribing and saying, "We walk by faith—and faith is an outward visible sign of an inward and spiritual grace." So sayeth the Good Book . . . [PAUSE] . . . And I can tell you this. If I, as Chairman of the California Institute of Social Welfare, if I didn't have faith, and if our thousands of members and friends didn't possess faith, the social welfare system here in California would be in such a mess of inequities, confusions and restrictions, that I seriously doubt whether anyone in need would want to be on the aid rolls regardless of what the consequences would be to their personal self.
> While our great cause is not religious, there is of necessity a certain

amount of kinship because our work is in behalf of the needy. We help those who cannot help themselves—we fight for the rights that some unscrupulous forces would like to see denied these folks who are considered too old to work. [January 3, 1952]

The religious theme is often used to bolster appeals for contributions and membership fees.

Yes, every day right here on this little old radio program at 3:45 P.M.—thousands and thousands of good, God-fearing people listen to my stories—they hear me give the public record of our achievements and our work of helping people—they have even from time to time heard the very person we have helped speak out on these broadcasts. And yet they have never once sent in one thin dime to help us in our cause—which is the cause of the Dear Lord—because it is the weak, the needy, the sick, the lame and the halt that He thought of first. [April 30, 1952]

The speaker as a martyr.—One impression created by the broadcasts is the indispensability of George McLain. A substitute speaker put the point clearly:

George has warned you time and time again—that the chambers of commerce would get you—if you don't watch out. . . .
George McLain was right.
. . . This "hymn of hate" against the needy . . . has now commenced to take on serious proportions—and the only man of prominence and in a position to oppose this vicious move is—George McLain—and the California Institute of Social Welfare. [January 9, 1952]

The language of the scripts is highly personalized. It has the shaming, petulant tone that an unappreciated head of a family might use to scold ungrateful dependents. McLain sometimes threatens to abandon his charges.

During these past eleven years—the saddest burden that I have had to carry in my heart, has been the knowledge, that out of 277,000 old age pensioners—whom I have helped to get $75 a month—only a "few" of them have appreciated my fight in their behalf—to become members of our organization. . . .
In the last few days—I have had a *double shock.* Because I have learned that even those who are members have "failed" to respond to this all-out fight that I am waging. . . .
It's bad enough when you don't respond to my plea for money. But what earthly alibi can you have when I am NOT asking for money—just an hour or two of your help—and you don't respond?!
. . . So I'm making it clear right now—as I have for the past eleven

years—if you are NOT with me—I can't go on. Because I can't hope to accomplish anything more in your behalf—unless you're with me, folks—all the way. And after all—I ask so LITTLE of you. . . . [PAUSE A MOMENT— THEN AS FORCEFUL AS POSSIBLE]: . . . I WANT 99,000 NAMES BY THE END OF THIS WEEK!

I don't want those names for George McLain. I have no use for them. I want those names to help every old-age pensioner in California, get a better way of life. Because by stopping the chambers of commerce—we're stopping the old people's worst enemy. . . .

Can't you understand—old folks, CAN'T you understand—that every day we don't have these signatures—it's costing us money—ALL KINDS OF MONEY! . . .

The lack of action on these petitions—seems to be the same lack of action I get when I send a letter out asking for money. Only about ten per cent response. It puzzles me—because I can't understand *why*. . . . Is it because you love the chambers of commerce? Is it because you don't think I've done a good job for all these years? Is it because you don't believe in the California Institute of Social Welfare, anymore? . . . . OR IS IT BECAUSE YOU DON'T THINK!

If it's because you don't think—and I sincerely hope that's the reason—you certainly have something to think about now. Because I have laid it on the line in this broadcast as I have never done before.

. . . I want those 99,000 names!

Or I am going to walk out the front door of this headquarters and I'm never going to come back. If you don't think enough of me and the work I am doing—to send me in just six little old names to those petitions—then I'm wasting my time. And you might just as well not have an organization or a Chairman. [January 26, 1952]

Two days later he drops his characteristic opening of the last ten years—"Are you with me?"—and refuses to use it again until listeners show that they are "with him." He also drops his usual phrase, "This is George McLain, the Voice of Freedom" because the "elderly people of this state—and their sympathizers have allowed the burning flame of freedom to die in their breast . . . and I refuse to make a mockery out of the sacred word: FREEDOM" (February 28, 1952).

The same tone pervades the following script:

On June 29th of last year—I underwent major surgery—and while recuperating—I had a divinely inspired vision—how the elderly or old folk's enemies could be stopped dead in their tracks. The weapon given to my brain—was a law to prohibit the county boards of supervisors from giving money to the chambers of commerce and other privately controlled organizations.

Before my convalescing period was over—I crawled out of my bed and took on a rigorous state-wide speaking tour—only a month after I had come out of the hospital. A speaking tour that meant talking three times a day and covering thousands of miles—from one end of the state to the other.

I put the idea of my brain before thousands of cheering people who promised to back me up. . . .

The sad truth was brought home to me—that cut into my heart like a knife. YOU FOLKS have been letting me down. And while you have been letting me down—you are letting your enemies walk in to destroy you. If you won't bestir yourselves to do the things that I ask you to do—then there is no sense in me asking you to do anything more—as I am only wasting your time and my time—and there might as well be a parting of the ways. . . .

Now of course, you know we can't operate without money. It is necessary for us to have a steady income every day to keep our work going—because we only exist day to day—according to your response. Yet if you will notice —this past week—I have not asked you or taken the time—regarding our money problems. This—in itself—goes to show to what length—I am willing to go—to assure the qualifying of these petitions against the chambers of commerce—which means so much to the cause I've been fighting these past eleven years.

Finally, the pension leader's long-suffering martyrdom has its religious parallel:

THIS is George McLain—pension advocate—who works for pensions— talks for pensions—sleeps and eats pensions. This fellow, McLain, seems to have nothing on his mind but old-age pensions.

How are *you* doing?

Are you satisfied to let poor old George McLain do *all* the work and you —nothing? I hope not. You can't expect one man to do all of the fighting and working—because one man can be snowed under and "buried" by numbers of the opposition.

Jesus found that out when He was crucified on Calvary. Only the Holy Mother Mary and a few close friends were there to openly mourn. In our work—just like that of Jesus—you are either for a cause WHOLE-HEARTEDLY —or you're not at all. [April 14, 1952]

Institute Meetings

Another regular device for reaching the members, and some potential members, is the fund-raising meeting. These gatherings vividly and poignantly epitomize the relation between the members and their leaders. CISW meetings are scheduled by headquarters for the primary and explicit purpose of soliciting contributions.

Since 1949 the number of such meetings throughout the state has fluctuated between a hundred and two hundred a month. Two full-time speakers, paid by headquarters, cover the meetings. In addition, area officers speak regularly, and occasionally other staff members as well. The full-time speakers travel from place to place, normally conducting two meetings a day, one in the late morning and another in the early afternoon. A secretary travels with the speaker, handling the money collected as donations, dues, and subscriptions to the newspaper. Meetings are held in American Legion halls, labor temples, churches, and sometimes private homes. Occasionally headquarters will be denied use of a hall and may be hard put to find an appropriate meeting place.

The speakers bureau at headquarters plans meetings well in advance, contracts for halls, and keeps an accurate record of attendance, funds collected, and overhead expenses. The collection may be as high as $1,000 in a Los Angeles mass meeting or as low as $15 in the little town of Lodi.

The report of one speaker showed that during December, 1950, a total of $1,862.92 was collected at twenty-three meetings, an average of $80.99 per meeting. In the following month $1,964.88 was collected at twenty-four meetings, an average of $81.87 per meeting. Dissatisfaction was expressed with the January record, for "January should have been a much better month."

Although, in some towns, meetings are held twice a month, and metropolitan centers with area offices hold them weekly, the monthly meeting is most common. Outside the metropolitan areas, attendance ranges from as few as ten to as many as three hundred. Approximately two-thirds of all meetings are held in the southern half of the state. The weekly meeting in Los Angeles, usually held in a movie theater, is the largest and most important. McLain usually speaks, and often has political candidates and other public figures address the audience.

Attendance is not consistent at meetings, nor have speakers been able to develop any rule of thumb for predicting attendance in advance. One generalization, however, can be made: when Mc-

Lain is scheduled to speak, attendance increases noticeably. A June meeting in Compton drew 90; in July, 51; in September, 90; in October, 61. In November, when it was advertised that McLain would speak, attendance jumped to 225. At Bellflower, in June, 52 people were present; in September, 25; in October, 26; but in November, when McLain spoke, 110 turned out.

The following account of a meeting in Pasadena describes fund-raising on an occasion when McLain spoke and the audience was comparatively large. This was a meeting in which some preparation, organization, and expenditure had been invested. It had been announced that McLain would be present at the meeting on September 5, 1951. Attendance was relatively high. There were 215 people in the audience: 130 women and 85 men; 6 of the women and 5 of the men were Negroes. The meeting was held at the women's club, a respectable meeting hall not far from the downtown district.

Before the meeting an accordionist played hymns on the stage and asked for requests from the audience. Charles Bender, the Institute speaker, opened the meeting with the Lord's Prayer and a salute to the flag, the standard opening for all Institute meetings. After three jokes had been told, the collection baskets were passed through the audience as the accordionist played "Bringing in the Sheaves."

Bender then announced that McLain would transcribe one of his radio programs from the stage of the hall. Bender asked the audience to clap very loudly when he introduced McLain on the radio program. After three practice demonstrations of applause, Bender expressed satisfaction with the audience's response. After the broadcast, Bender took up an "Old Gold" collection.[5] One person gave a gold tooth and a small nugget. Bender then asked if anyone in the audience wanted to join the organization, and two people raised their hands. Bender then introduced McLain.

McLain's speech claimed credit for the recent pension increase of $5 to the aged and the blind: "We were the only group in the whole United States to do anything." He regretted, however, that the increase was voted for a period of only two years and that it

---

[5] During the 1954 campaign, McLain had asked his followers to contribute any items of gold they might have to the campaign fund.

was not proportional to the increase in the cost of living. To illustrate his argument, he brought a woman member to the platform and gave her a pail containing twenty-five silver dollars. He said, "We are handing you $25 not once but every month for life." He was referring to the new pension bill the Institute was sponsoring which would add approximately $25 to the average California pension. McLain said that the silver dollars used in the demonstration were contributed by members and were washed and cleaned by people at headquarters.

McLain counted out thirteen dollars into a pail to show how much the old-age pension increase should have been to keep pace with the rise in the cost of living. He then brought out a sack containing another twenty-five silver dollars to show the medical fees the "old folks" would be able to pay if Proposition 11 passed, and added a piece of paper to symbolize the burial benefit of $150 included in Proposition 11. McLain said he had stopped a bill in Sacramento which would have permitted the sale of bodies of destitute pensioners to medical and embalming schools. "We've seen to it that you won't be put into a pauper's grave."

After his speech, McLain undertook the fund-raising himself, asking first for $100, then $50, and finally $10 contributions. Bender then went up and down the aisles taking the smaller contributions while the accordionist played "The Battle Hymn of the Republic," the audience timidly and halfheartedly joining in. As the money reached him McLain announced the names of the donors, and spurred the audience on: "I have $50! Who will make it $55?" People began to leave during the collection. Although more than half the audience had already left, the basket was again passed around to make up the difference between the $580 already collected and the $600 which would "break the record." The meeting ended with the singing of hymns. The audience, a rather well-dressed and apparently middle-class group, had contributed an average of about $3 each.

The members do not seem to resent the insistent fund-raising at meetings. On leaving a meeting in Glendale, one woman said to another, "Bender has left already." The other replied, "He got the money and that's what he came for." Neither woman appeared to be critical; both seemed to accept the speaker's fund-raising role and to take a measure of pride in his skill. Not only do members respond to these appeals, but some do not go to meetings unless they can afford to contribute. Others make the meetings the occasion for paying dues.

In contrast to the Pasadena meeting, with its large attendance and professional entertainment, a poorly attended meeting was held in December, 1951, in the home of two members of the Institute, at Buena Park, a small suburb about thirty miles east of Los Angeles. Only twenty-two people were present, fifteen women and seven men. The speaker, William Townsend, opened with the Lord's Prayer and a salute to the flag. Townsend told the audience that the meeting had almost been canceled because of lack of response. He urged the sale of the *Advocate,* discussed the petition drive, and gave instructions regarding the signing of petitions. He then addressed the meeting for forty minutes, arguing that taxes were high and that the McLain proposition would reduce them. The audience was quiet and even apathetic during the talk.

Townsend told them that the organization was always "up against it," but especially in December, when, because of Christmas and bad weather, contributions fall below normal. He asked for the renewal of memberships in advance, and for payments on life membership. He said that the new year might be a "make-or-break" year for the organization, and that everyone at headquarters was eager to start it with enthusiasm.

While the collection was being taken, a member from La Habra introduced members of his club from that city, a suburb of Buena Park. He told some jokes and read a poem, "I'm Not Dead Yet," written by a ninety-year-old woman. During the reading of the poem some in the audience began to doze. The La Habra member then gave a seven-minute recitation in German dialect, part of which he read. After the recitation, Townsend made another short speech in which he attacked the county administration. Later he complained privately that the collection had been extremely poor. Aside from the entertainment provided by the La Habra member and a few questions concerning the petition drive, there was no participation by members.

Letters

Perhaps the least effective of fund-raising and propaganda methods is the direct-mail appeal. This is true for the Institute as for most organizations. According to the usual McLain pattern, the letters and circulars predict catastrophe, stress the organizations' record of achievement, and appeal to the members' self-interest. Fund-raising letters are sent out at times associated with giving, especially Christmas, Easter, and McLain's birthday.

The following appeal for funds, printed on special stationery showing the picture of an infant, purveys the Christmas spirit.

To You Who Believe:

Dear Friend:

During this Christmas month most of our minds are on the spirit of giving.

While to some this spirit lasts for only thirty days, to we who work for the 277,000 elderly men and women who are dependent upon old-age pension payments to live, "we give" untiringly of our efforts and fortunes for them all year around.

This finds us at the end of the year as an organization, destitute and in dire circumstances because of the lack of money to carry us through. Even this month of December we are fighting desperately to exist. And unless more hearts and more minds turn to us in our hour of need, we will not be able to see the month through.

We know that the Good Lord is aware of everything we have achieved in behalf of His Children. So we ask you in His Image and Likeness to forsake us not, but to use the enclosed self-addressed, postage-paid envelope that you may put us on your "gift" list.

Beside our grateful blessings, you will find some Christmas Carols which we have printed here in the old folks' headquarters to show you how much we appreciate the help I know you will not fail to send us in this, our darkest hour.

"Give and ye shall receive—even a widow's mite will be blessed."

I remain spiritually in your cause forever.

> Faithfully yours,
> GEORGE McLAIN
> Chairman

LIGHTING THE WAY FOR BETTER LIVING

An acknowledgment of money received is appropriately decorated with a Christmas tree:

DECEMBER The Month of CHRISTMAS

"Blessed are they that put all their trust in Him."

Psalms 2:12

Dear Friend:

In giving us your help you have lived up to all of the things promised us the Holy Morn on which the Saviour of the needy was born.

May God keep you in His loving care not only this Christmas but always, and again my deepest appreciation.

Yours faithfully
GEORGE McLAIN

An Easter card, sent in March, 1952, displayed a picture of Christ with the caption, "And when the Angel rolled away the stone from the Sepulchre, a New Religion was born."

A "thank you" note ends characteristically.

Many thanks for your kind remembrance on my birthday. Your thoughtfulness was indeed welcome.

May God in His infinite wisdom grant like blessings on your house.

Yours in Appreciation,
GEORGE McLAIN

Interspersed in the cycle of holidays are requests for donations for specific purposes: lobbying, election campaigns, the defense of McLain when he was attacked by the Senate Interim Committee on Social Welfare, and court costs when the constitutionality of the law on the responsibility of relatives was tested in 1953.

Such letters are usually more hardheaded than the holiday appeals. During the 1952 election campaign 64,000 letters went out to members. Despite previous pleas, the letter says, the organization's financial needs are far from being met. McLain encloses ten "I gave" stickers, and concludes:

Please don't lose any time in contacting your grocer, druggist, landlord, business firm, friends and neighbors and ask them for a donation of at least one dollar. Some will give you $5 and others even more, depending on you and your approach. In this way I know you can raise $10 or more.

In the meantime, because of our desperate financial circumstances, WILL YOU ADVANCE US A $10 BILL ON THE BOOK, by using the enclosed envelope, and mailing the money to us RIGHT AWAY.

Sincerely yours,
GEORGE McLAIN

In a follow-up letter, dated January 15, 1951, to those who had not responded to an appeal for money dated eight days earlier,

McLain sounds the personally aggrieved note characteristic of the broadcasts:

Dear Friend,

Above you can see our legislative staff in action, working [McLain is referring to a picture at the top of the letter]—yet here it is January about gone and I haven't heard a word from you. I am frankly puzzled. What is wrong?

Just a short while ago, I wrote you a letter and even enclosed a return—self-addressed envelope.

I have worked so hard to help the pensioners. No obstacle has been too great for me to overcome because I have had faith in the oldsters and believe in their integrity and their willingness to join together in their own behalf.

Here in Sacramento I am putting everything I have behind the passage of our new pension measure, which will mean the final victory and a new way of life for each and every one.

However, because I haven't heard from you, I feel that in some way I have displeased you. Therefore, I am taking this valuable and important time out to personally write you.

Now when we are on the very threshold of success here in Sacramento, won't you let me know what I have done or the reason why I haven't heard from you?

Awaiting your reply, I am still

Faithfully yours,
GEORGE McLAIN, MANAGING DIRECTOR

In 1953 an especially elaborate form letter was printed to solicit renewals from those whose membership had expired. Its two pages (four sides) were printed in red, white, and blue. It began "IN THE YEAR OF OUR LORD, 1953," and ended "MULTILITHED BY THE OLD FOLKS." It was signed by Myrtle Williams as secretary-treasurer. The first page of text reads as follows:

Dear Friend:
What would you do . . .
How would you feel . . .
Where would you go . .
How would you live . .

IF YOU WERE A PENSIONER AND THIS WAS YOUR NOTIFICATION THAT YOUR NAME WAS TAKEN OFF THE PENSION ROLLS AND YOU WOULDN'T RECEIVE ANY MORE CHECKS?

WHERE WOULD YOU GO FOR HELP if as a pensioner you were notified that your monthly check has been reduced to $40.00 . . . ? Or even $25.00 a month as is now being endorsed by the U. S. Chamber of Commerce, the American Association of Physicians and Surgeons, and the California Taxpayers' Association among others.

If you were on the Blind pension, where would you go?

TO WHOM could you turn for help?

Where would you bring your grievance?

Who would listen to you once the fatal decisions had been made?

The answers are NO ONE . . . NOWHERE . . . YOU WOULD BE DESOLATE,— LOST! Because by that time it would be too late. The wild horses of reaction and "grab" would have long since high-tailed it down the road leaving you standing flat-footed on the last desperate miles of the highway of life without friends, funds, or strength to travel on.

In short,—YOU WOULD HAVE LOST YOUR PROTECTION—
    LOST YOUR SECURITY.

The letter goes on to recount CISW accomplishments in defeating antiwelfare bills in the state legislature. It also lists the services included in the $10 membership fee: a subscription to the *National Welfare Advocate,* membership in social welfare clubs, help with pension problems, and legal aid. The letter concludes:

We could go on and on. But the point is simply this:

YOUR MEMBERSHIP HAS EXPIRED.

BY LETTING YOUR MEMBERSHIP BECOME DELINQUENT

YOU HAVE PLACED YOURSELF IN JEOPARDY.

How can you expect us to put over our wonderful national and state campaign for $100 a month as a right without the help of everyone interested in a decent old-age pension system that is permanent.

If you believe in the fight for dignity and self-respect of our elderly citizens in a world of "Haves" rather than a world part rich and part needy, then you will act with all haste to renew your membership today.

Cordially yours,
MYRTLE WILLIAMS, Secretary-Treasurer
California Institute of Social Welfare

In response to McLain's radio appeals, headquarters receives an avalanche of letters, mostly from members and some from outsiders. The average amount of mail can be estimated at 15,000 letters a month, but there are extreme variations. The largest proportion of the letters from members is "money mail" (to use the jargon of headquarters) containing dues or contributions, usually in cash. Letters are often accompanied by excuses for the lateness or the smallness of the contributions, words of encouragement or gratitude to McLain, general comments on the pension or the state of the world, or bits of information about the pensioner's personal affairs. A small proportion of the letters are communications of a similar kind containing no money. Special occasions, such as McLain's birthday, bring a wave of "nonmoney" mail. In 1954, for example, McLain received about 5,000 birthday cards, most of them containing no money.

The tone of these letters tends to be personal. Most of them are addressed directly to McLain. About one-third of the members use the familiar "Dear George" as a form of address. The more formal "Dear Mr. McLain" or "Dear Mr. McLain and Mrs. Williams" are most frequently employed. Some letters begin with such phrases as "Dear Institute" or "Dear folks at headquarters," or simply McLain's own "Howdy folks." In spite of the emphasis on monetary matters, the "nonmoney" mail is not ignored, and the style of McLain's response explains the personal tone used by the members. Modern office equipment is used to give the illusion of a personal reply. All personal letters, whether or not they are accompanied by money, are answered with the help of automatic typewriters. To the member, the Institute is more than a protector, a pressure group, and a status-ascribing organization; it is, or can be, a good correspondent as well.

The "Advocate"

The Institute publishes a monthly twelve-page tabloid newspaper, the *National Welfare Advocate* (formerly the *National Pension Advocate*), which is distributed to all members. This is a fairly typical house organ, containing articles on pension issues, reports on McLain's activities, and routine information on scheduled meetings and broadcasts. The paper appeals to members for funds and for activity during petition and referendum campaigns, and some effort is made to increase the sense of member participation. The social welfare clubs are encouraged to compete for the honor of giving the largest donation to headquarters, and some human-interest items contribute modestly to community feeling. Activities of individual members and clubs are reported, as well as inspirational columns and stories of people helped by the organization.

About one-third of the space is given over to advertising, mostly by credit dentists, chiropractors, oculists, hearing-aid agencies, and other health services. Some of these capitalize on the medical benefits the pensioner is allowed under the law, featuring an "authorized" service or "free" product. The paper maintains that it will not sell space to "quacks" or to people who mistreat pensioners. One chiropractor was dropped because of complaints by members that they were badly treated.

From December, 1952, to December, 1953, the paper devoted its political space to attacks upon the enemies of Institute-sponsored propositions; criticism of the United States Chamber of Commerce pension plan; monthly coverage of lobbying activities in Sacramento; several extensive discussions of the relatives' responsibility law; a surplus-food plan offered by McLain that received some national publicity; news of the state convention and the attempts to put the organization on a national basis; and McLain's state tour beginning the drive for a $100 maximum monthly pension.

The paper usually includes a few news items on national pension issues or the problems of individual states. A rather bleak picture is drawn, and an occasional editorial comment stresses the need for organization and the success of McLain in California. Political issues are sometimes treated if they relate to pensions. During elections the candidates supported by the Institute are given publicity and the opportunity to present their views. On the whole, the pension issue dominates, and no broad social or political philosophy is promulgated.

Like most such papers, the *Advocate* is the spokesman of headquarters. There is no effort to make it a forum for individual expression of opinion by members or for debate on problems facing the Institute.

Social Welfare Clubs

In his first radio broadcasts in the summer of 1941, McLain called for the establishment of pension study clubs in each of the eighty Assembly districts of California. There would then be a pension counsel in each community to advise members on pension problems, to represent them, "and to conduct Dinners, Dances, Socials and meetings of interest." This reference to study clubs and socials was repeated in subsequent radio scripts, but no action to organize groups was taken. The subject was tentatively raised again by McLain in 1943, but was soon dropped.

During the next eight years the organization grew in size, wealth, and political power, reaching a climax with the successful 1948 referendum campaign to increase pensions and to reorganize the State Department of Social Welfare. Relying on his daily radio talks, the *Advocate,* and meetings throughout the state, McLain was able to mobilize the members sufficiently to circulate a petition, distribute propaganda, and raise funds. The organization apparently ran well enough without local clubs.

History.—The 1948 victory was almost too complete, for it was followed by some loss of membership and a spirit of crisis at headquarters. This gave new impetus to the idea of creating a network of local clubs to strengthen the organization, and the program was finally begun in 1949. Since that time the clubs have had a sporadic existence, with spurts of energy alternating with periods of lethargy. The club program has added little strength to the organization, but it does show something of the meaning of the Institute to its members and its leader.

A former organizational director of the Veterans of Foreign Wars was hired by McLain to set up the club program. According to the new organizer, the "membership was disintegrating." His functions were "to help run the Proposition 4 campaign . . . to change the administrative setup of the office," and to plan the organization of the clubs to assure that complete control would rest with the board of trustees, that is, with George McLain.

The plan originally proposed by this professional organizer sought all the benefits that could come from an active club program:

. . . the purpose of the plan to authorize subordinate units of the California Institute is: (1) to accelerate the rate of membership acquisition; (2) to conserve membership; (3) to provide means to control, direct, and coördinate activities in the fields; (4) to extend our membership potential by acquiring through local units complete lists of all pensioners, responsible relatives, small homeowners, and others; (5) to increase membership revenue sufficiently to provide funds for all home office needs; (6) to provide a local nucleus for precinct work; (7) to make free pension service available in each community; (8) to provide a workable means of expanding our operations to other states.

Every precaution was taken to assure control by the board of trustees. The plan called for social welfare centers whose elected presidents would serve on a county council. The presidents of the county councils would in turn serve on a council with members of the board of trustees. But the by-laws and constitutions of the centers and councils were to be set up by the board and could be changed only with the board's approval. Similarly, the center and council charters could be revoked by the board for a variety of reasons.

The plan was almost completely rejected. According to its author, McLain was "frightened to death of the program because of the possible loss of control, even though I told him it could be set up so that it always would be controlled." The original document has extensive notations in McLain's handwriting, almost all of which deal with forfeitures of membership and charters. However, even the extensive safeguards in this direction were not sufficiently reassuring.

Meanwhile the club idea was given publicity in the *Advocate*. The February, 1950, issue carried a story announcing the formation of these centers "intended to provide members with a wider social life and give them a service organization." Membership in the centers was limited to not less than fifty nor more than one hundred persons. The March, 1950, issue of the paper reported that "applications for charters flood in from all over the country," and, a month later, claimed that hundreds of applicants had come to headquarters. But nothing was done to make the proposal a reality.

Seven months later, in November, 1950, another attempt was made to set up the program. A new organizer was hired who had much experience in both Democratic and Republican party politics, and who had been associated with McLain in the Ham and Eggs movement. From November, 1950, to January, 1951, McLain and his staff worked on the by-laws, constitution, and programs.

According to the new club director, McLain was enormously demanding and wrote, rewrote, or edited every line of the constitution and by-laws. He continued to express anxiety lest the clubs get too much power.

At first, considerable effort went into organizing the clubs. The Institute had a list of 7,000 petition circulators who had worked in the 1950 campaign. These activists were asked to organize clubs in their areas. There was also extensive newspaper and radio publicity for the long-delayed venture. But in April, 1951, four months after the first clubs were set up, the club director was moved to a new position in the organization, and for more than a year the program was left without a staff member to direct it. Responsibility was left to a clerical employee. The clubs continued to receive the "Clubgram," but this too was suspended from January to August, 1952. In the summer of 1952 a new club director took over, issuing a whole series of new rules, adapted mainly from the ritual of the Moose lodges, where the new director had gained his organizational experience.

McLain's attitude toward the club program has wavered between using such a device for fund-raising and some political activities, and the fear that he might lose control of his organization. The sporadic attention paid to it by headquarters reflects the constant shifting of the positions of staff personnel, the high rate of turnover, and the repeated but discontinuous attempts to solve administrative problems by reorganizing and setting up new units. There seems to be little desire on the part of the membership itself to participate in a club program of any size.

In the fall of 1952 there were said to be 200 active clubs operating in the state with an average membership of thirty. These figures are probably too high. The October, 1952, issue of the *Advocate* reveals only 92 clubs listed in the club calendar.[6] Although it is probable that not all the active clubs sent in their meeting dates, it is unlikely that more than 100 failed to do so. There may have been as many as 125 clubs. The listings of club meetings in the *Advocate* up to July, 1954, show between 90 and 100 reporting. The clubs are scattered through the state; about 57 per cent of them are in southern California.

[6] The original goal stated in the news letter was 10,000 clubs.

Structure and activities.—According to the by-laws, the purposes of the clubs are:

A—to secure new members and the necessary income for the maintenance
of the California Institute of Social Welfare and to conduct an educational
campaign among tax payers, pensioners, responsible relatives and all other
citizens of the community; B—to make available information concerning the
services and benefits offered by the California Institute of Social Welfare
and where these services may be obtained; C—to advance our program for
better pension and social welfare laws in our state and nation; D—to conduct social and recreational activities for the members in your community.

It is clear that the clubs have been assigned no advisory role
and no function as formulators of policy. Neither do they have any
authority independent of that granted by the Institute, which
gives their charter and may suspend or revoke it "should any Social Welfare Club act in default or violation of these by-laws or
for any other good cause." Lest there be any misunderstanding
regarding the clubs' relation to headquarters, section 4 of the by-
laws, headed "Authority," states that "in order to maintain a uniform standard of operation, the clubs shall adhere to these by-laws
and future instructions from State Headquarters of the California
Institute of Social Welfare."

The club structure is extremely simple. Charters are issued by
the board of trustees whenever fifteen members in the same area
apply for a charter. Each club has four officers: president, vice-
president, secretary-treasurer, and chaplain. Every club is held to
by-laws established by the board of trustees.

Reflecting McLain's fear of a possible challenge to his leadership, the clubs are kept organizationally separate. Clubs in the
same area do not have a council; neither are they represented in
any state body of the Institute. Each club operates independently
of every other club, although there is occasional informal coöperation.

In the first days of the club program, membership in a club was
open only to members of the Institute, but this was changed in
May, 1951, when the clubs became open to "any citizen of good
reputation upon the payment of $1.00 registration fee." However,
only members of the Institute could become officers, and any offi-

cer who became delinquent in his Institute membership automatically ceased to be a club officer.

The limitation on club size clearly reflects McLain's fear of losing control. Originally, maximum club membership was set at one hundred, but in 1951 this was reduced to fifty. This limitation undoubtedly stems from a situation known to McLain in which a Townsend club with more than a thousand members grew powerful enough by virtue of its size and treasury to dominate the organization in southern California and ultimately to split away from it. Interviews with persons associated with the club program revealed that McLain specifically limited the club size to fifty because of his fear that the Townsend experience might be repeated in the Institute. As McLain explained, "This is my organization and I'm not going to let anyone take it away from me."

Club funds.—The problem of maintaining control affects the finances of the clubs also. The by-laws state that "not more than $10.00 shall be retained in the club treasury at any time." Any funds in excess of that amount are sent "immediately" to headquarters as a contribution.

The clubs have no monthly dues, and the only expenses permitted are for refreshments. Meetings are held at the homes of officers or members "except when other available meeting places may be desired and secured free of charge." Further, "Funds contributed at any Social Welfare Club meeting shall under no circumstances be used for a contribution to any purpose or cause other than the California Institute of Social Welfare."

One of the stated purposes of the clubs is to raise funds for the Institute. Two types of fund-raising are specifically called for in the by-laws: the general collection to meet the cost of refreshments; and donations and membership fees to the Institute itself, plus subscriptions to the *Advocate*. At some of the meetings, money has been raised by raffles, auctions, and penny-catchers.

The time and date of club meetings are also restricted by the by-laws. This might seem a simple precaution lest club meetings and regular Institute meetings inadvertently conflict. But the wording suggests that this control is meant to minimize the possible competition of club meetings with the Institute meetings, the latter being the more successful fund-raising device. The by-laws state:

The meetings of the Social Welfare Clubs shall be entirely separate from the regular public meetings of the California Institute of Social Welfare and in no instance shall the club meeting dates be held on the same dates as the regular public meeting dates of the Institute established by State Headquarters except by written permission from the State Organizer. The clubs are urged to aid in building the Institute's regular public meetings' attendance.

Lest club meetings be used for political purposes not acceptable to McLain, the by-laws state:

. . . the California Institute is a nonpartisan, nonsectarian organization. Partisan political talks or controversial discussions should be avoided. No candidate should speak at any club or other meeting of the Institute unless approved by State Headquarters and his remarks should be confined to a statement of his stand on the program of the Institute.

In practice the clubs often violate the by-laws, and there is little effective control from headquarters. Some meetings have had more than fifty members in attendance; political candidates not approved by headquarters have spoken at club meetings; and collections have been taken to assist a sick club officer. But on the whole these deviations are minor, and no important challenge to McLain has come from the clubs.

Club meetings.—Most of the clubs meet once a month, in spite of a change in the by-laws published August 1, 1952, that made a minimum of two meetings a month mandatory. Of the 92 clubs listed in the October, 1952, *Advocate,* 54 held one meeting during the month, 36 two meetings, and 2 met weekly. Clubs having more than one meeting monthly usually reserve one or two of the remainder for a "potluck" lunch. The clubs that meet more than once a month are, for the most part, the larger and more active ones.

Most of the clubs hold their meetings in the daytime beginning anywhere from 10:30 A.M. to 2:00 P.M. Of the 92 clubs mentioned, only 6 meet in the evening. The explanation for this, given by the Institute staff, is that the members "get tired early" and therefore go to bed early.

Somewhat less than half of the clubs gather in members' homes. The remainder meet in city parks, private halls, or churches. The practice of using private halls or churches where rent must be paid is in violation of the by-laws. But the clubs may be unaware of this, and headquarters ignores the infractions. Most of the homes are probably too small, and may be considered socially inadequate by the club members.

Because of the lack of direction from headquarters, the procedure varies considerably from club to club, reflecting members' common understanding of club life, or, where there is a dominant personality, his special background. In the absence of prior organizational experience, a club flounders in a sea of confusion and may eventually drown.

One club dominated by a disabled veteran married to a pensioner was conducted along the lines of the organization with which the leader had had the most experience—a veterans' group. His home, where the meetings were held, boasted a sign on the lawn reading "Social Welfare Post." The meeting itself was extremely informal, but whatever formality did exist could be traced directly to the leader's past experience. He referred on occasion to the "adjutant," by whom he obviously meant the secretary, and the salute to the flag seemed to have a deeper meaning than at other meetings of the Institute. No business was taken up; the entire time was devoted to a speech by an active club organizer from the southwest section of Los Angeles.

In direct contrast to this gathering, with its lack of formal procedure and business, was the very formal meeting, held in a park clubhouse, of a Yiddish-speaking club in a predominantly Jewish district of Los Angeles. The dominant figure in the club was the secretary, who apparently had a background in the labor movement or in "cause" organizations. The meeting, attended by nine men and six women, began very late, but the leader was at the hall an hour beforehand to fix the tables, arrange chairs, and generally set the stage.

Normally, the business of this club is conducted in Yiddish, but because of the presence of a guest speaker was conducted in English that day. First came the salute to the flag. The chairman then read a proposed agenda and asked for its acceptance. The agenda consisted of a report from the clubs' executive committee, the existence of which is itself distinctive; and a discussion of a party to be held jointly with another branch in the Boyle Heights area.

The agenda having been accepted, the leader gave the executive committee's report, which was followed by a rather lengthy discussion. There was a higher degree of participation than was observed in other club meetings, again perhaps because of the members' past organizational experiences in Jewish working-class groups. After the business discussion, the collection, and the payment of Institute dues and newspaper subscriptions, all of which lasted more than an hour, the guest speaker was introduced and heard. Sponge cake and tea were then served while the members listened to an "educational reading."

The entire meeting was conducted in a rather stiff and parliamentary manner. Questions were asked "through the chair," and the chairman, although obviously dependent for guidance upon the secretary, maintained order at all times. There was no confusion over organizational forms, and the conduct of business was well regulated.

Another contrast was the gathering of a dominantly Negro club in the home of a member. Here the combination of a strong leader and the members' shared experiences resulted in an atmosphere closely akin to that of a Negro church group. The members called each other "sister" and "brother" and punctuated the speeches with cries of "amen."

After the secretary had collected Institute dues and newspaper subscriptions, the meeting began with the singing of a spiritual, a lengthy Bible reading by the chaplain, a hymn, and the salute to the flag. The "business" included a discussion of the petition drive, a report on sick members, and a discussion of a party to be held jointly with another Negro club. Little attempt was made to channel the discussion, which centered on the relation between the church and "old people." A collection was taken and the meeting ended with a long prayer-blessing by the chaplain.

These meetings illustrate the lack of direction from headquarters and the influence of a strong leader upon a relatively small, unstructured group. Whatever reasons may exist for this lack of direction in the past, such as McLain's fear of the club program and the relatively minor amounts of money raised in this way, the results are easily observable.

For McLain the clubs have three main functions: they are a fund-raising instrument, a device to increase membership, and an action group.

As a fund-raising instrument the clubs are remarkably ineffective. In 1952 only about one-twelfth of the Institute's total income came from the clubs. This is probably due to several factors. (1) The total number of club members is small, and the number who attend meetings regularly is even smaller. (2) Fund-raising in the clubs is without efficient organization or professional guidance, in contrast to the Institute meetings, radio appeals, and direct-mail appeals. (3) Club members are faced with a conflict of loyalties. They have a limited amount of money to contribute. Confronted with the choice of donating anonymously through the clubs, or directly to "George," from whom they receive personal thanks (even if only in a form letter), they choose the latter. The club meetings are not understood by the members as a primary channel for giving money. This attitude, combined with the lack of professional fund-raisers, prevents the clubs from becoming an important source of income.

As a membership-recruiting device the clubs are similarly ill-equipped. Members of the Institute are recruited by McLain's radio program or, less likely, by a friend. Rarely do they join after having been taken to a club meeting. At club meetings little is said about recruiting, although the subject is sometimes discussed in very general terms. But recruiting itself can rarely take place unless, like fund-raising, it is organized. Here again the lack of direction from headquarters is apparent in this weakness of the clubs.

It is difficult to determine to what extent McLain has conceived of the clubs as action groups for political purposes. Certainly there has been no consistent or sustained effort to use them as such, though this may be a result of their weakness as much as a cause of it. In any case, the lack of direction in the club program makes them ill-fitted for effective action.

Successful mobilization requires a close similarity of organizational forms, in order that every group can be reached in the same manner, through the same device. For the social welfare clubs a variety of devices and forms would have to be used, and efficiency would thereby be lost. Even a deeply committed membership would be difficult to mobilize in the absence of appropriate organizational forms.

One of the remarkable features of the McLain movement is the existence of a large core of devoted members who spend long hours collecting signatures for petitions, distributing propaganda leaflets, raising funds, contacting other members, and helping in the office. All these activities are carried on despite advanced age with its limitations, physical and psychological. Yet rarely is this work related to membership in a club. The member relates himself directly to the Institute and its leader.

There have been two occasions when the clubs might have been used for action purposes by headquarters: McLain's congressional campaign in the spring of 1952, and the 1952 campaign to pass the Institute-sponsored propositions 10 and 11. The members did little to support McLain's campaign, and the clubs in no way provided a political machine. The campaign was conducted almost completely by paid workers. After his defeat McLain complained, "My own members didn't support me the way they should have, much less the rest of the pensioners in the district."

In 1952 the Institute had a proposition on the ballot for increasing the old-age pension. However, although there was a full-time club director, the lack of direction from headquarters was apparent, and the clubs were not effectively used. At some of the meetings there was much confusion concerning the use of campaign placards; literature was piled on a table at the beginning of the meeting and remained there at its end; and some of the campaign material already paid for by members' donations was sold back to them at club meetings as a part of the fund-raising work.

The lack of success in using the clubs cannot all be laid to poor direction. At one meeting the chairman, an Institute activist, had taken a great deal of time and trouble to map out the whole city of Glendale by streets for the purpose of distributing literature from house to house. At this meeting, attended by twenty people, he begged for volunteers to make these distributions, but only two or three people responded, and thousands of leaflets remained unused. Similar observations were made elsewhere. Many clubs probably had one or two activists who made such maps, posted placards, or distributed literature, but most club members did not participate.

Members as Clients

The Institute is distinguished from earlier pension movements by its more limited, practical goals. It offers no radical money reforms or panaceas. Rather, McLain has concentrated on "bread and butter" demands for increased old-age assistance and for specific changes in existing legislation. In this sense McLain does not have a "pension scheme," as his opponents often claim. His opposition to relatives' responsibility and to the public listing of those who receive assistance is shared by many other groups in the community. So too is his effort to gain more centralized control of the program for the State Department of Social Welfare. Debate stems mostly from differences over the amount of aid and from suspicion of McLain himself, especially of his methods and ultimate objectives.

A corollary of this emphasis on specific objectives is the effort to provide day-to-day service to the members of the Institute. This unique feature of the McLain movement deserves detailed attention. In 1949, during informal hearings before the Unemployment Insurance Appeals Board, McLain sought to convince the referee that the organization was purely a service organization and met the requirement that "no substantial part of the activities . . . is carrying on propaganda, or otherwise attempting, to influence legislation." [7] McLain, under questioning by his own attorney, testified to the early activities of the organization.

What we did at that time was, we welcomed, put ads in the paper and invited all elderly people who were dissatisfied by their treatment from the County welfare to come in and explain their cases, and we did that all over Southern California, to find out what their problems were, and that was one of the things that gave us the desire to go ahead because we found that the elderly and blind recipients of old-age aid were being mistreated by the County Welfare Department. . . .

. . . for a long time we didn't have any money, and I did practically all of the work myself, interviewing the cases, handling the cases, going before

[7] Unemployment Insurance Appeals Board, Tax Decision no. 701, June 16, 1949, Sacramento.

the County welfare officials, appearing before the State Social Welfare Department. I did practically all of the work myself, and only when we started on the radio did we start receiving money, and add more girls to handle the necessary functions of the organization.[8]

Attorney Raiden asked, "Has this welfare work continued . . . ?" McLain: "It has never ceased." "Has it increased?" "Yes, it has and if we could afford it, we would have more welfare workers." [9]

When McLain went on the radio for the American Citizens' Pension Association, welfare work was part of the three-point program he repeatedly outlined: "A Pension Counsel in each community to advise members how to secure the present pensions and intercede for speedy action." [10]

Such a counseling and advisory service, backed by intercession with the county and state administration, might well have considerable appeal among the aged. Many people lack the skill to interpret administrative forms, or at least feel impotent when confronted by them. Poor health, failing eyesight, and other mental and physical disabilities increase the difficulty. Often there is a sense of embarrassment or even shame connected with applying for or receiving the pension, and the applicant or recipient is all too willing to let the social worker decide everything.

Why do people come to the Institute for help? The prospective applicant may come before applying for aid because he has a generalized fear and distrust of bureaucracy. Getting old-age assistance is not a matter of merely walking into an office, stating one's age, and automatically receiving a check. Forms, interviews, birth certificates, proofs of residence, and names of relatives must be produced, and a multitude of other technical details must be cleared up before the magical check is forthcoming. All this is known among the indigent aged, though in a vague and fear-provoking way. For some applicants, therefore, the trip to the Institute office may well be a step into a charmed circle where all problems will be solved.

Once the application has been made, the prospective pensioner may come to the Institute because he is suspicious of the judg-

---

[8] Unemployment Insurance Appeals Board, Hearing, February 9, 1949, Sacramento.

[9] *Ibid.*

[10] Broadcast, August 18, 1941.

ments regarding his budget of needs, property requirements, relatives' responsibility, limits to earnings and savings, or other items that affect his eligibility and his grant. Often he is afraid to challenge administrative judgments for fear of losing all, and cannot easily be convinced that this is an unwarranted fear. In the light of these problems, the Institute's claim that it gives advisory and legal service to its members is an important one. An organization that did nothing else, yet did this well, might have great appeal for pensioners.

Extent of the program.—Judged by the amount of money spent on it, the welfare service is *not* one of the major activities of the Institute. The Senate Interim Committee found that, during 1947, only about 8.5 per cent of the salaries paid went toward welfare work ($2,604.80) and less than 9.5 per cent in the first half of 1948 ($1,416.51).[11] This may not be a fair indicator, in part because of the wide variations in salary paid to staff members. According to the *National Welfare Advocate*, there were, in 1950, three welfare consultants at the Los Angeles office, all of whom contributed columns to the *Advocate* advising readers on legal and administrative aspects of old-age assistance as well as technical and legal problems of the blind.

In addition to the service performed by the central office, all speakers are instructed in the mysteries of the pension laws and are expected to help members at the various clubs and meetings they address. It is impossible to say how much of this is actually done. More important, perhaps, is the work of the area offices. At one time or another, welfare consultants have been active in San Diego, Fresno, Sacramento, San Francisco, and Oakland; although this work is somewhat sporadic, it is clear that McLain considers the service important enough to keep a minimum of two staff members assigned to it regularly.

The Los Angeles office keeps a record of the number of cases handled daily, and the number of mail inquiries received. The total is impressive; it suggests that the service is important to the members and that roughly 10 per cent of them use it each year. Consultations (mail and personal interview) at the Los Angeles office in 1952 and 1953 averaged 10,220 yearly. If we add to this

---

[11] Weybret Report, p. 87.

the minimum estimate of similar services rendered at the Oakland field office, alone, we have at least 1,000 more instances of personal consultation each year. Of the total an undetermined number are "repeat" calls, since a single member may write more than one letter or call more than once. Even assuming that one-third are repeats, the adjusted total of 7,480 consultations is still more than 10 per cent of the membership of 68,000. The percentage would be higher still if we included the services rendered by speakers in the field; and we cannot estimate the usefulness of the *Advocate* columns or of the occasional information mailed to members concerning changes in the assistance laws and related matters.

George McLain, in his broadcasts and his *Advocate* column, at various times has claimed a monthly average of 1,000 cases handled. This figure is somewhat high, but apparently not greatly exaggerated. The records in the Los Angeles office show that in 1952 a total of 5,516 calls were made at the state headquarters asking for advice and assistance. Records are kept both by the main receptionist and by the welfare department, and were in substantial agreement. In the same year, 5,581 letters were received. The year 1953 showed 4,399 calls and 5,345 letters. For the period December, 1951, to May, 1952, there were more than 20 calls a day, six days a week, at the Los Angeles headquarters, and about 500 mail inquiries each month handled by the department.

Most personal consultations occur in the early part of the month, immediately after the assistance checks have been received and when complaints or problems are most likely to appear; 40–50 recipients a day may come to the office at this time.

Written records cover only cases requiring follow-up action with county and state agencies. The great majority, requiring only advice, are not recorded separately, however, but only as part of the total number of cases handled daily and monthly. For this reason it is not possible to determine accurately the percentage of repeat calls. The consultants themselves believe that the number who return after the first call is "fairly small" and restricted to "the folks who just like to have an excuse to come in and talk."

The steady flow of welfare mail is in marked contrast to the cyclical excitement stirred by political agitation and political crises in the organization as a whole. From December, 1951, to May, 1952, the monthly average of 503 welfare-service letters varied by no more than 70. But the gap between the highest and the lowest amount of *all* letters received was 11,173. In 1952, there were only two more letters in the welfare service in May than in February, while 10,000 more letters in all were received in February than in May. Evidently a sustained need is met here, however adequately.

The service is described as free to all, but in practice the policy is similar to that of other organizations doing practical work for members. As in a trade union or chamber of commerce, the service is free to members, but not to those who do not share the financial burden. The Weybret Report raised an eyebrow at the claim of free service available to all who need it; since then, McLain has made the position of the organization explicit. In the *Advocate* (September, 1953) he explained that "while our service was free, it was free to members of the Institute." An earlier headline in January, 1951, read, "He joins us: wins $1,200 back pay. . . . The five dollars he gave as membership dues to get our free service was strictly a gamble on his part. He didn't believe anything could be done."

Character of the service.—Most of the work of the welfare service consists in giving information and advice to members on budget problems. The bulk of such advice concerns old-age assistance, but some destitute mothers eligible under the Aid to Needy Children program have also been helped.

The Institute at times intervenes actively on behalf of its members with case workers, supervisors, and administrative officials of the county and state welfare departments. If some decision seems incorrect or unfair to the Institute staff, an appeal is made to the State Social Welfare Board. Such an appeal involves a formal hearing before a referee, and the Institute acts as counsel for the member.

The record of success in these appeals appears to be high. Frank Gardner, who directs the Institute welfare service, states in the May, 1954, issue of the *Advocate* that, over a three-year period, 82 per cent of the appeals cases were won by the Institute, and that a total of $19,729.01 was recovered for clients. In 1951, 14 out of 17 cases were won; in 1952, 18 out of 22; and in 1953, 22 out of 27. Not only were pension payments recovered, but many members were restored to the pension rolls. These figures do not include the cases settled directly in negotiations with welfare officials.

This good record in appeals cases is due in part to the skill and experience of Gardner himself. According to both state and county social workers, he knows the laws thoroughly and represents his clients in an able and responsible manner. Although totally blind, he conducts interviews with the aid of a secretary who reads the relevant documents to him. His handling of the pensioners is sympathetic and patient, and he is personally effective in his appearances before the welfare authorities.

Another reason for this success is the responsible manner in which the welfare service is conducted. At present the Institute does not attempt to appeal cases unless it is convinced that the complaint is legally defensible. Over the years, increasing attention appears to have been paid to the legitimacy of the cases appealed by the Institute.

The advice given to recipients is based on knowledge of the law and its limits. Social workers are not berated during the consultations; on the contrary, if a member attacks his case worker for some action, the Institute staff will often come to the latter's defense if the action was necessary under the law. Only once in the history of the organization did the Institute officially complain about the behavior of a case worker. As a result of this complaint and a subsequent investigation, the worker was transferred to a job requiring no contact with recipients.

County and state social workers are not considered enemies by the Institute consultants. Indeed, over a period of years a certain community of interest has developed between the Institute welfare staff and some of the case workers and supervisors in the county offices. A complaint brought to the Institute is often handled in an informal way and treated as a problem which both groups have a common interest in solving quickly and without fuss. The Institute staff can protect the county office by informal negotiation, though it can also communicate the implied threat of pressures by McLain: "If George finds out what's happened here, he'll raise hell with your office over the radio." County workers who have learned from experience that the Institute staff will protect their interests are more likely to seek a solution for the pensioner than they would if every error was immediately called to the attention of McLain and was given unfavorable publicity.

Attitudes of official welfare bodies.—The Institute welfare service is regarded with mixed feelings by the heads of county and state social welfare departments. Because of the wide variation in county practices and standards, as well as the differences in opinion among county leaders, McLain has a history of sharp conflict with some counties and fair relations with others. A negative attitude toward McLain usually means that the office will insist on purely formal, official relations rather than informal coöperation, although some counties have refused to deal with the McLain organization on any level. Usually, however, even a hostile office will process complaints and queries from the Institute as quickly as possible. As the organization is a potent political pressure group, its communications will normally be given special treatment and come to the personal attention of the district director.

Differences in professional training and experiences seem to affect attitudes toward McLain among the county personnel. While it is rare to find a county worker who wholeheartedly approves of McLain, the professionally trained case workers are more likely to understand the social roots of his strength and to be correspondingly more tolerant. The nonprofessionals, on the contrary, tend to regard McLain much less favorably. Professional workers have a better understanding of the role that pressure groups can play in influencing the administration of complex government programs. They know that some of this influence is salutary, if only because McLain can act as a spur to speedy disposition of difficult cases.

The officials in the State Department of Social Welfare do not always share the attitudes of county workers toward McLain. In Sacramento, McLain is regarded as a *product* of the old-age assistance problem; county officials tend to view him as the *creator* of the problem. Since the state personnel have a vested interest in control of the program by their department, an objective which McLain has championed, they see him as something of a mixed blessing. Because the administration of the program is in the hands of the counties, they bear the brunt of McLain's attacks, while the state office emerges relatively unscathed. Moreover, in his lobbying activities McLain often finds himself supporting the state administration, which becomes at times his uneasy ally.

Role of the welfare service.—Although it brings in only a small portion of the Institute's income directly, the existence of the welfare service is useful to McLain in raising funds and supporting morale. He mentions the work frequently in his broadcasts; the newspaper runs stories of its activities; and it is "sold" to the prospective member as an example of what the organization can do for him. McLain places a high value on the service, even though he occasionally complains about the expense it entails. To be sure, he has attempted to make it a "paying proposition." Pensioners who seek advice must join the Institute; donations are solicited from members when they are given assistance. When a case on appeal involving a sizable sum of money is won, an even greater effort may be made to get a contribution, sometimes through Mc-Lain's personal intervention. And at one time the welfare staff received a commission on all donations made as a result of their efforts. This practice has been discontinued, however, and the trend has been toward acceptance of the activity as an important and distinctive function of the Institute that sets it apart from other pension organizations and should not be required to pay its own way.

Chapter V | *The Followers*

THE Institute plays a great role in the lives of its more devoted members. For many of them, not a day passes without their remembering "George" and the Institute at 3:45 P.M., when McLain's program goes on the air. Yet most of the members are rather uncertain about the year they enrolled or the circumstances surrounding this event. They seem to have drifted into the fold by listening to McLain's program and occasionally sending a contribution. Since headquarters makes it a practice to issue membership cards to contributors who send the equivalent of the yearly dues, many may have acquired membership without actually intending to do so. The following quotations are typical of the responses of signature collectors to queries concerning their enrollment:

"I guess I joined by mail. I was living in the mountains at that time on some mining property that I owned. This was before I was injured, before I even figured on getting a pension. I was always for the old folks. I had friends in the mining camps that were old-age pensioners."

["When did you join?"] "1947 or so." ["How?"] "Heard George over the radio; kind of got in the habit of hearing him." ["Know anybody who belonged?"] "No. We were asked by a friend to manage her rest home for a week while she was away; there were several ladies on the same floor. They would sit in the main room talking away to each other; then every day exactly at 3:45 they would all get up and go to their private rooms or cubicles, where most of them had radios, and would listen to George. As soon as we left there we went down and joined. We didn't miss a meeting till I had a heart attack."

Some learn about the Institute by hearsay as they cast about for means of solving their financial problems. Its welfare service is known, by reputation at least, to people in the pensioners' environment, and many join for the purpose of obtaining a consultation. One of the respondents, not yet sixty-five years of age, became a member when she was faced with the problem of providing for an aged aunt.

"I needed help for my aunt's pension. I went to talk to Mrs. . . . at the Institute." ["How did you hear about it?"] "One of my friends told me. He knew through another friend who was on pension. He's a businessman in town. He has his own folks, whom he takes care of. He built a home for them on his place. He knew my case was different, and he advised me about the Institute."

Joining the Institute is not an act of conversion. Rather, it is a way of implementing long-standing inarticulate desires for organization and participation. (See chap. iii.) Nor does the existence of the organization come as a surprise to the pensioners who join it. In our nonmember sample, 75 per cent of the respondents were aware of McLain and his group. This figure may be artificially large, owing to the self-selection of our respondents, but an estimate of 50 per cent is probably conservative.

Moreover, the pensioners who do not belong to the Institute have a fairly good opinion of McLain. Of nonmembers, 33 per cent who know his name believe that he has the best group for old people, while only 16 per cent designate it as the "worst" group. In appraising the organization, 62 per cent of those who judge it favorably say that they believe McLain gets laws passed for the benefit of the old people, and 60 per cent think that he makes the country aware of the problems of the aged. McLain's critics among the recipients commonly believe that he "exploits the old people" (57 per cent), but a relatively small group (23 per cent) thinks that he "spoils the older people's chances to get better laws passed for their benefit." It may be inferred that the reputation of McLain and his Institute is better among the people with whom the pensioners come in contact than it is in the press and, perhaps, among other sectors of the citizenry. The signature collectors report that they encountered very little resistance when approaching strangers for their signatures; they felt that "everybody is for the old folks," and most of them could recall no more than one or two refusals.

In view of the political and social attitudes current in the pensioner's milieu, the transition to membership involves no emotional strain. The recipients experience no contradiction between their basic striving for status and respectability and their adherence to a movement which has had an exceedingly bad press in the community. Newspaper opinion has little effect on some groups, as many election results have attested.

Friends and Enemies

Although the road from nonmembership to membership is a smooth one, participation in the Institute results in important changes in attitude. The members develop a greater interest in the legal technicalities and the politics of welfare administration, and, as a result, their world becomes complex to the point of confusion. In turn, this complexity generates feelings of insecurity and a need for protection. With these go heightened feelings of distrust. These changed feelings and attitudes serve to strengthen the members' attachment to the organization.

We have found that such changes in attitude are directly related to the amount of money a member donates. *The more money he contributes the more likely he is to display the patterns of behavior and the beliefs and attitudes that are most characteristic of the organization.* The heavier a member's contributions, the more likely he is to accept the ideas conveyed by McLain, to display distrustful attitudes, and to participate in the activities of the Institute. It thus appears that money contributions are a rather trustworthy indicator of involvement in the organization. We have, therefore, consistently classified the members according to the size of their financial sacrifices.

The classification of members by pecuniary sacrifice overlaps widely the classification by membership type. On the average, life members make higher contributions than do the highest contributors among regular members. Moreover, life members feel that they have a special stake in the organization by virtue of their investment and their long-continued participation. Those who are making payments toward life membership contribute $60 per year and often make additional voluntary contributions. The two groups of aspiring and actual life members were therefore considered as the groups most involved in the Institute.

An attempt was made, further, to divide our nonmember sample into groups which would in some sense parallel the involvement classification. These pensioners do not contribute to the Institute; the only criterion for gauging their nearness to the organization was their acquaintance with the name of George McLain or that of the Institute of Social Welfare. Thus, while members are classified by the vigor of their response to McLain, nonmembers are classified by their accessibility to his propaganda.

The sample groups, according to degrees of involvement, are as follows:

A. Nonmembers

1. Those who do not indicate that they are acquainted with any organizations of or for the aged.
2. Those who, although acquainted with old-age organizations, do not indicate that they know about McLain.
3. Those who indicate that they know McLain.

B. Members

4. Those who state that they are not members of the Institute and (or) have not contributed to the Institute during the past three months, but whose names appear on its roster.
5. Those whose yearly contribution to the Institute (subscription to paper or donation) amounts to $2.00 or less.
6. Those who contribute between $2.01 and $10.00 per year in dues, subscriptions, or donations.
7. Those who contribute $10.01 or more per year.
8. Those who are making installment payments on a life membership.
9. Those who hold life memberships.

Responses were obtained also from a group of ninety-three presidents of social welfare clubs whose addresses were taken from a special list of the club department; they do not form a part of the random sample of members. The club presidents may be regarded as the most deeply involved Institute members.

By making comparisons between the various groups it will be

possible to gain a clearer view of the CISW. In particular, observation of the groups of members having different degrees of involvement may give an idea of the changes a person undergoes as he moves from the periphery toward the center of the organization. This is not to say that all members, or even a substantial number of them, travel the road from lesser to greater involvement, for many never get beyond the threshold. Even so, the various categories may be regarded as stages in the development of committed members.

Status-anxiety and the search for information.—The unorganized pensioner's world is simpler than that of the McLain follower. The ways of the welfare administration may be mysterious to him, but he feels no strong urge to understand them. He may have grateful feelings for "the welfare" which protects him from destitution; or he may, if he is somewhat deviant, scornfully accept the morsels that are thrown to him. Whatever his feelings, his relations with the administration are easily defined. Under the impact of Institute propaganda, McLain's followers develop a lively interest in welfare law and administration. Anxiety about their status drives them to inquire more insistently into the rules and practices which seem to have far-reaching effects upon their lives.

The members' preoccupation with the details of welfare legislation is remarkable. When interviewed, many of the members exhibited their knowledge of such details as the number of persons on OAS in California or the comparative sizes of average grants in various states. When asked about the benefits derived from Institute membership, they invariably mentioned information as the most important gain.

A female respondent, in explaining what she liked best about Institute meetings, stated: "We have a bright man who leads the meetings. He understands these things well, and . . . well, some of us are slow; he explains patiently to us. Every day I listen to McLain's broadcast. I like the information he gives us—how things are going; keeps us informed."

Other respondents expressed a need for a broader understanding of pension politics.

["What is the most important thing you get out of the Institute?"] "I get the truth about the Sacramento legislature. You don't get it from the papers.

I listen to the broadcasts most of the time, when I'm home." ["What do you like best about them?"] "The legal parts, the legal troubles. George McLain helps these people. People are sometimes cheated. He helps them even if they are not members. It is wonderful that there are so many better-to-do people interested in this work."

"Those who aren't in the Institute are missing a good thing. You get the facts from Mr. McLain—you know what's going on. McLain has kept them from letting us starve to death—if he hadn't been up there they would've cut the pension to $62. . . ."

"Belonging to this organization helps you to know what the law is. I'll tell you how they treat some of these older people that don't know the law: they reject them everything. . . . There's an old woman told me (that was when they were paying $80) told me how this welfare woman came to her house and told her how it was cheaper to buy cabbage . . . and how to cook it. . . ."

Negativism.—The member's great desire to understand leads him to realize the complexity of the law. Often he accuses the law and the social worker of confusion and bureaucratic arbitrariness. In chapter iii we showed, by combining the antithetical terms in a check list of adjectives describing the pension law and the social worker list, that the orientation of members and of nonmembers is basically similar. (See pp. 75–77; also Appendix I, table 8.)

When the responses to specific words in this list are tabulated separately, however, striking dissimiliarities emerge. In their reactions to the pension law (fig. 6), members and nonmembers are at opposite poles.[1] Between one-quarter and one-half of the members describe the law as "full of red tape," "humiliating," "confused," and "tricky"; similar proportions of nonmembers call the law "generous," "kind," "respectful," and "efficient."

The same word list was used in order to test the recipients' feelings about the social worker.[2] In this instance the contrast between members and nonmembers is not nearly so sharp, and many terms receive large votes from both groups. Among members the most frequent choices (about 25 per cent) are "respectful," "kind," and "full of red tape"; nonmembers most frequently select the words "kind," "respectful," "efficient," and "clear."

These choices suggest that members consider the existing wel-

---

[1] See table 29.
[2] See table 30.

fare law a threat to their status ("humiliating") and a tangle of bureaucratic obscurity and arbitrariness ("full of red tape," "confused," "tricky"). The two appraisals are closely related. The protest against the obscurity and inconsistency of the law doubtless

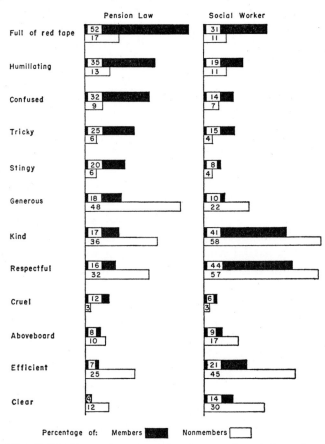

Fig. 6. Feelings about pension law and social worker.

has its root in the feeling that the law, as administered, does nothing to define and secure the pensioners' position in society.

Nonmembers tend to disagree with members on this point: they regard the law not only as "kind" and "generous" but also as "respectful" and "efficient." Since nonmembers are almost as preoccupied with status problems as are members, we must conclude that the disagreement in appraisals of the pension law reflects differences in the method of *handling* status-anxiety. Nonmembers tend to persuade themselves that the pension law does protect such status as they may ascribe to themselves, whereas members regard the law as the source of their status problem.

A similar disagreement between members and nonmembers occurs in appraisals of the social worker. The largest differences between proportions of members and nonmembers occur in the choices of the terms "full of red tape" (a 20 per cent difference) and "efficient" (a 24 per cent difference). Members are more prone to feel confused and frustrated by both the law and the social worker than are unorganized pensioners. Probably a considerable amount of hostility is associated with the members' bewilderment; yet the words which would imply evil intent on the part of the legislator or of the administration ("stingy" and "cruel") are chosen less frequently than any of the other negative terms. That most members do not impute ill will to the welfare administration is plain from their appraisals of the social worker. More than 40 per cent of the members select the words "kind" and "respectful" to describe the social worker; 31 per cent regard him as "full of red tape"; while only a small proportion of the members think of the social worker as stingy or cruel.

Instead of outspoken hostility directed at specific personalized targets, we find a general negativistic attitude. This can best be shown by ratios describing each respondent's appraisal of the pension law and of the social worker; these ratios are computed by taking the number of adjectives which imply a positive attitude as a proportion of *all* adjectives selected by a given respondent. Unfavorable appraisals are much more frequent among members than among nonmembers.[3]

In appraising the pension law, 55 per cent of the members but only 21 per cent of the nonmembers check only unfavorable adjectives; conversely, 26 per cent of the members and 61 per cent of the nonmembers check none but favorable adjectives. In judging the social worker, 27 per cent of the members and 11 per cent of the nonmembers select only unfavorable adjectives; and 48 per cent of the members and 75 per cent of the nonmembers use exclusively favorable words to describe the social worker. Thus

[3] See tables 31 and 32.

organized and unorganized pensioners disagree less in judging the social worker than they do in appraising the pension law. Participation in the Institute seems to bring about a considerable increase in negative feelings toward the *institutions* of society, but not nearly so large an increase in negative feelings about *persons*.

That participation in the CISW is associated with negativism can be further documented by comparing the classes of members.[4] The more deeply involved a given group is in the Institute, the more likely is it to make negative appraisals. This holds true both for each particular adjective and for the ratios of positive and negative adjectives.

The question might be raised whether these negative feelings about the welfare adminstration are a result of unpleasant experiences that members have had with welfare agencies. In responding to our questionnaire, 31 per cent of the members stated that their grants had been stopped or reduced at some time in the past. This figure is 10 per cent larger than the one for nonmembers. The 10 per cent difference does not account for the much larger difference (36 per cent) between the proportions of members and nonmembers appraising the welfare law negatively. The interviews with petition circulators were analyzed with this problem in mind. Of the forty-two signature collectors interviewed, nine felt that their social worker had not treated them fairly and four felt that the State Welfare Department had mishandled their cases; the remainder either had no personal experiences to report (seven individuals) or had no negative feelings (twenty-two individuals).

We believe, therefore, that the members' negativism, which occasionally erupts into open hostility, cannot be viewed as stemming from individual unpleasant experiences; such negativism seems rather to result from the perception that the welfare system is exceedingly complex and therefore threatening. In several interviews the connection between the perception of complexity, the demand for information, and negativism was openly displayed. The following statements are indicative:

"He [McLain] informs us of legislation. He tells us how to vote. He tells us how to elect our friends and defeat our enemies."

---

[4] See tables 29–32.

"I'm able to keep in touch with what's going on. I'm able to know my enemies. I know what the old folks are doing. I'm able to weigh both sides of the problem."

["How do you feel about your membership now? Do you think it does a lot for you to be a member? In what way?"] "I didn't understand the pension laws and I knowed that this County Welfare was a pretty rough outfit— they don't care whether you live or not. It was either McLain or a lawyer. I got McLain so I didn't need a lawyer. He wrote me a letter and told me they'd take care of everything with the county. . . ."

Fewer members than we expected make a wholesale indictment of "the welfare"; most of the members confine themselves to accusing the administration of inefficiency and bungling. Yet it is of interest to record some of the more extreme statements about the welfare administration.

"I've never seen anything so rotten in my whole life. They try every way they know to be mean. They try to drag every dollar out of you. You're not allowed something for this or something for that. People that are running it aren't interested in the pensioners. They want the pension cut. They'll probably vote against it."

"Seems to me I did hear about somebody, a social worker gives them everything and then recalls it the next month. Says you don't really need a phone. It shouldn't be so hard on them. They should get a few extras. 'Course, twenty-five years ago they got very little. McLain has helped them."

"There are things pertaining to the legislative body that I can't coincide with. They don't do it for good but for money. They'd hold back our rent if they were on their own. They try to grab everything. They can't make me believe that relatives' responsibility is constitutional."

The most common complaint of the more negative members is that the social worker pries into their private affairs.

"I don't see any sense in sending out snoopers, prying around to see what people are buying and spending." ["To you?"] "They haven't bothered me too much."

"Well, I don't know anything about the main part of the welfare department. Of course, there've been big changes in welfare workers. George has helped to do this. They used to snoop around. When I first got the pension, one asked me once to see in my purse. But it's all right now. I won't see a welfare worker but from time to time. I just get a card and I go down there and they check me out and I get my pension."

"I'll tell you how people are these days. There are so many stool pigeons. I know an old man about ninety-three down on San Pablo. He knows some guys, see, and he tells them he's workin' a little. A couple days later the County Welfare guy comes and tries to get this old guy off the rolls. The old man told me he really wasn't workin', but that's how it is with stool pigeons. . . . You can't talk—the County Welfare dictates—tells me how I have to do and think. I says, this ain't Russia yet, I says, the old people ain't livin' in the Dictatorship yet, I says, you may have a dictatorship with the older people but that don't give you a right to order me. I never had anybody dictate to me, see? I bought a TV set and a watch—they said that I abused the funds."

Perception of hostility.—In the recipient's view, society becomes divided into friendly and hostile sectors. This inference can be drawn from the responses to a check list consisting of public figures, political officeholders, organizations, and minority groups. The respondents were asked which of these they regarded as friends and which as enemies of the pensioners. They were instructed not to check the names of persons whom they regarded as neither friendly nor inimical. Members were much more prone than were nonmembers to regard groups or individuals as friends or enemies.[5] On the average, of the 22 items listed, members checked 12.16 items; nonmembers, 8.66. This tendency increases sharply with the members' involvement. A similar tendency of the more involved members to check a larger number of items shows up also in the responses to the check lists concerning the pension law and the social worker; but the rate of increase is not as great as on the "friends-enemies" question.

Not only do the members tend to perceive the social world as black-and-white; they are also prone to believe that groups or individuals are enemies of the pensioners and other old people. On the average, slightly more than half of the responses of a given member designate some group or individual as an enemy; for nonmembers, this average is less than one-quarter.[6]

The detailed list of recipients' responses to the "friends-enemies" question is given in figure 7. Only the proportions of recipients distrusting a given individual or group are shown, and the items

[5] See table 33.
[6] See table 34.

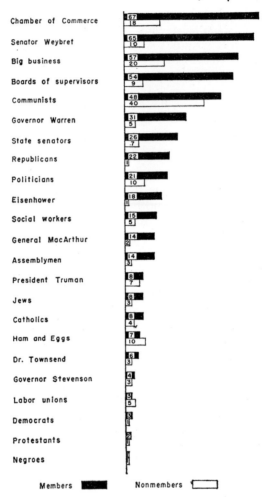

Fig. 7. Number of individuals and groups designated as enemies.

are arranged in the order of the frequencies of "enemy" responses among members.[7]

Six items at the top of the list elicit "enemy" responses from 31 to 67 per cent of the membership. Three of these—the Chamber of Commerce, State Senator Weybret,[8] and boards of supervisors

---

[7] See table 35.

[8] The late Senator Fred Weybret was for some time chairman of the state Senate Interim Committee on Social Welfare. He conducted the investigation of the California Institute of Social Welfare shortly before the 1949 elections.

—have been fairly constant targets of McLain's propaganda attacks. Big business, a fourth item at the top of the list, is not consistently under McLain's direct attack; but his frequent derogatory references to "the interests" may account for part of the unpopularity of big business among the members. Another McLain target, Governor Warren, is sixth on the list, after the Communists. The next seven items draw "enemy" responses from 14 to 26 per cent of the members; of these, six are names of individuals in political life or generic terms for political figures, and one is the social worker. The remainder of the list consists of Democrats and individuals identified with the Democratic party, pension and minority groups, and labor unions; none of these is perceived as an enemy by more than 8 per cent of the members.

How membership affects the recipients' perception of threats can be most clearly seen from a comparison of members and nonmembers and an observation of the relation between involvement in the CISW and proportion of "enemy" responses. On all items which draw a heavy "enemy" response from members, the proportion of members giving this response is at least twice, and usually a much larger multiple of, the corresponding proportion of nonmembers. The only exception is the Communist item, to which 48 per cent of the members and 40 per cent of the nonmembers respond with the term "enemy." The reason for this similarity is, undoubtedly, that Communists have been designated officially as enemies of everything that is considered worth while in American society. To the extent, then, that members and nonmembers belong to the same society, they share their enemies. The fact that certain enemies are *not* shared leads to the inference that, to some extent, members do not belong to the same society as nonmembers. Participation in the Institute has produced some degree of dissociation from society and its generally accepted views and doctrines.

There are obvious resistances to such dissociation. We have repeatedly drawn attention to the members' intense desire to be part of society. Even in the absence of such specific desires, they must overcome shared social beliefs before they are able to think of a "respectable" group of citizens or a well-known public figure as their enemy. This conflict between the common beliefs of society and the special beliefs of McLain's organization can best be seen by examining the five items at the top of the list (not including the Communists), which are McLain's special propaganda targets. The five items are almost a popularity scale in reverse. Governor Warren, whose popularity with Californians was very great, receives the smallest "enemy" vote of all five targets. Supervisors enjoy some popularity simply by virtue of being local people known by name and reputation to some of the recipients. On the other side, the Chamber of Commerce has been under fire not only from McLain but from many labor and liberal groups. Senator Weybret would be totally unknown to the pensioners if it were not for McLain. In his radio broadcasts and in the *Welfare Advocate*, McLain has described both the Chamber of Commerce and Weybret as representatives of moneyed interests bent upon destroying him and his Institute politically. Since any opinions which might counteract McLain's indictment of the Chamber of Commerce and of Senator Weybret are relatively weak— and particularly so in the pensioners' environment—the proportions of members considering these two as "enemies" are large and about equal in size.

In examining the relation of "enemy" responses to involvement, we find that the five targets of McLain's propaganda show a particularly steep increase in proportion to increasing involvement. The differences between the two extreme groups on the involvement scale—nonmembers who have heard of McLain, and club presidents—range from 48 per cent to 76 per cent.

The way in which common social beliefs and specific CISW beliefs bid for the members' loyalty becomes apparent when the pattern of "enemy" responses is examined more closely. How many of the members believe that all four of McLain's chief targets— Senator Weybret, the Chamber of Commerce, county supervisors, and Governor Warren—are enemies of the aged? How many consider only three of these as enemies? The combinations of "enemy" responses made by individual members are revealing.[9]

The responses follow a definite pattern. Members who regard Warren as their enemy tend to consider the other three McLain targets as hostile also. Those who do not believe Warren to be an

---

[9] See table 36.

enemy but think of supervisors as enemies of the pensioners regard the remaining two targets as enemies. The most distrustful member will check all McLain's targets as enemies; as distrust declines, the least vulnerable targets drop off the members' lists successively. Enmity was most easily imputed to Senator Weybret.

There is a clear relation between these response patterns and involvement in the organization. Only 22 per cent of the regular members express distrust of all four propaganda targets, but among life members 49 per cent do so. The more deeply a pensioner is involved in the CISW, the larger is the number of groups and individuals he distrusts; and the specific objects of this widening distrust are designated for him by the counteracting forces of Institute ideology and community opinion.

The technique described above can be used also to investigate whether distrust spreads, in the same ordered fashion, to other objects. It is possible to demonstrate the existence of definite relations between distrust of Senator Weybret and of state senators, and between distrust of the Chamber of Commerce and of big business. Nearly all members who regard state senators as enemies also distrust Senator Weybret; but distrust of Weybret does not necessarily imply distrust of state senators.[10] Moreover, there is a strong relationship between these response patterns and involvement. We can therefore say that distrust of Weybret is primary and distrust of state senators is secondary: the perception that these individuals are inimical to the pensioners spreads from the former to the latter.

A similar, although not quite so definite, relation exists between distrust of the Chamber of Commerce and of big business.[11] The belief that big business is unfriendly to the aged appears to develop as a result of the belief that the Chamber of Commerce is an enemy of the pensioners. But the degree of relationship between response patterns and involvement is lower than that found in the Weybret–state senators pattern. Distrust of big business cannot be explained as an exclusive result of the members, feelings about the Chamber of Commerce; rather, it is also a consequence of fairly widespread popular feeling. Figure 7 shows that distrust

[10] See table 37.
[11] See table 38.

of the Chamber of Commerce and of big business is rather frequent among nonmembers as well. The members' feelings regarding these two items can therefore be explained, in part, as conformity with opinions popular among the general pensioner population.

A more complete picture of the similarities and dissimilarities which distinguish members from nonmembers emerges from the list below.[12] The items used in the "distrust" question are ranked according to the degree of relationship between Institute membership or nonmembership and the choice of the terms "friend" and "enemy" to describe the individuals or groups listed. On items at the top, members are unlike nonmembers in their choices; most members describe the groups and individuals as enemies, while nonmembers describe them as friends. Members and nonmembers make the same choices on items at the bottom of the list; that is, approximately equal proportions in each sample regard these groups as friends and as enemies.

The first ten items, which show the greatest discrepancies between members and nonmembers, are all "Republican" items or identified with state or county government. In all these items the discrepancy between members and nonmembers means that members give more "enemy" responses and nonmembers more "friend" responses. On none of the other items is there substantial disagreement between members and nonmembers.

There appears to be a clear anti-Republican bias on the part of a substantial number of McLain's followers. This bias is combined with an antipathy toward state and local government which is not unusual among Democrats. Does this mean that the CISW is essentially a Democratic organization? According to the recipients' expressed political preferences, Institute membership is more strongly Democratic than are pensioners in general. About 40 per cent of the members describe themselves as Democrats, whereas 30 per cent of the nonmembers prefer this party; 39 per cent of the members are Republican, as against 49 per cent of the nonmembers. Moreover, McLain considers himself a Democrat and has run his personal political campaigns under the Democratic

---

[12] For details see table 39. The sequence in the list was determined by the sizes of the contingency coefficients.

DEGREES OF DISAGREEMENT AND AGREEMENT BETWEEN
MEMBERS AND NONMEMBERS IN DESIGNATING
GROUPS AND INDIVIDUALS AS FRIENDS OR ENEMIES
(Disagreement highest for items at top of list)

Board of supervisors
Republicans
Chamber of Commerce
State senators
Warren
Social workers
Senator Weybret
Eisenhower
Assemblymen
General MacArthur
Labor unions
Ham and Eggs
Big business
Politicians
Catholics
Jews
Communists
Townsend
President Truman
Governor Stevenson
Democrats
Protestants
Negroes

label. Nevertheless, the Institute cannot be regarded as essentially
Democratic. No more than half of the members with a clear political preference are Democrats. We can say only that the Institute
proves somewhat more attractive to people of Democratic background than to Republican voters. Because of the role played by
the Democratic party during the New Deal and Fair Deal administrations, Democratic voters are probably more inclined than the
Republicans to give their support to the improvement and expansion of welfare programs.

The finding that Democratic voters tend to respond more
strongly to the Institute's appeal than do Republicans is not in
itself particularly revealing. The interesting fact is that Institute
membership reinforces Democratic (and by the same token anti-
Republican) convictions but does not appear to have the same
effect on Republican convictions. There is great distrust of the
Republicans on the part of some of the Democrats in the Institute,
but the Republicans in the Institute develop no such distrust of
Democrats.

The perceived "enemies" of Institute members are thus not entirely of McLain's making. Big business and the Chamber of Commerce are unpopular with the more interested pensioners both inside and outside the Institute. Republicans and representatives of state and county government (who also tend to be Republican in California) are likely to be distrusted by Democrats. McLain is bound to profit from such preëxisting political attitudes. His propaganda reinforces available political beliefs by making the targets of distrust more specific. He does not revolutionize the attitudes of the members nor does he turn them against society. Rather, he encourages some attitudes and discourages others; and he puts emphasis upon some aspects of the recipients' background at the expense of others. This exploitation of predispositions—a technique common to most political and advertising campaigns—also imposes limitations upon McLain: he cannot get the support of his members for political positions or campaigns which run counter to their preëxisting beliefs.

It is difficult to say to what extent the members' distrust of certain individuals and groups can be regarded as hostility. It is a common experience that outward aggression may become disguised as a feeling of being attacked. An understanding of racial and religious prejudice, as well as international hatreds, needs this psychological theory of projection. Before making a judgment regarding the members' hostility we should note, however, that there is no evidence of any desire on their part to destroy or damage other social groups or society as a whole. It is reasonable to assume that the pensioners' many frustrations result in hostile feelings. So far as this is true, we can say that the movement causes the members to focus their hostility upon specific targets. However, the most extreme form which hostility takes among the pensioners is the formulation of strong accusations.

Moreover, the expression of hostile feelings is restrained, even if the feelings are directed against persons unknown to the members. During his 1952 congressional campaign, McLain asked his members to write letters to Philip Murray, then president of the Congress of Industrial Organizations. They were to complain about the chairman of the Los Angeles County CIO Council, who had refused to endorse McLain and had made derogatory remarks about him in a press conference. More than five hundred members responded to McLain's appeal and wrote letters to Philip Murray. In most of these letters they extolled the virtues of their leader as a fighter for the aged and the needy, and expressed their perplexity as to why a CIO leader would see fit to attack a "friend of labor." They asked Mr. Murray to "investigate" the situation. Only a few letters asked for specific sanctions against the local trade unionist.

If there is hostility, it is kept under control. It is doubtful that McLain could, for example, induce his members to disrupt the meetings of other organizations or to infiltrate other groups. (There is no evidence that he would wish to do so.) His efforts to keep the members isolated probably grows out of the correct perception that their convictions are not strong enough to stand up under pressure. McLain might have entertained the idea of encouraging his members to go into the recreation centers for older people which have been developing in several California cities; there, they might have been able to recruit new members or even to exploit city facilities for their own political purposes. Instead, McLain has made an effort to keep his members out of the recreation centers. When the Oakland Recreation Center first got under way, one of McLain's speakers told his audience: "Don't go there. They'll be nice to you all right. But you know who's behind it— the Chamber of Commerce! The first time you go they'll give you a free hot dog, and the second time you go they'll tell you what a *scoundrel* George McLain is."

Independence and the Need for Protection

How do heightened distrust and the perception of more clearly defined threats affect the member's ability to deal with his problem of psychic dependency? One of the consequences of status-anxiety is a desire to counteract impotence and to preserve or achieve independence. But does not distrust *enhance* the desire for a protective dependency?

The members tend to prefer reliance on strangers (the social worker and other officials) to reliance upon their families and close friends. McLain is even more remote than the recipients' case worker, since to most of the members he is only a voice over the radio, a picture in the *Welfare Advocate,* a signature on a letter, or at best a figure on the rostrum. According to remarks made during interviews, some of the members feel that they have hired McLain to work for them, as one would retain the services of a lawyer or a physician. In contributing money to the organization, members may feel that they are helping themselves by hiring a capable representative. Such remarks were often made by respondents who were trying to defend McLain.

"A lot got it in for him [McLain], of course, for having a fine house and all that, like they say. But my lands, he's a lawyer and he can't work for nothin'. Nobody can be expected to. If it weren't for him, the old wouldn't be gettin' nothin'."

"The papers like the *Times* [Los Angeles *Times*] keep hollering about McLain. They say he's got a mansion. Well, it's just a cottage, but I guess billionaires like the Chandlers [owners of the Los Angeles *Times*], they'll call it a mansion [smiles]. And what if he did have a mansion? For what he does for the pensioners we couldn't pay him nohow. We couldn't hire a better man."

"I once heard one say, 'I think he's a grafter.' I told him how much do you think the Standard Oil Company would pay him to work as hard for them as he works for us? [Respondent kept asking me this question and tapping me on the shoulder insistently.] We should pay him that much anyway." ["Pay him how much?"] "I don't know how much we pay Mr. McLain and I don't care. Whatever he gets he earns. I want him to live in the best hotels and eat the best food."

Similar references to McLain's status as a hired professional occur in discussion of the benefits of membership:

["Do those who are not members miss out on something?"] "I think this way about it. They get the things that benefit us. They should string along with us and join. After all, McLain has to eat. That man is worth $15,000 a year to us. I think they're missing out on helping to repeal the relatives' responsibility clause . . ."

["Do those who are not members miss out on something?"] "Yes, in the first place they're missing out on the sociability which means a lot to older people who don't get around much any more. Then they're not helping themselves. They're waiting for others to do it, for George to do it as they say." [Laughter at this point]

Members often justify the desirability of membership by the services the pensioner gets for his contribution. Confidence in the welfare service of the Institute may to some extent derive from the fact that the service is *not* entirely gratuitous but is rendered only upon payment of membership dues. The *quid pro quo* relationship so established may be more palatable to many pensioners than one in which advice is given free. The fact that the service is not free adds a dimension of self-help to the act of using the Institute.

While a striving for independence doubtless motivates the behavior of many members, the followers' dependence on McLain as a person is much more conspicuous. McLain is seen by his followers as the *only* protector of the pensioners, without whom they would be utterly lost. He is the very image of righteousness being persecuted by evil forces, such as the "interests" and the venal press.

Descriptions of McLain by members in preliminary interviews were condensed into a questionnaire check list. The respondents were asked to mark the words which, in their opinion, came closest to their personal view of McLain. The most frequent designations were "friend" (47 per cent), "protector" (44 per cent), and "good shepherd" (38 per cent). The terms "brother," "political leader," and "teacher" were chosen by only 8–15 per cent of the members.[13]

The terms "protector" and "good shepherd" are very close to one another in meaning: the more religiously inclined members tended to select the phrase "good shepherd"; the others preferred "protector." Of the members, 4 per cent (about four-fifths less than would be expected on chance) checked both terms; this proportion was largest among those paying on life memberships (18 per cent), the group containing the greatest number of fundamentalists. Over-all, 78 per cent of the members checked either "protector" or "good shepherd" or both.

The responses clearly indicate that only a few of the members regard McLain as the leader of a political movement. Rather, they think of him as their benefactor—a term which perhaps sums up most adequately the meaning common to the three terms most frequently selected: "friend," "protector," and "good shepherd." This implies a certain lack of intimacy between the members and

---

[13] See table 40.

McLain and a rather one-sided relationship in which McLain is seen as the provider.

The members' images of the organization lead to similar conclusions about their feelings of dependence. Almost two-thirds of the members selected the term "service organization" to describe the Institute.[14] Only 7 per cent regarded it as a "political group"; and, although the word "union" probably comes rather close to describing its actual functions, only 14 per cent selected this term. The fact that 34 per cent of the members think that the Institute is "like a family" may be surprising in view of the very small amount of informal interaction which takes place between members. For 12 per cent of the members the Institute is a club, and for a similar 12 per cent it has enough of an aura of holiness to be described as a religious group.

The emotional significance of the Institute and of McLain's protective role far exceeds the utility which members derive from them. The members' fervor increases with involvement. Interviews and letters are studded with such phrases as: "We are for George all the way," "I'm for George and the old folks," or "We just like McLain." Frequently, the interviewer had to listen to a torrent of laudatory phrases about McLain before he was able to begin the actual questioning. A few quotations will give the flavor of the members' enthusiasm for their leader:

"I think George McLain is doing wonderful work. If'n it weren't for him we wouldn't have no pensions."

"I have a great deal to be thankful for. I feel that the Institute is the service of the Lord. It's a great security to have that check coming in. I'm not as active as I was ten or fifteen years ago when I was better off. That's when I was able to get up and around."

Some tell touching stories about their leader, taken chiefly from his "autobiography" and other Institute literature, and embellished by bits of folklore.

"His [McLain's] mother was the first white child in California. His father was a construction man. They say that out on the West Side on the sidewalk you can see the McLain name. He went broke in the early depression. Gee, that must have been an early depression, because when my husband

---

[14] See table 41.

came here they were just recovering from a depression. Well, they went broke and his father got a pension of $12. I don't recollect exactly, but I think it was $12 and then they found out that he was a Christian Scientist and he didn't need medicine and they took $4 off for his medicine. So George got out his war clothes. . . ."

"He takes care of people of all religions and black and white. There are no distinctions. I knew him before he went in. Do you know how he went in?" ["No."] "He went in through a friend of Myrtle Williams who was kept waiting [for relief]. That's how it was. Not only her, it was not only her that was kept waiting. I had a friend who was kept waiting too. Well, you see, Myrtle Williams went with this lady and she didn't have any success in getting in to see the people who would take care of her pension, so Myrtle called George. He went with her and, you know, he took care of it. Well, you know, he's a good talker and it worked. You see, prestige means something. So Myrtle Williams said to herself, 'I'm going to devote my life to helping the old. . . .' "

["What sort of things should McLain try to do?"] "Well, like yesterday he went to see an old man in the hospital. Seems that he saw that he was taken care of. He didn't live long, the old man, only two days, but at least George saw that he was taken care of during his last hours and he saw that he had a decent burial instead of being thrown in Potters field. And like children. Well, I've heard that George sees to it that people with needy children are taken care of. It's not all just old people that George does. It's charitable work."

"I think he's helped us. He's a very fine man. He and his wife work together. They have a little five-room house and the man was raised good. He was raised good. He and all his brothers were raised good. They were the sons of a Baptist minister."

Frequently the members worry about the amount of work their protector is doing and express fears for his health. A constant theme is "If it weren't for George, where would we be?" or "Without George, we wouldn't get any pension." In many variations, the members tell how the Chamber of Commerce, the Taxpayers' Association, the county supervisors, and the rich in general attempt to stop George McLain and the old folks, and how hard McLain has to work to withstand their assault.

"These people listen to too many lectures. The people in high finance pay a lecturer to lecture against McLain."

"They hate him. They tell all the lies they can. They don't want the people to get it [the pension]. They think it's all right to raise their own salaries." ["Who thinks that way?"] "Why, the supervisors. If they didn't have to they wouldn't help the old people. They don't want him to help the people. They weren't against him before he started all this."

Feelings that are probably widespread among the recipients are neatly summed up in the following comments of a former salesman, who, throughout the interview, distinguished between the "House of Have" and the "House of Have-not": "My landlady is friendly toward it [the petition], but her husband is an engineer. He won't sign it. He's afraid of taxes going up. The House of Have don't approve of it. They never approved of Jesus Christ or George Washington or Abraham Lincoln neither."

In the minds of many there is no great gap between the stilling of hunger and the salvation of the soul. To mention in one breath Christ and George McLain may seem sacrilegious to the sophisticated; and to them pressure groups and religion may lie in two different spheres. But fundamentalists look for real miracles in a real world and for the filling of real stomachs. George McLain can be called a "good shepherd" because many of his followers literally picture their Lord as a shepherd who leads the members of his flock beside still waters and into green pastures. Unconditional trust in the leader becomes the complement of a widening distrust of society. Dependence on relatives and close friends is replaced by dependence upon the distant George McLain.

If the relation between McLain and his members is understood as one between shepherd and flock, it becomes clear why there is no trace of democracy in the Institute. We have found members who were dissatisfied with McLain—but mostly because they think him too demanding. Not one of the members interviewed expressed a wish to participate in the decisions of the Institute. Our interview guide contained a series of five questions designed to elicit some expression of democratic interest. The following quotations show the typical reactions to such questioning:

["Should members have more to say?"] "Well . . . be all right for them to say, but sometimes they have funny ideas. Our leaders are prepared, qualified. What they need mostly is for people to help them. If every pensioner gave $1 a month—just think what he could do." [Note the shift from "our leaders" to "he."]

"Well, too many hands in any organization like that couldn't do so much —too many heads and hands in the pie. It won't work so good."

["Should members have more say?"] "I don't know. After all, I think it takes a person with more knowledge than what we old folks have who go to meetings. Why, there's not one down here—yes, there's not one who would be able to go to Sacramento and do the needed work."

"Well, I think the Institute tells the members what to do. That's the way it is, I think. They got smart people down there."

[Do members make suggestions?"] "I don't know. I know people cut out clippings and take them to meetings and discuss them. But I imagine the leader sees them long before we see them in the paper." ["Should members have more say?"] ". . . people are always whispering in meetings, it irks me to death! People should pay more attention." ["I mean suggestions about running the organization."] "They have heads that are perfectly capable. We have capable leaders. They are just like school-teachers, you know. We don't know too much about it all and they have to tell us. Mr. McLain and the people under him are good leaders."

Of the forty-two signature collectors who were interviewed, only three believed that members should have more say. But they did not construe this as membership participation in policy decisions; rather, it would be a manifestation of greater interest.

The Cost of Protection

Protection comes high. For all practical purposes, the operation of the Institute of Social Welfare is financed by the dues and contributions of members. Money from other sources—for instance, the sale of address lists for campaign purposes—is relatively unimportant in the total budget. The yearly outlay for all activities (radio and television time, newspaper, speakers and other personnel, overhead, etc.) almost certainly exceeds $12 per member, even in periods when the organization is numerically strong. Besides making contributions, members are expected to attend meetings and help collect signatures during initiative-referendum campaigns. However, from McLain's point of view, all membership activities are subsidiary to the raising of money. The members may be dimly aware of this. In any event, McLain's speakers and local lieutenants note that attendance dwindles toward the end of each month, and they attribute this to the fact that the members feel embarrassed when they have no money to drop into the collection basket.

Compared with the heavy financial demands, other Institute activities are for most members only a small sacrifice and often prove rewarding in themselves. McLain himself has been repeatedly surprised by the members' ability to collect large numbers of signatures on petitions; both in 1948 and 1952 he retained the services of a professional signature-collecting agency, but soon found that he could rely on his members to collect all the signatures needed. Obtaining long lists of signatures gives the individual prestige and the pride of achievement. Signature collecting is clearly related to involvement.[15]

McLain's radio program is attractive to the members. The more involved the members are, the more faithfully they listen.[16] The motivation for listening probably combines self-interest and vicarious enjoyment of McLain's fight against the enemies of the pensioners. The radio topics "pensions" and "the work of the Institute" draw the greatest audience interest; the topics "how the pensioners live," "religion" and "McLain's appeals for help and contributions" are much less popular. Nevertheless, listening is an ambiguous burden on the member in that it forces him to expose himself to McLain's often caustic criticism of the indolence and ingratitude of the members and to his insistent requests for more money.

Attendance at meetings, for all the positive values that members may derive from it, constitutes an even greater sacrifice than does radio listening. Here the appeal for funds is made face-to-face, and contributions are difficult to avoid. Moreover, there are transportation costs and physical handicaps to cope with. About 29 per cent of the highly involved regular members and 42 per cent of the life members state that they attend "nearly all" the meetings.[17] While such reports may be exaggerated, the increase in attendance with deepening involvement certainly conveys a true picture. When asked why they attended meetings, most of the signature collectors mentioned either they enjoyed the social aspects or that

---

[15] See table 42.
[16] See table 43.
[17] See table 44.

they appreciated the information they received; a few added that the purpose of the meetings was mutual aid or that they enjoyed being among like-minded people. Not one of the respondents said that attendance was necessary in order to strengthen the movement and help in fund-raising.

McLain's motivations differ from those of his members much as do those of the sponsors from the listeners in commercial broadcasting. Sponsors finance programs for the sake of the commercial, but audiences tune in programs for the sake of their content. Like any commercial advertiser, McLain must overcome resistance in order to get his message across to his customers. It is plain that the customers have no wish to listen to the commercials; they do not go to meetings in order to be able to contribute to the cause; nor do they listen to the radio in order to hear about deficits and the impending doom. Only 22 per cent indicate that they pay "greatest attention" when McLain asks for help and contributions, and most of the listeners checking this category are equally interested in two or three or all of the other items.

Making contributions and paying dues clearly yield no direct psychological satisfactions to the members. These are the sacrifices they must make in order to enjoy McLain's protection. The contributions which, according to their own report, our respondents made during the three months preceding the survey are presumably somewhat exaggerated. Even so, it seems that contributions to the Institute take a rather high proportion of members' income.[18] About 58 per cent of life members report contributions of more than $5 during a three-month period; among those paying on life memberships (i.e., among individuals making regular payments of $5 a month) 30 per cent report contributions of similar size. The amounts contributed by regular members cannot be so easily estimated, since it is obvious that the more involved regular members are overrepresented among our respondents. If, however, we assume a response rate as high as 75 per cent for the most involved group of regular members, this would mean that at least one-sixth of regular members had made contributions of more than $5 during the three months preceding the survey.

While the figures given by members as their contributions for

[18] See table 45.

the last three months may be inflated, contributions of as much as $5 a month are not unusual. We have talked to enough members and seen enough letters to believe that a substantial number of members make regular gifts of $5 a month. The most significant finding to emerge from the members' reports on their contributions is that nearly one-sixth of the regular members are about as highly involved as are life members if involvement is measured by voluntary contributions.

As in most political or "cause" organizations, the financial burden is shared very unequally among the members. A comparatively small number make disproportionately large voluntary contributions. The 772 life members in our sample claim to have contributed a total of $8,395 during the three months preceding our survey; this amounts to an average contribution of $10.87. Of this total amount contributed, nearly one-half came from 16 per cent of the life members, who gave more than $20 each. The 514 highest contributors among the regular members included in our sample contributed a total of $4,704, the average contribution being $8.95; 38 per cent of this total sum came from that 13 per cent of regular members who had contributed more than $15 each during a three-month period.

A few members make extraordinary financial sacrifices for the organization. An example is Mrs. D., who shares a flat with three other old ladies. Mrs. D. listens to every one of McLain's broadcasts, she goes to every meeting, and has participated in every petition drive, gathering several hundred signatures each time. And, according to her story, she sends the larger part of her assistance check—$50 a month—"to George." Mrs. D. is not privileged in any real sense. She owns no property, she has no income other than Old Age Security, she buys what she needs for herself in the local stores, and her monthly check amounts to exactly $80. When asked how she can possibly send such large amounts of money to McLain's headquarters, she explained that she does not need the money. Her share of the rent is $13.50; although she is in excellent health, her appetite is not very great and she does not like to eat anything but bread and milk, which costs her about $10 a month; she has all the clothes she thinks she will need in this life, does all her own washing and mending, and has made all the installments on her burial expenses. Thus $30 a month pays for her food, shelter, utilities, and incidentals, leaving a full $50 to be invested in the cause.

Mrs. D. does not feel that she is depriving herself. She congratulates herself upon her good health, and participates in the CISW because she feels that others "less fortunate" than she need her help. Being a rather cheerful and vivacious person, she evidently enjoys her Institute activities; and she is rather proud of her ability to live so economically and use the major portion of her meager income for "something worth while."

To be sure, very few of McLain's followers present so cheerful a picture. Most of them perceive their contributions as a rather heavy, although necessary, burden. Nor can we be entirely sure that even in cases such as that of Mrs. D. there are not hidden costs of membership.

Guilt and resentment.—What keeps the members contributing and working for the Institute irrespective of their past contributions and of the success or defeat of its campaigns? Slightly more than one-half of the members believe that neither they themselves nor other members are doing enough for the organization.[19] In stating this, they are echoing the opinions of McLain, who in his radio talks consistently declares that he feels "let down" by his members. McLain is eminently successful in generating feelings of guilt among the members. The frequency of such guilt feelings bears very little relationship to the effort which people actually exert for the Institute. Among those making contributions toward life memberships (and thus engaged in an especially strenuous effort for the Institute), 64 per cent feel that they are not doing enough; this percentage is slightly higher than the corresponding one for regular members. While it might be expected that members with very low involvement are less likely to feel guilty (49 per cent) than other members, it is significant that life members also have a particularly low proportion of individuals who feel that they are not doing enough (48 per cent). For a relatively high proportion of the life members (about 44 per cent), the attainment of life-membership status does seem to result in release from guilt.

[19] See table 46.

By making the members feel remiss in their duty toward him, McLain can hold his followers more strongly attached to him than does the commercial advertiser who must rely on his customers' feelings of gratification. The customer feels little obligation to buy; but McLain's followers feel an obligation to pay. In order to gain insight into the habits and motivations of contributors, we examined 650 letters[20] which were received at headquarters between February and November, 1952. Of the 650 letters, 623 contained donations. The average contribution was $5.12. Of the 623 contributors, 566 give a reason for sending the money. Among these, 383 express some sense of duty either to pay previously assumed obligations (dues and pledges) or to support "George." The remaining 183 are responses to McLain's appeal.

Besides feelings of obligation, the letters accompanying contributions contain direct expressions of guilt feelings. An apology of some sort was contained in 242 letters. The most common reason for apologizing was the smallness of the contribution. Typical statements are: "Wish it could be 1,000 times this much," "Sorry this is so little," "Had to pay the doctor and can't send more," "Have been to the hospital and couldn't mail this," or "Unable to get out last month, so this is late."

APOLOGIES IN "MONEY MAIL"

Smallness of donation	163
Lateness of donation	52
Lack of participation	16
Lack of attendance at meetings	11
Total	242

There is little doubt that the members feel under obligation to contribute and some are mortified lest their contributions might be insufficient or belated. For these, the guilt feelings so generated may be regarded as a hidden cost to the members.

Most of the members who believe that they are not doing enough for the Institute also point an accusing finger at others.

[20] The letters were collected as follows. The personnel in charge of the mail in McLain's headquarters were asked to preserve each tenth letter that had been processed. When this procedure began to create administrative difficulties for McLain's staff, the method then followed was for a member of the research team to drop in at McLain's headquarters and pick up all letters which, on a given day, had been processed but had not yet been destroyed.

More than half of those who believe that they are faithfully discharging their duty believe that other members are not doing their share; among life members, almost two-thirds of those who are satisfied with their own performance accuse others of being slackers. This response pattern ("I am doing enough, but others are not") shows the clearest and sharpest relationship to involvement; the opposite pattern ("I am not doing enough, but others are"), which occurs rather rarely, shows a decrease in frequency with increasing involvement.

The members' criticism of those who do not do their share is full of acrimony:

"They ought to be ashamed. It's not right to let just a few bear the brunt. They figure they're going to get it [the pension] anyway."

"Some will go there and never give one penny! Of course it's none of my business, but it irks me! [Story about an old woman who said she could not afford to give money since she was paying $58 rent a month.] Now, she doesn't have to pay that much. And she isn't supposed to. The budget says a lot less. She could move. She didn't want to give anything. I heard later she was a Jehovah's Witness—and they say they don't believe in giving donations. I heard of some people who quit the Institute because they joined the Jehovah's Witnesses." [Note that this respondent cites the budgetary rules of the welfare administration to support her views.]

People who do not belong to the Institute are often judged with similar harshness.

"I think the people that aren't in it are slackers. They don't help a bit. They may miss all of their pension and cause the rest of us to lose all that we've won. They're endangering their future and the future of others."

["Are nonmembers missing out on anything?"] "No, I don't know as they are missing anything. They're just not holding up their end."

"If they're not in for the services they'd better get in there. If it weren't for the Institute what would we do? If they're not in there they have no one to turn to. But still some people . . . there's a group of pensioners, old men, who live around here. They just can't be bothered. They're always saying they have no money, don't even have enough for the paper. They finally get our paper between them. They collected some twenty cents a week until they had enough money."

We have commented on the recipients' disinclination to identify with members of their own generation. (See chap. iii.) If anything, Institute membership reinforces such feelings. The lack of success of the club movement may be attributable not only to McLain's failure to give it content and direction but also to the members' inability to get along with one another. Some members who had joined in the belief that the Institute would satisfy their needs for social exchange complained about the lack of spontaneity in meetings.

"The most important thing I get from the Institute is meeting people—but it's not like it used to be. The membership is falling off now."

["Do you have any personal friends in the Institute?"] "No . . . [pause] no, I don't have any friends there now. Some of those people in the meetings aren't very sociable. Others go in little groups. I don't think it was like that in Townsend's. In Mr. Townsend's group everybody was very friendly. He didn't ask for money all the time. We used to go on picnics, someone made the potato salad, some cooked the chickens. It was real nice."

["Do you have any personal friends in the Institute?"] "No friends. Of course, I'm getting so old I don't socialize any more. People around here don't associate with one another. I'm quiet and tend to my own work. I know a couple of people that aren't in the Institute. They live about seven or eight blocks from here. Once in awhile we visit . . ."

The typical Institute meeting reflects this lack of spontaneous sociability. Although some of the members begin to gather long before the appointed hour, there is a minimum of personal contact. During the meeting itself there is little opportunity for audience participation—except the inevitable passing of collection baskets and hats.

The favorably inclined nonmembers' image of the Institute tends to be more realistic than that of the members.[21] The members believe that the organization fulfills all sorts of functions, including that of providing recreation, equally well. Nonmembers rarely believe that the Institute provides entertainment; they think of it chiefly as a propaganda and lobbying organization, and they are less convinced of its efficacy in helping and advising pensioners or of the selflessness of its aims.

It is possible that a misreading of the Institute's function is important to the pensioner's emotional economy. His misperception shields from view the large disparity between the gain derived

---

[21] See table 47.

from membership and the sacrifice it entails. McLain's organization serves specific ends, primarily in acting as a pressure group to advance recipients' economic interests. But the financial price which some members pay is so large that they cannot admit to themselves that the organization is as restricted in scope as it actually is. Not only must they believe that the dangers threatening their economic well-being are very great; they must also believe that the Institute fulfills the important function of giving them a place in the esteem and affection of other people.

This illusion cannot always be maintained; when it breaks down, it leads to much questioning and confusion and eventually to bitterness. McLain's "dead file" of addresses from which no response has been forthcoming for some time is about half the size of his active file; and, although many of the members listed as inactive may have died, there appears to be much movement in and out of the organization. Five of the forty-two signature collectors —who had just engaged in a campaign for the Institute—expressed doubts and were critical of McLain. One lady kept anxiously asking the interviewer whether "we would be getting the pension without McLain."

"Tell me something, would the elderly people get the pensions taken away if it wasn't for McLain?" ["No, the state would continue to pay you your pension."] "Well, some people say McLain is taking the money from us for himself . . . but you've got to have proof of a thing like that. People are getting tired of giving him money. They haven't got it to give. He seems to think we should keep paying in. Now he's after buying television and he wants money for that."

Complaints about the amount of money which McLain requests from his members also occur in interviews with members who are, on the whole, very favorable to McLain.

["How often do you listen to McLain's radio program?"] "Well, he's on five days a week. I usually hear him every day." ["What do you like best?"] "Just the general information. Sometimes I get disgusted, say I won't give a dime. I can't come out and say I don't like the guy. . . . Two years ago McLain started howling about $20 or $30. Well, I wrote him. You know yourself that McLain is making a good salary out of the deal. If McLain had no income but the $80, then he would realize what $10 or $20 means to the pensioners. He'd ask us for a dollar instead. The man has done an awful lot of good. I'm for him. He has to have money to run things. But make an appeal for a dollar instead of asking for life memberships."

["Is it easy or hard for pensioners to contribute?"] "Some it's hard on. 'Cause there's some as has to go to the doctor. I go every other month myself. I have high blood pressure and I have to go. He [respondent's husband] does too."

One of the more disillusioned respondents expressed similar thoughts in these terms:

["What do you like about the Institute?"] "There's not too much I like about it. They're always asking for money. I realize they have to have it. I want to listen to them the same way I listen to news. I want to get information." ["Have you heard about the television program?"] "Yes, I've heard about it. No, I haven't seen it. I don't really care about television. There's too much advertising on it. If it costs McLain very much to put it on it's sure not worth it. Even though there are a lot of people that see it. Of course, all people don't think like I do."

Another put it even more forcefully:

"Well, I tell you, I think that initiative is going to go through this time, yes, I do. And when we get that extra money they're going to come and get the money right out of us. They are going to want more and more money." ["Who?"] "McLain and that bunch. I oughn't to say that, I suppose, but I'm disgusted, to tell you the truth. I have paid in and paid in. I'm a life member."

The same pensioner later in the interview accused one of the officers of the organization of having appropriated handicraft objects that had been made by a member for the purpose of being raffled off at an Institute function.

One signature collector expressed concern and disillusionment for reasons other than monetary demands.

"I don't want to talk about George McLain. I think he's got a seat in Washington. A great many people around here don't like McLain because he says so much about the Chamber of Commerce. In a way, I think he hurts the old people by talking against the Chamber of Commerce. . . ."

["What do you like about Institute meetings?"] "In the beginning it was wonderful, but it seems to be falling off now. People haven't got the money to give—that's what they do at the meetings, keep asking for money. There were only about twenty-five people at the meeting last Saturday. I used to like the meetings, but now it's stale. People don't have the money to give."

There is no place within the Institute where resentments against McLain can be expressed and translated into concerted action. The disillusioned member must either hide his feelings or withdraw from the Institute.

One possible price that the followers may pay for McLain's protection is psychological isolation. This isolation may exist even when there are many contacts; the devoted follower neither gives nor expects genuine affection. As members' involvement increases, even the belief that they are the objects of McLain's affection tends to wither. The more involved members are less likely to think of McLain as a "friend" or "brother." Instead, he assumes more and more the role of a distant "protector" or "good shepherd."

The followers' isolation is compounded of fear, guilt, distrust, suspicion, and resentment. The member is left alone in a peculiarly distorted world in which physical presence passes for companionship, salesmanship for solicitude, and passive submission for active participation.

The Core Group

To the person with experience in voluntary organizations, the most impressive feature of McLain's movement is the substantial core of devoted followers he has been able to create. This core, although perhaps not too stable in composition, makes possible a large budget, and provides energy for petition drives. Because the great majority of members behave like customers whose patronage depends on the exigencies and the whims of the moment, it is doubtful whether the CISW could exist without a core of devoted members. These are to be found among the high contributors, the life members, those making payments on life memberships, and the club presidents.

Types of devotion.—Among the thousands who make extraordinary sacrifices for McLain, there is at any time a relatively small group of dedicated members. What are the characteristics of this group? People who become attached to an organization may be strong supporters of the goals for which they think the organization stands; or else they may be loyal to the organization and its leader as such. Both types of attachment can be discerned among the more involved members of the Institute. The recent acolyte is more goal-oriented. He enters the core group because he hopes that the organization and its leader can somehow change the circumstances of his life which he holds responsible for his dissatisfaction. He may be mistaken about the Institute's aims and methods; having entered the inner circle only recently, he is less well informed than core group members of long standing. The older member of the core group is more likely to know all the answers which are "right" by Institute standards; yet his enthusiasm may have suffered in the process of habituation to the organization's routine. In his mind, the very existence of George McLain and his movement may have become more important than the goals for which they purport to strive. Relatively few will succeed in retaining an emotional attachment along with an organizational participation which has become part of the daily routine of living. These, however, are the most valuable members from the standpoint of the organization.

The three types of core-group members (emotionally committed, organizationally involved, and a combination of the two) are unevenly distributed over the four classes of members of which the core group is composed. Those making payments toward life membership seem to include the largest proportion of neophytes emotionally involved in the organization. Both high contributors and life members tend more toward the organizational type of attachment. The club presidents, generally, are characterized by both emotional and organizational attachment.

Among life members and club presidents one can hardly expect to find any neophytes. Practically all life members have gone through a novitiate of at least eighteen months, and it would be very unusual for anyone to become a club president without previous experience in the organization. Of all the core-group members, those making payments on life memberships have been in the organization for the shortest time; on the average, they have belonged to the organization for 3.6 years.[22] For life members the

[22] Many members have difficulty in recalling when they joined the Institute. The questionnaire answers are of limited value, since there is a high proportion of nonresponses. Moreover, nonresponse rates vary considerably (61 per cent for the least involved members, 15 per cent for life members, none for club presidents). The figures given in the text are estimates based on the assumption that about one-third

average length of stay in the organization is 5.3 years; for club presidents, 4.5 years; for high contributors, 3.9 years.

There are some suggestive differences in the demographic characteristics of the most involved groups. Nearly two-thirds of those making payments toward life membership are women, although in the Institute as a whole women account for 53 per cent of the membership. The proportion of women is also somewhat high among life members (59 per cent). The opposite is true for club presidents, of whom only 36 per cent are women, and for high contributors (46 per cent). Among the club presidents, 71 per cent are married, and 49 per cent of the high contributors still have their spouses living. These figures are higher than those for the groups paying on life memberships (41 per cent married) and for life members (45 per cent married). The proportion living in cities with populations of 100,000 or more is only 16 per cent for club presidents and 43 per cent for high contributors.[23] Of those paying installments on life membership, 49 per cent live in large communities; and among life members, 40 per cent.

Thus, in each of the four most involved groups, there are appreciable differences in the comforts and economic advantages derived from married life in less urban environments. In this respect aspiring life members are least fortunate, life members are somewhat more comfortable, high contributors still more so, and club presidents head the list. But these differences do not show up in the same way when we consider the other two indices of comparative advantage: home ownership and source of income. Here, only the club presidents include a consistently higher proportion of privileged members. In general, only the club presidents are more privileged than the average Institute member; when slight privilege is measured by cumulative advantages, the differences among high contributors, aspiring life members, and life members disappear.

The primarily emotional attachment of aspiring life members manifests itself in a fairly high dissatisfaction level and in roman-

---

of those not answering the question actually do not recall when they joined the organization, while the remainder joined so recently that they either are not sure whether they are members or else wish to conceal the recency of their joining.

[23] See tables 22, 24, and 25.

ticized images of McLain. These members are less inclined than are other members to think of the CISW as a service organization. Having not yet learned to give all the "right" answers, they express their negativism in demands upon society rather than in distrust of the pension law, of the social worker, and of McLain's "opposition." The activity scores of aspiring life members are about as low as those of life members, and there is a fairly wide gap between actual activities and activity aspirations.[24]

The attachment of high contributors and life members to the Institute is more organizational than emotional. In neither group is general dissatisfaction particularly high, nor are the demands on society numerous. Both groups tend to give the "correct" answers in expressing distrust of McLain's "enemies" and in describing McLain and the Institute. However, life members are more deeply committed to its official ideology than are the high contributors, but the latter tend to lead more active personal lives, with the result that their interest in the organization is somewhat diluted by other interests. (It will be remembered that there is a fairly large proportion of men among the high contributors.)

The club presidents are both emotionally and organizationally committed to the Institute. They display high activity and activity aspirations. They evince strong dissatisfactions, particularly of an ideological sort. At the same time, they are very negative in their feelings about the pension law, the social worker, and the "enemies" of the Institute. However, their image of McLain and of the Institute is less romantic than that of the aspiring and paid-up life members.

The most active followers.—The most active member is not necessarily the one with the strongest attachment to the organization. It will be remembered that some of the signature collectors were quite critical of McLain and the Institute. In order to gain a sharper view of the highly active members, we have examined a selected group of 110 followers. These were all the people in our sample who had made voluntary contributions of more than $5 during the preceding three months, attended all the meetings,

---

[24] Comparisons in this and the next two paragraphs are based on data in tables 15, 17, 19, 31, 32, 34, 40, and 41.

listened to McLain's radio program at least four times a week, and participated in all signature collection campaigns.

Of this group, 22 were club presidents; 73 were life members, 13 were making installments toward life memberships, 23 were regular members, and 1 was without clear membership status. We estimate that these 110 persons in the sample represent at most 1,500 Institute members who are similarly active. Slightly more than half of these would be regular members.[25] Clearly, it would be incorrect to assume that the core group consists chiefly of life members.

The special character of these most active members is best understood when they are compared with the average members and the club presidents.[26] These people are neither particularly high nor particularly low on the scale of slight privilege. They express a higher degree of general dissatisfaction than any other group in this survey; their average score is .71, compared with .55 for the membership as a whole, and .64 for club presidents. The activists resemble aspiring life members more than any other group of highly involved members.

Their demand scores, however, are about the same as those for the membership as a whole (3.83 as compared with 3.86). Instead of subscribing to demands upon society as a whole, they direct their feelings against the pension law. Of these very active members, 85 per cent check only adjectives unfavorable to the pension law; in this respect they exceed even the club presidents, of whom only 76 per cent take so completely negative a stand; among the total membership, only 55 per cent describe the pension law in only unfavorable terms. Similarly, the most active members make the highest proportion of entirely negative judgments of the social worker (51 per cent as compared with 41 per cent for club presidents and 27 per cent for the membership as a whole).

The key to high activity is apparently this single-minded focusing of all negative feelings upon the welfare law and institutions. Along with this negativism, activists exhibit a considerable amount

---

[25] Because of the sampling rates applied in our survey, the regular members are underrepresented in the active group.

[26] The data discussed in the following paragraphs are shown in table 48.

of distrust, which is about as high as that of club presidents (.62 for activists, .60 for club presidents, and .51 for the general membership).

The most active members have the most highly sentimentalized image of McLain. In no group is there a higher proportion of individuals calling him "protector" (56 per cent, as against 46 per cent for presidents and 44 per cent for the general membership), "good shepherd" (49 per cent, as against 43 per cent for presidents and 38 per cent for members in general), or "brother" (28 per cent, as against 20 per cent for presidents and 15 per cent for members in general). Few activists, however, regard McLain as a political leader (11 per cent as against 20 per cent for presidents and 14 per cent for members in general).

It is of particular interest that only one-third of the most active members designate McLain as "friend"; this is the lowest proportion of "friend" responses observed in any group. Among the general membership, 47 per cent regard McLain as a friend; among club presidents, 39 per cent. As we have seen, the proportion of members who think of McLain as a friend decreases with increasing involvement in the CISW. This generalization carries over to the most active members. They need to think of "George" as a somewhat remote protector or an almost divine being; or else, in a curious but typical reversal, some of them see themselves in a very intimate "brotherly" relation with McLain.

Participation in the Institute leads to estrangement from the social world and to an unrealistic view of experience, but *increased* participation in the organization is accompanied by estrangement from McLain. This paradoxical result is to be attributed to the structure of the CISW and the procedures employed by McLain. The members who are capable of developing an institutional attachment are not given a sufficient chance to do so, for there is not enough of an organization to identify with. Consequently, McLain must rely mostly upon persons who are seized by sudden enthusiasm and who throw themselves into his campaigns with abandon. From the point of view of continuity in the organization, these are the least desirable core group members. They cannot be relied upon to stay with a job. They have ambivalent feelings about the organization and its leader. More than any other group, they project guilt feelings upon the rest of the membership (93 per cent say that others are not doing enough; this compares with 69 per cent for the average membership and 89 per cent for club presidents); and thus coöperation within the Institute would seem to be difficult. Their belief in the organization and its leader requires constant bolstering, and their zeal calls for continuous reinforcement.

This is perhaps one reason why the Institute is a crisis organization. The kinds of people from whom McLain is capable of getting most useful support must constantly be brought back into line; they must be bullied or wheedled into action. They must hear strong language presented in a single-minded fashion before they will bestir themselves on behalf of the cause. So long as McLain must count on this part of the core group for much of the necessary funds and labor, he cannot refrain from the use of "high-powered" propaganda techniques to which some segments of the community object.

Chapter VI | *Political Action*

McLAIN's primary political task has been to organize the constituency. He has had to reach out into the old-age population and create a new political enterprise. Consequently, a very large part of the organization's activity has been directed inward, toward the members and potential members, rather than to the general community.

At the same time, the possibility of organizing the "old folks," and sustaining the organization, has required a program of continuing action in the larger political arena. The struggle for increased pension benefits is the major device for recruiting new members and reinforcing the commitment of old ones. It is the key to fundraising, lending credence to the urgency of financial appeals and to the recurring "crises" from which the organization must be saved. The McLain movement is an exercise in political mobilization; it has no other basis for survival.

For the most part the Institute has used the normal means available in California for pressure on public policy. This consists primarily of lobbying activities in Sacramento and direct appeals to the electorate through the initiative procedure. However, the Institute's activities have also been a vehicle for furthering the political ambitions of McLain himself.

The long-term political effectiveness of an organization depends in large part on its community relations. A secure base of support can be found among like-minded groups; communication with other forces can produce temporary alliances; and the organization may thus earn the esteem of disinterested elements who value what it does. Moreover, good community relations may inspire enough respect among opponents to sustain rational controversy. The extent to which the CISW has succeeded or failed in establishing such relations in the community is a major theme of this account.

Since the organization directs so much of its activity toward the single purpose of survival, its external effectiveness is inevitably hampered. The spokesman himself, by his own psychological make-up, is limited in his dealings with other people. The members are hampered by declining health, lack of status, and psychological withdrawal. Because of its structure the Institute cannot provide a political and social training ground for community participation. Leader and follower alike have a none too clear perception of the political world in which they live. Such an organization has many difficulties when it engages in political action, especially when it does so in a hostile environment.

Getting on the Ballot

For groups lacking other political tools, direct legislation provides an opportunity to apply political pressure. An analysis of the issues which have appeared on the California ballot as initiative statutes or initiative constitutional amendments shows three groups supporting such measures: groups which are geographically diffuse, have no organization, or whose common interests arise only sporadically; groups with a small constituency struggling for social recognition; and groups making large demands on the public treasury.

The Constitution of California provides a remarkably effective instrument for pension politics. In 1911 an initiative procedure was established, giving to the citizenry direct legislative power equal, in some respects, to that of the elected state senators and assemblymen. By the use of the initiative, amendments to the state constitution can originate from private citizens as well as from the legislature. In either case, a simple majority of those voting on the proposed amendment is sufficient to make it part of the constitution.

Amendments resulting from the passage of an initiative are well protected. The governor cannot veto such measures nor can the legislature amend or repeal them unless the measure specifically provides for such amendments. Only another popular referendum, originated by the legislature or the people, can alter or revoke direct initiative legislation. Thus direct legislation by the people, acting through organized interest groups, is a constant political factor in California state politics.[1]

Despite the power of the direct legislation provided in the state constitution, the ability to use the instrument is now greatly limited. Any citizen or group wishing to initiate direct state-wide legislation must have large resources. In 1954 the valid signatures of more than 300,000 votes were required merely to qualify an initiative constitutional amendment or statute for the ballot. Since many signatures are invalid, well over 400,000 must be collected initially—a formidable task for any group.

As a result there has been a growing tendency in the state to hire professional organizations specializing in the collection of qualification signatures, at an estimated cost of $75,000. A group unable or unwilling to spend this sum must make large-scale use of volunteer petition circulators. But this requires a sizable organization. Since World War II, the California Teachers Association has been the only interest group able to rely solely on volunteers to qualify an initiative.

For the CISW the problem is not entirely one of cost. Petition drives supply an immediate purpose and a sense of participation

---

[1] We are concerned here with only one aspect of direct action by the registered voters—the initiation of legislation. In addition, there is the referendum, which provides for the suspending of acts passed by the legislators (with certain exceptions) until the voters have a chance to approve or veto it. Another direct-action instrument of the voters is the recall, whereby a public official can be forced to undergo an election during his term of office. All three actions can be either local or statewide; all require petitions with varying numbers of signatures and all three have been frequently used.

See Winston Crouch and Dean McHenry, *California Government* (Berkeley and Los Angeles: University of California Press, 1949), pp. 100–112; W. Crouch, *State and Local Government in California* (University of California Press, 1952); W. Crouch, *Initiative and Referendum in California* (Haynes Foundation, 1950); California State Chamber of Commerce, *Initiative Legislation, 1950; California Election Code, California State Constitution.*

for the members, whose advanced years sharply curtail their other activities. The McLain organization, in combining voluntary and professional circulators, reflects the restrictions placed on the organization by its own character and by the political system within which it operates.

Qualifying an initiative has been one of the characteristic political weapons of pension groups. For these groups, the running of qualification campaigns has a number of functions. Once the measure is on the ballot, there is always the possibility that the climate of the times will bring approval by the voters. Moreover, a qualified measure can be used to raise campaign funds for the passage of the measure or for other organizational purposes. Finally, the campaign serves to reinforce the members' commitments by involving them in activity.

Even a defeat at the polls may still demonstrate such potential voting strength that the future demands of the organization will have to be taken into account. In the past, all three of the major pension groups in California—Townsendites, Ham and Eggs, and the CISW—have qualified initiatives for the ballot. But only the Institute has had an initiative passed to become part of the state law.

Petition campaigns.—In its petition campaigns, the Institute is hampered by the fact that its volunteers are aged, untrained, and in some instances physically handicapped. But the reliability of the members more than compensates for these disadvantages. Most of the difficulties met by professionals in recruiting reliable workers do not exist for the Institute. On the average, more than 70 per cent of the signatures collected have been valid, and in the 1950 campaign the percentage rose to 80 per cent.

Institute members are probably able to obtain a better response from voters than do professional petition circulators. They are fighting their own battle, and the public perceives this. Passers-by on the streets, shoppers in supermarket parking lots, and housewives in their doorways seldom refuse to sign the petitions. Some members have collected as many as 1,500 signatures. One collector reported:

It only took me about four hours to fill in a petition with about twenty-five names. Once in a while I'd meet a person who was hostile. These people were sore at McLain. They called him an old buzzard. I told one guy that said that, "Tomorrow we'll shoot him before breakfast." You should have seen him hightail it!! I was surprised at all the young people. They weren't yet here in the county. They wanted to sign it though. I wouldn't let them do it. McLain is fighting for us. The old people sponsor McLain. They're not working for him; he's working for us.

The most popular method of collection is door-to-door canvassing; this is supplemented by collections in commercial establishments, on the streets, or through personal contacts. Some collectors have used a combination of methods.

I'd meet them door-to-door. I'd go to the public places. I asked all the registered voters. First I'd ask them if they were in favor of it and if they were I'd gladly let them sign. I didn't go to all the houses along the street. I didn't want to walk too far to the ones that were in back. I went down to the stores like the laundry. I went up to the head man in the store. I asked him if he was in favor of the old folks getting a pension. I don't remember asking any customers for their signatures. Somebody else got the petition to the big stores before I did. Toward the last, pretty near every other person I asked had already signed the petition.

The signature collectors sometimes find the citizenry more than willing to coöperate. One said:

Everybody was anxious to sign. They came here, they came to the house. A few were afraid, of course, because of taxes. That's all though, just one man. A lady didn't sign, for religious reasons, I think. She was a—now what's that? I never can remember these names—oh yes, a Jehovah's Witness. And then there might be some for that other church, what's that the television . . . Oh yes, the Four Square Gospel signed, too.

Another reported:

The first place I tried said that it would increase taxes. I asked him if he hollered when they raised the pay of supervisors. I asked him if he hollered when they raised the pay of the governor. He said no. I asked him why he should holler about raising our pension.

McLain is sometimes the subject of argument between the collector and the potential signer. One woman collector reported:

Some were pretty snotty. There was one guy I could have slapped in the face. He was snotty. He asked if it was George McLain that was behind the petition. I said "yes." He said, "He's just hogging people out of everything."

Her experience differed from that of the man who said:

They were all friendly. I talked to one colored lady and she said no, she wouldn't give no money. I said to her, "Do you get a pension?" She said yeh. . . . I said, "Why don't you sign?" Well, maybe some people are nervous because the county welfare service runs around here all the time with papers to sign . . . that's no way to do . . . but I told the people, "Mr. McLain will help you."

In McLain's hands, petition circulation itself has become a political instrument. Beginning in 1941, when he made his first attempt to qualify an amendment,[2] through 1954, McLain succeeded in placing four initiative measures on the ballot. Only the 1948 measure passed, an unexpected success that was immediately followed by a bitter campaign to rescind it. In a special election an anti-McLain referendum was passed, revoking most provisions of the McLain proposition.

The successful 1948 measure was qualified for the ballot by a professional signature-collecting company which gathered 215,530 certified signatures, 10,000 in excess of the number needed for qualification. The collection cost, according to the October, 1947, issue of the *Advocate*, was "approximately $75,000." It was impossible for the Institute to raise this sum from membership contributions, although $25,000 was borrowed from the members.[3]

The 1948 initiative contained far-reaching revisions of the state's old-age program. In addition to increasing the maximum allowable grant from $60 to $75 per month, reducing the eligibility age, and liberalizing other eligibility requirements, it removed the control of the program from the counties and placed it in the hands of an enlarged and centralized State Department of Social Welfare. The most controversial of its provisions specifically named Myrtle Williams the first elected director of the Department of Social Welfare. Mrs. Williams was secretary-treasurer of the Institute and one of McLain's close collaborators.

---

[2] McLain prepared an initiative in 1941, but made no real attempt to have it qualified. Its titling by the Attorney General—a purely automatic process set by law—was hailed as a victory by McLain. The amendment was read in full over the air, and copies of it were apparently sold to the members.

[3] "We have raised this $25,000 in loans. Yes, we accepted loans from our members in amounts over $50, for which we issued notes payable to the bearer on demand after 90 days" (broadcast, February 13, 1948).

To the surprise of everyone, the 1948 initiative passed by a 2 per cent margin: 1,837,805 voted for the measure, 1,800,513 against. But immediately after its passage a campaign to repeal the measure began, ending with McLain's defeat in the 1949 special election.

After the 1949 repeal of the 1948 measure, the organization, exhausted by its fight against repeal, was heavily in debt and was losing members. But within six months McLain bounced back with another initiative petition plan. For this new referendum he decided to use the indirect method, requiring valid signatures equal to only 5 per cent of the votes cast in the previous gubernatorial election instead of the 8 per cent required for the direct method. McLain this time planned to use the members as volunteer signature collectors, with professionals supplementing their work.

To qualify the initiative in the fall of 1950, prior to the election, was undoubtedly advantageous. The use of the indirect method reduced the number of required signatures; moreover, there was every reason to believe that the 1950 vote would be extremely large. McLain thought that his 60,000 members might reasonably be expected to gather the 127,910 valid signatures without great difficulty.

McLain had much to gain and nothing to lose from qualifying the initiative which would reach the new legislature in January, 1951. There was little expectation that the legislature would pass the bill; but its existence would give direction and emphasis to McLain's lobbying activities. He could anticipate using the measure during an entire year as a fund-raising and organization-building tool.

McLain had learned a great deal from the 1948 passage and the 1949 repeal of his initiative and had used that knowledge in writing the 1950 measure. One of the weakest parts of the 1948 initiative, which had made it highly vulnerable to sustained attack, was the naming of Myrtle Williams to the post of welfare director. The 1950 proposal included no such provision. The new measure also called for state administration of the welfare program, but avoided the wholesale reorganization contemplated in the 1948 proposal. In other respects the 1950 initiative was very similar to the earlier one. One totally new provision was included: the amount of the assistance payment was to be adjusted to the cost-of-living index.

To validate the 1950 initiative, half of the signatures were gathered by professionals. The remainder were collected by the members. More than 327,000 names were filed, of which 249,202 were validated; this amounted to nearly twice the number needed. After validation the measure was sent to the legislature. There, as had been anticipated, no action was taken and it was placed on the ballot for the 1952 election.

The year of McLain's most ambitious attempts to gain power via the ballot box, was 1952. In the same year he ran for Congress.[4] He also successfully carried out a much more difficult campaign to qualify a second initiative measure only indirectly related to the pension issue. This initiative, prohibiting certain uses of public funds, was directed against the chambers of commerce and the County Supervisors Association.

The public-funds measure originated from charges made in the state legislature that county boards of supervisors were distributing county tax funds to lobbyists (mainly representing the State Chamber of Commerce), who then used the funds to influence legislation. A bill to prevent this practice had been introduced in the legislature and defeated.

McLain took up the issue and gave it extensive publicity on the radio and in the newspaper. It is not unlikely that he conceived of a second initiative dealing with this matter as a diversionary maneuver; he could hope that the chambers of commerce would concentrate their fire upon this second issue and correspondingly invest less effort in the fight against the pension measure.

It was not only the large number of signatures that made the task of qualifying the amendment so difficult. The issue itself required a sustained attack upon the Chamber of Commerce, an organization not usually identified as evil by the general public. Further, since McLain's own members did not easily connect their own welfare with the necessity for defeating the chambers of commerce, the pool of volunteer signature collectors was rather small. The exceptionally severe winter and the fact that McLain refused,

[4] For a description of the congressional campaign see below, pp. 236–243.

despite professional advice, to wait until the end of the holiday season were added factors in making the qualification of the Chamber of Commerce initiative the most difficult of McLain's campaigns.

The collection effort began in November, 1951, when the proposed amendment was titled. Professional petition circulators were employed, but McLain made a great effort to mobilize and use his members. By mail and radio, at Institute and club meetings, the members were asked, urged, and cajoled into accepting petition blanks, which were available in one hundred-name, twenty-five-name, and six-name sizes. The six-name petition, dubbed the "family" size, had never before been used in any campaign in California, and may be one of McLain's original contributions to the art of collecting signatures.

For the first time, too, McLain was assisted by other groups in his attempt to qualify the amendment. Both the state AFL and the CIO endorsed the campaign and circulated petitions. No accurate count was kept of the number of signatures gathered from or by union members; but both labor organizations and McLain agree that this number was very small.

Finally, after great effort, in March, 1952, 460,000 names were filed, 327,526 of which were found to be valid. Professionals had gathered approximately 80,000 of the total. The petition had qualified.

Both of McLain's measures, the previously qualified old-age benefit increase and the Chamber of Commerce measure, were defeated in the 1952 election despite a spirited campaign. The benefit increase lost by a vote of 2,619,927 to 2,021,038 and the Chamber of Commerce measure lost even more decisively by a vote of 2,467,604 to 1,776,367.

During the summer of 1953, a national pension of $100, to be paid by the federal government, was given priority in Institute's propaganda. McLain advised his members that it would take time to achieve this goal. He toured the state, ostensibly to see whether the membership wanted to place the $100 pension measure on the state ballot in 1954. Presumably they did, and the new campaign was launched.

To put this measure before the voters, a large number of valid signatures (303,687) was again required. Several factors helped ease the task of collecting signatures. Since the measure dealt specifically with their own problems, the members were more willing to spend the necessary time. And public response, which determines the ease and speed of signature collection, was favorable. The amendment was simple, uncluttered with such technicalities as cost-of-living indices, responsible relatives' problems, changes in administration, and excess-needs payments. This, said McLain, would prevent the opponents of the amendment from using their "favorite means of attack—which is to pretend to sympathize with the need for an increased pension payment but to find fault with any proposal to effect such an increase because of some other provisions contained in the measure" (*Advocate,* January, 1954).

Once again the family-size petitions as well as the larger ones were successfully used. Interviews in 1954 with a sample of the volunteer petition circulators disclosed an almost unanimous opinion that the 1953 petition campaign had been the easiest, by far, of all the CISW efforts.

The December, 1953, *Advocate* had announced that 400,000 names were to be collected by volunteers. But McLain was evidently not satisfied with that goal, for in April, 1954, two weeks before the final filing date, he stated that 450,000 names had already been collected but that 500,000 were needed. To achieve that end, professionals were to be hired. At the first filing, 550,000 names were turned in, of which 392,484 were valid, giving McLain a margin of 88,979.

The total of 550,000 names was one of the highest ever collected in the state in a short period of time; but it did not represent an omen of things to come. The 1954 election continued the pattern established in 1949; the voters again rejected McLain's amendment by a vote of 2,030,132 to 1,688,319.

Referendum Campaigns

McLain has generally found it easier to mobilize the membership for a petition campaign than to convince the voters to pass the amendment. Although there is considerable support for welfare legislation in California (McLain's propositions always receive a sizable vote of approval), all but one of his measures have been defeated. The vote for the propositions is, however, large enough to encourage the members and make them help qualify another amendment and work for its passage.

Amendment campaigns require a complete shift in the Institute's orientation. During the period of qualifying an amendment, internal problems are paramount, for success depends almost completely upon the carrying out of a specific task by the members. But, after qualification, referendum campaigns require an external orientation. It is no longer the members alone who must be convinced of the legitimacy of the Institute's demands, but the public as well. During the campaign, McLain has a difficult double task to perform: he must attempt to persuade the electorate while simultaneously making demands upon the membership.

McLain's internal organizational efforts during the campaigns are carried out through his radio programs, special mail appeals, and Institute meetings.

The radio broadcasts are directed primarily toward the members. McLain recognizes that his listening audience, beyond his own membership, is not large. The broadcasts present all the standard campaign arguments concerning the proposition, together with limited, inner-circle organizational information and instruction.

How many of you members are planning to attend our great big, second annual convention at Long Beach? To be held there on September twentieth for a two-day session of great importance to all of us! I know a lot of you are going but we must know how many to count on, so we can make our arrangements for hotel accommodations and for luncheon and banquet. [Broadcast, September 10, 1954]

The fund-raising appeals to members increase in tempo and length during the campaign broadcasts.

Each day we've fallen a little farther behind—and each day I've prayed that the miracle would happen tomorrow—that enough of our friends would remember us so that we could square our shoulders with confidence and give this campaign everything we got in this last fateful month. Won't you do your part to make that miracle a reality before it is too late? It's for your own security, your own well-being and peace of mind. Let us hear from you today. Send your donations—whatever you can afford. . . . [Broadcast, October 1, 1954]

The radio campaign is seen by McLain primarily as an instrument to reach his own membership and exhort them to greater effort on his behalf. The campaign broadcasts simply continue the pattern of the daily program.

Similarly, mail campaign appeals and meetings extend and intensify the normal organization pattern. Fund-raising is the primary function. All three instruments—radio programs, mail, and meetings—are used to reach the membership and spur them on to greater efforts during the preëlection period.

Public appeals.—It is impossible to judge the relative effectiveness of McLain's attempts at mass persuasion. He avails himself of the usual propaganda devices—billboards, posters, automobile bumper stickers, handbills, direct mail, and, in 1954, television.

In the weeks before the 1954 election, the face of the elderly gray-haired woman who became the campaign symbol was seen on thousands of buildings, telephone poles, and boulders, and in the homes of pensioners as well as in Institute meeting halls. Prior campaigns had used the picture of an aged couple in the same way; the poster people always looked genteel, slightly shabby, but very clean and a little pathetic.

In some of the earlier campaigns, direct mail was used extensively. One mailing in the 1952 campaign amounted to two million pieces at a cost of $30,000 for postage. During the 1954 campaign, however, there was no large-scale, state-wide postal coverage. The expense of the method and the fact that McLain's state-wide voters' list was no longer up to date have made direct mail a less important campaign technique.

However, special mailings to specific interest groups have been an integral part of every campaign. McLain's 1952 letter to the chiropractors is a good example:

Dear Doctor,
Upon reading the other side of this letter, you will realize how important it is to you personally for Proposition 11 on the ballot to pass into law on election day.
The passage of this payment to aged persons measures means an important and new source of income for you.
It is interesting to note that 70% of the 273,000 old age pensioners cannot now avail themselves of much needed chiropractic treatments because of the

limitations placed on them by the small monthly pensions payments they are now receiving.

Under Proposition 11 the State will provide them with up to $25 a month to take care of their health needs, paid direct to the practitioner.

Because Chiropractors are eligible to receive this new income the Medical Doctors are contributing toward the fight against us, saying "it opens the doors for quacks."

At the suggestion of Dr. Palmer, we welcome your help in this campaign which will be of considerable benefit to you and the aged.

Can we count on you for $10 or more to pay for much needed radio and television these last few days before the election?

The enclosed envelope is for your convenience.

Very truly yours,
GEORGE McLAIN

We cannot assess the effectiveness of such appeals upon voting behavior. According to McLain's own statements, financial appeals directed outside the organization have brought little or no response.

Television broadcasts were used for the first time in the 1954 campaign. The programs lasted fifteen minutes and were televised on Sunday afternoons or evenings over nine stations, including outlets in Los Angeles, San Diego, and San Francisco. McLain dominated the programs, using them in part to explain and defend his own role as the leader of the organization. He discussed his family background and official history in some detail. In one telecast he held up his weekly paycheck of $100, before deductions, and showed it to the viewers. Next, he exhibited a bank account showing that the McLains' combined savings amounted to only $2,529.22. He described how the McLains had for years lived in a small apartment above the CISW office while Mrs. McLain was working. The telecast displayed a photograph of the "modest four-room bungalow" which the McLains had purchased. The opposition charge that this was a "lavish" home was derided; McLain carefully explained that he had installed a swimming pool because his wife preferred the pool to a car: it was less costly and they could both enjoy it on weekends.

All the campaign arguments were presented on the television programs. At first the word "contribution" or any suggestion of fund solicitation was studiously avoided. Until September, only letters of encouragement were requested. Then the listeners were urged to join the organization and (or) make contributions. Finally, by October, the television pleas closely resembled those which McLain was making to his members on the daily radio program.

> In these final days between now and the November 2 election, we desperately need funds to give our campaign that final boost to victory. A five, a ten, a twenty, or whatever donation you can give—may well mean the difference between slow starvation and security for the needy. Believe me, the monied interests are spending hundreds of thousands of dollars to keep the old folks from getting 66¢ a day—we must ask for donations of any amount—to help bring our message to the people. [Telecast, October 10, 1954]
>
> With big business pouring all these hundreds of thousands of dollars against us—can you imagine them having the nerve to criticize us because we ask for small donations to help in letting the public know why they should vote yes on Proposition 4? [Telecast, October 17, 1954]

Campaign themes.—Whatever the media, the campaign themes have always been the same. From the 1948 sketch of a blind man sitting on his bed in a barely furnished room and asking, "Who will wash my face this morning?" to the 1954 poster of the elderly gray-haired woman hopefully looking for assistance, pity is the chief emotion to which the Institute has appealed. This theme appears in all the campaign propaganda. The pensioners are frequently described as "weary oldsters," "needy Californians," "enfeebled oldsters," "discouraged to the point of tears," who are asking only for an "increase of a meagre 66 cents a day."

The specific arguments fall into three major categories: "facts" concerning the physical condition of California's aged, attacks upon opponents, and demonstrations to business and professional interests that the small tax increase necessary to finance the measure would be more than outweighed by the increased purchasing power resulting from additional grants.

The factual part of the CISW propaganda deals with the condition of California's aged. The position of the state's pensioners is compared with that of pensioners in other states: "California is in fifth place. California does not rank first in the nation in the amount of its old-age assistance payments. The foes of the aged would have you think so—but their propaganda is false! The truth is that California ranks fifth."

The $80 monthly "budget of needs" prepared by the state is compared to the Welfare Department's survey of "average need" of $100.02 a month. "This means, of course, many thousands of old people required a much higher income to meet their needs— which of course were not met." McLain describes a "typical" recipient: "(1) a widow, age seventy-five years, who is paying rent; (2) has lived in California for the last thirty-one years; (3) has an outside income of only $18.96 a month, which is deducted."

State Welfare Department studies are quoted to explain the financial condition of the pensioners: "The hardship forced on helpless oldsters is best illustrated by the present budget of needs allowances. In the two most vital categories, food and rent, these allowances are only $28.50 and $15.00 respectively per month, creating widespread malnutrition and misery."

The tax-cost problem also receives attention. The Institute points out that

. . . between July 1950 and July 1953, combined state and county costs declined by $8,612,650; even though the maximum aid payments were increased during this period. As more and more people become eligible for federal OASI benefits, the state and county old-age assistance costs will continue to decline even though aid payments are increased.

The opposition does not reveal the fact that the Federal government now pays more than $180,000,000 to California each year for its aid to the needy aged. All this money, which would otherwise be contributed to other states, is spent with merchants and other local businessmen in the recipients' own communities. Proposition 4 would further increase this purchasing power on the local business level, and at an annual increase of only 2½¢ on the county tax dollar.

Great emphasis is placed upon the benefits accruing to merchants and businessmen from increased purchasing power. A county is cited "where they have 1,202 old-age pensioners who receive from the Federal, state, and county government a total of $84,232 a month [at a cost to the county taxpayers of] only $6,175 a month. . . . [Proposition 4] would increase purchasing power $21,768 a month at a cost to the county of $1,610 a month. That's only 2½ per county tax dollar."

Even more direct appeals to self-interest are made. A characteristic example was the letter to chiropractors which pointed out that they had an occupational stake in the passage of the proposition.

The Institute rarely advances arguments for a proposition without attacking its opponents.

Strangely enough, there is never any opposition to the state legislators voting themselves and their dependents fat pensions, at the taxpayers' expense, or giving the governor an old-age pension of from $10,000 to $18,000 a year. The judges receive a big pension—and the Los Angeles County supervisors and sheriff receive $1,000 a month, but when a small pension based upon need, mind you, is proposed for the senior taxpayer, it is a horse of a different color. [Telecast of July 18, 1954]

Similarly, when the Institute argues that larger grants would increase purchasing power it will, at the same time, attack the "interests." "Here is real purchasing power little realized by the merchants and businessmen of the community—who have for too long been misled by the false propaganda of the state chamber of commerce and their big business allies." This attack upon big business is always present in McLain's propaganda. Why were the big business interests against his 1948 measure?

Well, friends, it's simple—in the drafting of this pension measure, I took a tax of $20,000,000 a year off the home owners and county property owners and transferred it to the state. You see, most people don't realize, but for the past fifty years the big business lobbyists have been successful in shifting from their own shoulders to the county taxpayers' shoulders, a great share of the burden of running our state government that rightfully belonged to them. [Telecast, July 1, 1954]

A letter asking for contributions declared: "Although this measure will only increase pension payments by $20 a month or 66¢ a day, state chamber of commerce, and the big business interests (see other side) are steadily opposing its passage through the newspapers and other powerful means at their disposal." The "other side" referred to in the letter listed some of the corporations contributing to the campaign against McLain. The amounts of these contributions appeared under the headline "MONEY BAG$ $UPPLY LUH FUND AGAIN$T NEEDY."

McLain's combative posture may be accounted for in part by the large amount of personal criticism launched against him. The ease with which McLain's opposition has been able to follow this pattern, with the general support of the press, reflects the low public status of McLain and his organization. Since his followers invariably respond better when McLain "turns on the heat" and is under attack, it becomes clear why his campaigns deal so extensively with the evil ways of "the opposition." McLain is forced to fight on the battleground chosen by his enemies. Two important consequences are that the real issues raised by Institute propositions are often pushed into the background and do not come to the attention of the voters; and, because of its character, the campaign propaganda has greater appeal for Institute members than for average voters. Cut off from the public at large by a screen of adverse propaganda, the Institute has less opportunity to develop campaign themes which might have meaning for the general public.

This limitation is reflected in the few ineffectual attempts of the Institute to influence the press or voluntary organizations in the community. Instead of advancing arguments for his proposition, McLain is kept busy in attempts to discredit his opponents. In 1954 a long letter was sent to every newspaper in the state; it pointed out that the organization handling the anti-McLain campaign was being sued by McLain for allegedly libelous releases. The letter clearly implied that any newspaper using this material might also face a lawsuit. No defense of the proposition was made in the letter, which concluded: "It is one thing to oppose a measure on its merits; it is an entirely different matter to engage in libel and to involve others."

The California Federation of Women's Clubs received a letter from McLain in September, 1954, advising them that "their club would be addressed by Mr. N. Bradford Trenham, General Manager of the California Taxpayers' Association, speaking in opposition to Proposition 4." The letter pointed out that CTA is "big business," and listed the names and business affiliations of the executive committee members, including the president of the Southern California Gas Company. The company was attacked in the letter on the ground that it was requesting a rate increase at the same time that ". . . we find these big business interests who 'put on the poor mouth' before the State Utilities Commission, now spending their time, money, and effort against the old and helpless."

A letter to members of the Democratic state and county central committees stated: "It is the State Chamber of Commerce and their big business affiliates who are financing the campaigns of the Republican candidates and incumbents. The same selfish interests are also putting up the money to fight Proposition 4, a measure which will give the needy elderly an increase of $20 more a month or 66¢ a day."

Role of Institute members.—During campaigns McLain sees his membership primarily as a source of funds, and expects little work from them. Raising the large sums necessary for the campaigns calls for extra effort on McLain's part. Although the devices used are much the same as those employed during noncampaign periods, there is a sharp difference in the character and tone of the fund-raising. It is, first of all, more urgent. The radio broadcasts become saturated with pleas for funds; the *Advocate* dins the same message in every issue. Institute and club meetings are interrupted constantly by a variety of fund-raising appeals. Second, there are more publicity devices during the campaign. Buttons are sold, window stickers distributed, and the members are asked to become financial "sponsors" of McLain's television programs. McLain endeavors to convince the members that their contributions will result in an immediate financial gain through the passage of the amendment.

The social welfare clubs themselves became "gimmicks" in 1953–1954, when they were styled the "100-clubs"; they were so named for the proposed amendment which would have raised the maximum grant to $100. Each club member was urged to raise $100 in campaign contributions. Account cards were to be issued and "Upon receipt of a total of $100, the holder [of the account card] will receive an appreciation award in the form of a $100 Aid-to-the-needy-aged century bond; not of any monetary value but of great intrinsic value for the holder" (*Advocate*, June, 1954).

In addition to requests for funds, other less successful demands are made upon the members. Each campaign sees elaborate plans to utilize members in the distribution of literature, in house-to-house calls, and in getting out the vote. And each campaign finds the members doing very little of this work. The lack of membership participation shows up sharply in the contrast between the great activity carried on at campaign headquarters and the effects actually produced upon the members of the organization. During the 1952 campaign, speakers addressing club and Institute meetings took with them quantities of printed cards and pamphlets, which were stacked on tables at the meetings, but remained undisturbed. In the same campaign the club director merely expressed a "hope" that club members would be organized for the tasks of placing literature on card tables near points of heavy pedestrian traffic, conducting telephone campaigns, watching the polls, and counting votes (*Advocate,* November, 1952).

Near the end of the 1952 campaign, prizes were offered to members in whose precincts the highest percentage of "yes" votes would be cast. First prize, a trip to headquarters, was to be given to the member personally responsible for a *unanimous* "yes" in his precinct on both propositions 10 and 11. No mention of the contest was made after the election was over, nor was any winner ever announced.

Evidently no one won the 1954 contest either, although the campaign was organized better that year. The state was divided into northern and southern areas with a campaign director for each. Volunteers were sought in almost every precinct to distribute publicity material. Managers, selected for each county and assembly district, were made responsible for creating an organization that was to have as its base a volunteer in each precinct. In the 1954 contest the earlier first prize of a trip to headquarters was replaced by something more tangible—a new stove, a refrigerator, or a television set.

Supplementary prizes of one-cup coffeemakers were offered to member contestants "responsible for majority votes on Proposition 4 in their precincts." All awards were predicated on state-wide passage of the proposition. Since a fund-raising drive was going on simultaneously, McLain perhaps felt impelled to explain the contest by saying that it "doesn't mean we have any surplus money with which to buy expensive prizes—but we must make certain that pensioners get $100 for life. And if we have to give away prizes to do it, we will" (*Advocate*, September, 1954).

To enter the contest the members had only to mail in a form indicating that they would be responsible for certain precincts. In this fashion the organization attempted to recruit precinct workers and gain some idea of the precincts covered during the campaign. It was apparent from observation of both the 1952 and 1954 campaigns that precincts not covered far outnumbered those in which an active Institute member was working. McLain's image of a state-wide political precinct organization of the aged is likely to remain a dream. For it is obvious that his ability to mobilize the membership is limited to specific tasks. The members will collect signatures to qualify an initiative, but are far less interested in carrying on the more general campaign to pass the amendment. They may well feel that their efforts are indeed significant in getting on the ballot but that it is beyond their power to affect the final outcome.

The vote.—Even in defeat, McLain's measures have had the support of a large number of voters. The Institute's sole victory in 1948 was achieved by a vote of 1,837,805, giving the proposition a slim majority of 37,292, or 1 per cent of the total vote. In 1948, a presidential election year, more than 4,000,000 votes were cast in California. Of the registered voters, 80.5 per cent participated in the election, and 89.2 per cent of those casting ballots voted for or against McLain's Proposition 4.

In 1949, the year of the special election in which Proposition 4 was repealed by Proposition 2, only 61.1 per cent of the registered electorate cast ballots, but 97.1 per cent of them voted for or against repeal. It is obvious that almost everyone who voted understood that the function of the special election was to deal with McLain. The Institute's margin of loss in 1949 was 408,155 votes, or 13 per cent of the total vote.

In 1952, McLain had two measures on the ballot. The first, Proposition 10, dealing with the expenditure of public funds, lost by 691,237 votes, or 14 per cent. Proposition 11, increasing payments to the aged, lost by 591,889, or 11.5 per cent, although a higher percentage of voters cast ballots both for and against Proposition 11 than for or against Proposition 10.

McLain's margin of defeat dropped to 8.4 per cent in 1954 when his Proposition 2, increasing OAS payments, lost by 341,813 votes. Of the registered voters, 69.7 per cent participated in this non-presidential election, but 90.7 per cent of them voted approval or disapproval of McLain's proposition.

A number of significant facts emerge from the election figures. A McLain proposition has never received less than 1,000,000 votes, and, with one exception, he has always had close to 2,000,000 ballots cast in favor of his proposals. This sizable McLain vote, achieved in the face of bitter opposition, is an indication of the reservoir of welfare-oriented voters in the state.

Over the years, the vote for and against CISW propositions has followed a fairly consistent geographical pattern. The accompanying maps show areas of strength and weakness of the pro-McLain vote. California's Central Valley, consisting of the predominantly agricultural basins of the Sacramento and San Joaquin rivers, has given the least support to McLain. His areas of strength lie in the northern and eastern mountain countries, which are relatively thinly populated and rely chiefly on lumbering and some mining; in the southern counties, whose economy is based on fruit and vegetable growing and a large variety of relatively young industries; and in two industrial counties in the San Francisco Bay Area, Contra Costa and Solano. The other counties of the Bay Area, including the cities of San Francisco and Oakland, have tended to be among the districts least favorable to McLain.

The geographic analysis of the vote shows fairly clearly that there is very little relation between the vote for CISW propositions and McLain's campaigns. In the Bay Area counties which have consistently given McLain a heavy vote, no intensive campaign for the propositions has ever been noted. The geographical distribution of the pro-McLain vote appears to reflect exclusively the predispositions of certain voters. The nature of such predispositions is, however, somewhat obscure; the populations that align themselves clearly with McLain or with his adversaries are neither rural nor metropolitan, neither industrial nor agricultural.

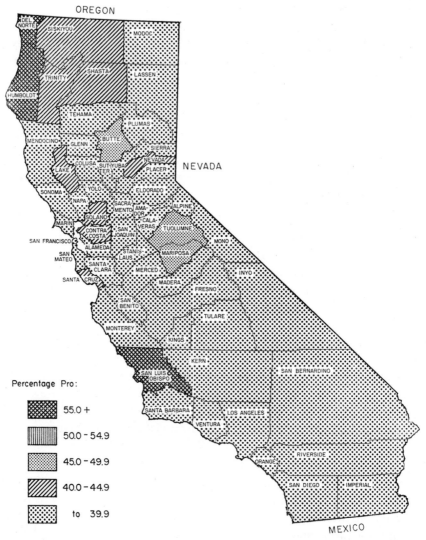

Map 1. Percentage of votes in favor of Proposition 11, by counties, 1944. Retirement payments and gross income tax measure, sponsored by Ham and Eggs.

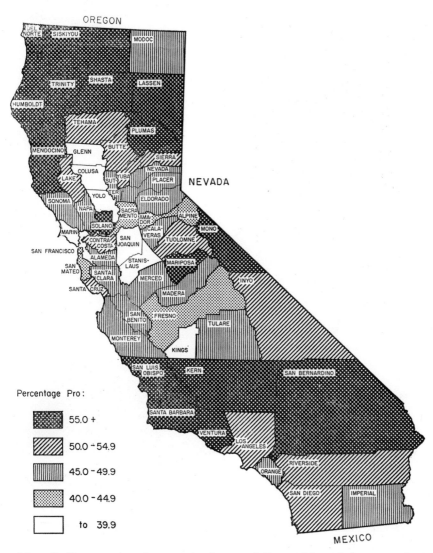

Map 2. Percentage of votes in favor of Proposition 4, by counties, 1948. Constitutional amendment sponsored by McLain.

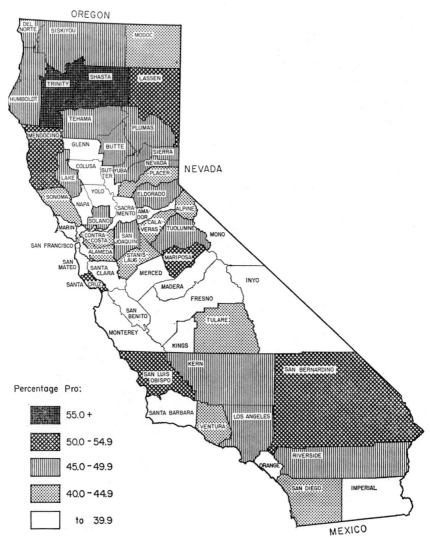

Map 3. Percentage of votes *against* Proposition 2, by counties, 1949, to repeal Proposition 4 of 1948.

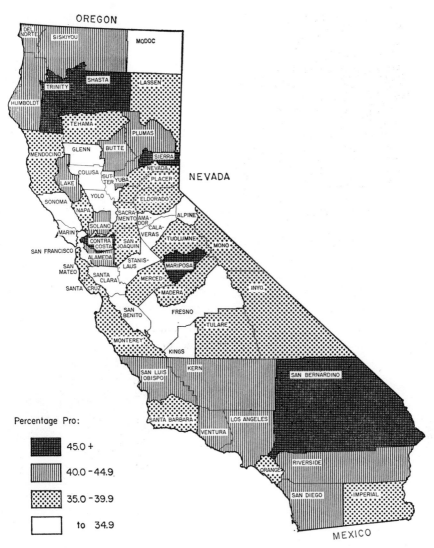

Map 4. Percentage of votes in favor of Proposition 10, by counties, 1952. Constitutional amendment prohibiting certain uses of state funds.

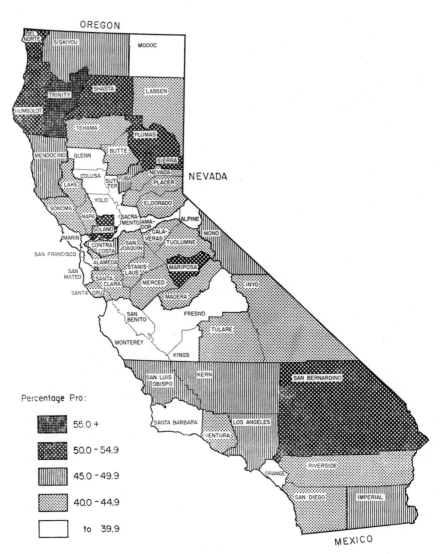

Map 5. Percentage of votes in favor of Proposition 11, by counties, 1952. Constitutional amendment increasing payments to the aged, sponsored by McLain.

This suggests that the appeal of the Institute hardly reaches the voters. In the urban centers it is drowned out by the vociferous attacks of the press upon McLain, and it is doubtful whether it reaches the smaller and more remote counties (some of which give McLain a sizable vote). In spite of its considerable propaganda effort, the CISW is cut off from the voting public. Its margin of victory or defeat seems to depend exclusively on the intensity of the campaign *against* the propositions, and not on the Institute campaign in favor of them.

No more campaigns?—Over the years, the proposals submitted to the voters by the CISW have become more and more responsible. The features which might have given McLain some political control in state affairs have been gradually eliminated. At the outset, McLain may have regarded the initiative campaigns as springboards in his personal struggle for political power. But repeated defeats at the polls seem to have modified his ambitions.

In private conversations during 1955 McLain indicated that he did not plan to run any campaigns in the future. This would be hard to explain if he saw the initiative campaign only as a device for rallying his members and justifying to them the existence of the Institute. It is evident, however, that McLain does not measure the success of his campaigns by these criteria alone. In the course of time, winning must have become more important to him than merely mobilizing the members.

If a shift toward more responsible methods does occur, McLain will probably have to abandon the use of the initiative and referendum procedure as a political tool. McLain as "the pension promoter" has become a stereotype in the minds of many Californians. The business groups who have fought McLain in each of his campaigns have made every effort to keep this stereotype alive. Any new initiative campaign would be used by them to reiterate what has been said about McLain and his pension organization for many years.

The "Interests" Against McLain

McLain's adversaries are strong and well organized. Most of their money comes from business interests, as McLain has correctly charged. Although it is impossible to make an accurate estimate of the total amounts spent to defeat McLain's propositions, it is clear that large sums are available for this activity. More than twenty contributions of over $1,000 each were listed in the Office of the Secretary of State during the 1954 campaign. Heading the list were the Pacific Gas and Electric Company with a $7,950 contribution, and the Bank of America with $7,500.

While business has supplied the money, the actual conduct of the campaign has been placed in the hands of professional organizations, supported by chambers of commerce, taxpayers' associations, and the County Supervisors Association of California. The professional campaign organizations issue press releases, buy television and radio announcements, place large advertisements in the metropolitan dailies, and distribute pamphlets under the auspices of *ad hoc* committees such as "Californians against Pension Dictators," the "Committee to Defeat Proposition 4," or permanent groups such as the State Chamber of Commerce. In 1949, McLain's opposition was able to muster many influential community organizations to fight for the repeal of the proposition which had elected Myrtle Williams to the post of state welfare director. No such wide mobilization against McLain has been possible since that year. As McLain's referenda have become more respectable, the opposing coalition has become more and more restricted to business and taxpayer groups.

"The opposition."—Prior to his 1948 election victory, McLain was virtually unknown in the state. Overnight he catapulted into fame as the business community suddenly realized that the state's OAS program was in his hands. The campaign to destroy him was begun immediately. The year 1949, during which Myrtle Williams was in office, was a legislative session year and McLain was very much in evidence in Sacramento.

McLain's behavior was closely observed, and many likened him to his predecessors, the Allen brothers of Ham and Eggs fame. His political future was still before him. According to a widely told story, McLain once sat in a restaurant at Sacramento and drew up a complete slate of candidates for the coming election—with himself as governor. The table napkin on which he had listed the names was purchased by one of the publicity men working for the opposition, and the story was given wide coverage in the press.

The possibility that McLain might become governor was enough to frighten most businessmen. The business community had no contact with McLain, no channels to him, no common points of reference. He was a stranger from another world. Mixed with this fear, distrust, and dislike of McLain was the business community's attitude toward the OAS program and the recipients. There is a pervasive concern lest the remains of the charity concept be replaced by the belief that old-age assistance is a right.

The alliance among the groups that McLain came to call "the opposition" first took shape in the 1949 campaign to repeal Proposition 4. This campaign began almost immediately after the passage of McLain's measure whereby Myrtle Williams was elected to the post of state welfare director. The same amendment had abolished relatives' responsibility, lowered the eligibility age, raised the benefits, and shifted administration of the program from the counties to the state.

The fight began when several business groups attempted to persuade the governor to call a special election for the sole purpose of submitting to the voters the repeal proposition, which had been qualified by the spring of 1949. But the governor took no action and left the problem to the legislature, which called for a special election on a school bond issue. This unusual move made it possible to put before the voters all pending propositions, including the repeal proposal.

Publicly, the repeal campaign was conducted by the California Council for the Blind, but privately it was in the hands of the State Chamber of Commerce. Both groups were opposed to McLain's proposition, although for very different reasons. The alliance allowed the Council's name to be used for prestige purposes while screening the Chamber's role in raising funds and conducting the campaign. The anti-McLain forces spent more than a million dollars to repeal Proposition 4.

The work of the California Council for the Blind was carried on by a small group under the leadership of Newell Perry. The Perry group was deeply concerned with raising the level of training and assistance for the blind, but they believed that the blind could best be helped by a program which concentrated on making them self-sufficient rather than dependent on a state grant.

McLain had contact with the Council through Frank Gardner, who headed a group affiliated with the Council. Gardner was opposed to what he called the "paternalistic attitude" of Perry and his group toward other blind people. He felt that the Council was "railroading through" its program for the blind, though it did not represent the entire group of sightless people in the state.

Bad feeling had existed between the Council and McLain ever since his appearance at a Council meeting in 1944. Perry looked upon McLain as an intruder, and clashed with him immediately. After an unpleasant session, McLain attacked the Council over the air, and Gardner and his group withdrew from the Council to join forces with McLain.

The Council had strong objections to Proposition 4. Although they were satisfied with the aspects of the proposal which dealt only with the aged (state administration, the flat grant system, and the abolition of relatives' responsibility), they were opposed to the naming of Myrtle Williams as director and to the first lien on tax funds for the aged. Their strongest objections concerned the sections of the proposition dealing with the blind. It had long been the contention of the Council that the problems of the blind and the problems of the aged were completely different, and the Council had always fought to separate the two programs, whereas the McLain proposition joined them.

The Council felt that inherent in McLain's proposition was an image of the blind as helpless. McLain's propaganda for the proposal reaffirmed this belief. Especially irritating and disturbing to the Council leadership was a cartoon in McLain's paper of a blind man sitting on his bed in a shabbily furnished room, asking, "Who will wash my face this morning?" For all these reasons, the Council leadership consented to spearhead the repeal campaign which had been initiated by the business groups.

Propaganda against McLain.—The campaigns against McLain have a number of characteristic themes. Appeals to business groups point to the cost of the CISW measure; warnings of tax increases are addressed to property owners; teachers and parent-teacher associations are told that McLain's proposal would drain funds away from education; the general public is made to fear that indigent aged from all over the country will flock to California to collect the high pensions. McLain's real or imagined political ambitions, his control over the Institute, and his personal life are bitterly attacked. In presenting these ideas to the voters, the anti-McLain forces have had a most effective ally in the press. The overwhelming majority of California's newspapers have been strongly opposed to McLain.

The State Department of Social Welfare, under Myrtle Williams, was charged with waste, inefficiency, and corruption. "We have frozen in power a pension dynasty answerable to no one, headed by promoter George McLain who directs the whole thing from behind the scenes without benefit of official office or the check rein of responsibility," editorialized one paper (Chico *Enterprise Record,* October 17, 1949). "Should McLain obtain the passage of new laws he is now seeking in the legislature, he will be Artie Samish, Governor Warren, and the legislature rolled into one," wrote another (San Diego *Tribune Sun,* October 21, 1949).

Although none of McLain's later propositions would have permitted him to obtain the political power he had through Myrtle Williams, the charge against him persisted. His two measures in 1952 were "designed to carve out a new empire for the pension dictator," claimed the opposition. And the ballot argument against the 1954 proposition said, "Proposition 4 is really another grab for political power by George McLain."

The opposition presented the picture of the helpless needy in its propaganda. The theme in the 1949 campaign was, "Protect the needy from the greedy." "There should be no necessity for paying a membership 'fee' in any organization to obtain a pension. The exploitation of the aged and blind by unscrupulous promoters will end when Proposition 2 is adopted at the polls on November eighth," was the theme of an opposition pamphlet.

"Protecting the needy" by attacking McLain and his measures continued in 1952 and 1954. In those years the charge was made that he was not only bleeding the poor but also endangering the pension system by making it too liberal. McLain's proposal was attacked because "it could result in drastic tightening of pension eligibility rules—chopping thousands of needy pensioners from the rolls and forcing them on county relief—hurting instead of helping our elderly citizens." The ballot argument against the measure used large print to state again: "Proposition 4 threatens to destroy one of the most liberal aged aid systems in the United States."

During the 1952 campaign, when McLain had two measures on the ballot—the Chamber of Commerce measure "to restrict the expenditure of certain public funds," and the increase in OAS —the opposition attacked them simultaneously with, "Smash both schemes; they're poison for California." The cover slogan on this inflammatory pamphlet was "This 'black-jack' is aimed at you."

> That pension politician is back again . . . with more poison for California. . . . The "double entry" scheme is designed to carve out a new empire for the pension dictator and to punish those organizations which have opposed him in the past. . . . The McLain black-jack is swinging. The man who gave us Myrtle Williams and has tried many other cock-eyed schemes seeks to hold off respected organizations with Proposition 10, while he takes another big bite out of your paycheck!

According to the pamphlet, the measure endangered many other worth-while projects and programs: new industries, 4-H clubs, rehabilitation programs, veterans' organizations, tourist and convention industries, and the jobs of teachers who belonged to parent-teacher associations.

McLain as an individual has always been a special target of the opposition. The first organized personal attack came in 1949 when a well-timed Senate committee hearing was arranged to investigate both the State Welfare Department under Myrtle Williams and McLain's campaign organization, the Citizens' Committee for Old Age Pensions. There can be no doubt that the investigation and hearings were an essential part of the campaign against McLain. The first public session was held a scant two weeks before the election, and subsequent sessions were scheduled on seven of the fourteen days preceding the election. All the witnesses were unfriendly to McLain, and most of them were disgruntled former employees.

The hearings were sensational, and the daily newspapers carried in rich detail the charges made against McLain and the Citizens' Committee. Typical of the manner in which the press handled the preëlection attacks upon McLain was an editorial in the Oakland *Tribune* on October 26, 1949: ". . . the McLain forces and the state social welfare director, Myrtle Williams, took a terrific drubbing in the transcript of testimony during the initial week of the hearing. Witness after witness testified to McLain's domination of the State Department now operated by the former secretary of his former pension organization, his political ambitions, his boasts of power." The front page of the Los Angeles *Times,* on the same day, described ". . . a long day of interesting testimony as to the operation of the McLain pension machine, the machinations of McLain and his efforts to put over legislation to give him greater control in the field of social welfare legislation."

It was not until well after his defeat in the election that McLain was able to fight back with "exposés" of the witnesses who had testified against him. At that time, when it was too late to affect the election and when his audience was limited to his organization's membership, McLain charged that the principal witness against him had been a member of the Ku Klux Klan, and that three of the other chief witnesses had been involved in bad-check charges and police reports (December, 1949, *Advocate*).

The hearings, which continued after the election, have been a fertile source of material to be used against McLain in every campaign. A three-part feature story, with one installment based on the investigation by the Senate Interim Committee in 1949, was sent out in 1954 by the anti-McLain group in northern California. The title of the story was, "The Pension Man Is Here Again." Throughout the articles are quotations from the committee report on McLain's money-raising "antics" and "gimmicks," his "messianic" posture, his callous and opportunistic attitude toward the aged, and his possible "intimidation of the elderly." The feature concludes with a summary which is typical of the personal attack upon McLain.

By constantly reiterated appeals for contributions and over a network of radio stations from a variety of "gimmee gimmicks" at mass meetings, from dues and subscriptions, from sales of "life memberships" costing "only" the amount of one month's pension, from sales of vitamin pills—even, it has been claimed, from commissions on burial insurance—the George McLain promotional ventures have reaped a golden harvest year after year out of the pockets of pensioners. . . .

Three legal actions occurred as a result of the 1949 hearings. In the first, a state assemblyman was indicted for bribery after it was revealed that he had been on the payroll of the Citizens' Committee while attending the legislative session. Following a lively trial in which the star witness, a former employee of McLain, was himself accused of accepting bribes, the jury was dismissed after an eleven to one vote for acquittal. The second legal action, accusing McLain of bribing the assemblyman, was dismissed under an immunity law which bars indictments based on a witness' own testimony before a legislative committee. The third action concerned McLain's refusal to submit his books and records to the Senate committee. McLain won this case when the appellate court ruled that the committee had not established the materiality of the records it sought from McLain. McLain's legal victories have not prevented the opposition from continuing to portray him as a "pension promoter" callously using "gimmicks" to collect money from the aged.

Marginal leadership and political vulnerability.—It has not been difficult for McLain's opponents to frame their fight against the propositions as a fight against an individual. McLain has done nothing to prevent this. He has never attempted to divorce the propositions from his own political personality. He was, for example, the star of the television program. He has never been successful in finding a group of citizens less vulnerable to attack who might have sponsored his proposals.

In public campaigns, McLain's complete domination of the organization and his insistence on giving an extremely personal color to all the Institute's work has been a political liability. Since McLain has sometimes used the organization for furthering his own political ends, it is not surprising that he should insist on holding the spotlight.

McLain's lack of contact with community groups greatly hinders the success of the campaigns. Since the Institute is isolated from the community, it has few campaign contacts with other organizations. McLain has increasingly realized the importance of winning support from other groups, but he has had very limited success. Some elements in the labor unions and the Democratic party, a few liberal political groups, and assorted organizations of minor political influence have supported McLain in the more recent campaigns. These groups have given him little more than nominal endorsement. McLain cannot expect financial help from them, since they are too much concerned with their own electoral problems or too poor to contribute to his campaign funds. The only known instance of direct aid to McLain occurred in 1952, when a CIO union printed a leaflet favoring the proposition prohibiting the use of public funds for lobbying purposes.

Prior to 1948, the year of its only successful campaign, the Institute had relatively little outside support. During the 1948 campaign McLain did try to erect a façade of community support. He listed endorsements by "committees," most of whom were filled with Institute staff members; a defunct organization that McLain had founded in 1936—the Natives of California—was exhumed and its ghostly presence thrown into the battle; and eleven labor groups were listed as supporters, although McLain had received no important labor endorsements.

Beginning in 1949, McLain began to obtain endorsements from labor and the Democratic party. Within the labor movement, the support of McLain's proposals is no longer limited to endorsement by an executive committee. In recent years the issues raised by the amendments have been brought to the membership at union meetings and in the labor press. More and more assistance has been given in the collection of signatures on petitions. Labor support of the referenda has become much less critical as the proposals have become more responsible.

The change in the character of McLain's propositions, from the original "pork barrel" proposal of 1948 to the much less self-interested proposition of 1954, has gained him an increasing amount of organizational support within welfare-oriented groups. Perhaps the best illustration of this is the change in attitude of the California Council for the Blind. It will be recalled that the Council was greatly perturbed by the fact that programs for the aged and those for the blind had been combined. In 1949 the Council was used to spearhead the campaign against McLain. In all the referenda following his 1949 defeat, however, McLain avoided the mistake of combining programs for the aged with those for the blind. Consequently, the Council endorsed McLain's proposals in 1952 and again in 1954.

Bid for Congress

McLain's relations with labor and minority elements are well illustrated by his campaign for the 1952 Democratic nomination in the twenty-third congressional district. His success in gaining the support of labor and other groups was due primarily to the traditional positions taken by such groups on welfare issues. But a congressional campaign requires more than sympathy on ideological grounds; it calls for coöperation and compromise. In these arts McLain has usually failed. This failure probably results more from his inability to understand the necessity and the techniques of coöperation than from a refusal to compromise on principles.

The campaign to gain a congressional nomination in 1952 provides the most clear-cut example of the personal, political use McLain has made of the Institute. McLain justified the use of the organization by stating that he would be better able to serve the interests of his members as a congressman. But the justification was an afterthought. By 1951 the House of Representatives had become his most coveted goal. All the internal drives which had in the past led him to seek election as mayor, assemblyman, state senator, and United States senator were now focused on this congressional primary.

Never before had McLain seemed to want anything as much as he did this nomination, in a safe Democratic district. One observer commented, "Months before the election, McLain could taste the bean soup served in the House restaurant. In his fantasy world, Institute chairman McLain became Congressman McLain, and McLain devoted every waking hour to making the fantasy a reality. His single-minded devotion to the election was incredible. He was truly a man obsessed with his own future." There was an almost frenetic quality about McLain's election attempt, somewhat pathetically emphasized when, a few months after his failure to win the congressional nomination, he sought unsuccessfully to be elected water commissioner in the small town of Lynwood, California, where he lives.

To achieve that future, McLain leaned heavily on the Institute's financial resources. The kind of campaign McLain waged would have been impossible without the Institute's money, technical facilities, staff members, mailing lists, and volunteer workers.

The new twenty-third district where McLain decided to run had been created in 1951 by division of the old eighteenth district. Before the split, the eighteenth had been extremely heterogeneous, both in population and in voting habits. It had included the strongly Republican residential areas of North Long Beach and Long Beach; the Democratic industrial, middle-class, and working-class areas of Southgate and Compton; and the Negro community of Watts. As a result of the legislature's action, the predominantly Republican areas of Long Beach and North Long Beach became one district, virtually guaranteeing the Republicans an additional seat. The new twenty-third district was an overwhelmingly Democratic area, and Democratic nomination meant almost certain election. The population of the district includes primarily lower-middle-class trade-union members, Negroes, and a fairly high percentage of old-age recipients.

The social composition of the population and the high Democratic registration were not the only factors that attracted McLain's attention to the district. For some time there had been persistent rumors in California political circles that Clyde Doyle, the incumbent Democratic congressman from the old eighteenth district, would not run again. He was tired of campaigning, it was said, and was no longer interested in political life. If Doyle did not run, McLain would not have to fight an incumbent for the nomination, always the most difficult type of congressional primary to win.

McLain privately began his campaign plans in the fall of 1951. His first step was to purchase a lot in the new district and begin building a house. At Institute meetings in the district, McLain told the members that he and his wife had picked the Lynwood area for their home after having looked in almost every district of the city and finding nothing they liked better. At that time nothing was said of his congressional ambitions.

Campaign activities began almost nine months before the primaries. By October, 1951, two Institute staff members were working full time on the campaign. One handled publicity and public relations; the other mapped the new district and attempted to contact influential persons and organizations within it. The publicity man was carried on the payroll of the Williams Advertising Agency, while the other staff person was on the payroll of the Institute itself.

By the beginning of 1952 the planning of the campaign was almost completed. As a first step, McLain had sent Christmas cards to the thousands of registered Democrats in the district. The fact that he intended to run was more and more widely known, although he had made no official announcement.

One problem remained unresolved—Doyle's plans. McLain was spending a great deal of time in the early months of 1952 seeking the support of the groups which had aided and supported Doyle in prior elections. In the absence of an official statement from Doyle, McLain's overtures were resisted, ostensibly on the ground that no endorsements were possible until Doyle had put his intentions on record. The Democratic party and its organized labor support feared that, in the absence of Doyle, McLain would win the nomination and the election. Doyle's silence was very welcome to the many groups who sought to avoid endorsing McLain but recognized him as the strongest alternative candidate.

As the weeks went by without official word from Doyle, McLain attempted to take precautions against the contingency that Doyle might run again. He promoted the idea that the Democratic party make either no endorsement or a split endorsement in the primaries. When Doyle finally announced that he would run again, the political and labor groups in the district were much relieved. A troublesome and embarrassing problem had been solved.

Reacting angrily to the announcement, almost as if he had been betrayed, McLain denounced Doyle and sent telegrams to other Democratic congressmen asking that they "do something" about the situation. But, with Doyle's decision made, McLain could not receive official support for his candidacy. In fact, he now had to fight Doyle among groups which had always supported the congressman in the past and were glad to do so again.

McLain's belief that Doyle would not run may have been wishful thinking, or it may have been based on what he thought was a commitment from Doyle. If he had not been very confident, in the early days of campaign planning, that Doyle had no intention of running, McLain would hardly have decided to run in the twenty-third district, since he must have known that Doyle would be assured the support of official Democrats and the unions.

Conduct of the campaign.—Any seriously contested congressional primary campaign is costly. But McLain's expenditures for the 1952 campaign, estimated by experienced observers at $75,-000–$100,000, were five to ten times as high as the usual outlay. Doyle spent less than $20,000 to defeat McLain and used a paid staff of only five in comparison with McLain's staff of twenty workers. Dean McHenry, of the Political Science Department of the University of California (Los Angeles), spent approximately $20,000 in the same year to win the Democratic nomination in a district much larger than McLain's.

Where did McLain get his campaign funds? Most of the money came directly or indirectly from the Institute itself. Staff members at work on the campaign, who were paid either by Institute or Williams Advertising Agency checks, estimated that a high proportion of the funds came from the Institute treasury. Additional funds were collected, by mail, from Institute members, who were invited to join McLain's finance committee by making donations to the campaign.

Funds were not the only Institute contribution to the campaign. The voters' mailing list was used at least three times, and the print shop turned out any campaign material that McLain felt did not require a union label. Because of high trade-union consciousness in the district, only letters or mimeographed material came from the Institute's presses. With the exception of the welfare service, the Institute's organizational machinery was focused on McLain's campaign. Meetings, club activities, the speakers bureau, the newspaper, and the radio program all reflected McLain's efforts to achieve office.

But McLain's congressional ambitions met with no real response from the Institute membership. The number of campaign volunteers was not large; nor did such volunteers work more than sporadically. Few members attended any of the election meetings held in the district, and little participation came from the clubs in the election district. Their apathy and the lack of direct involvement in the campaign were characteristic of the organization. The clubs were not designed to function as political action units in the manner of local clubs of political parties. According to some club leaders, many members may have feared that they might lose McLain if he went to Congress.

If the membership did not participate actively in the campaign, the staff did. Of the twenty paid workers, eleven were Institute personnel temporarily placed on full or part-time work for McLain's election. Since the staff members simply transferred their functions from the Institute headquarters to campaign headquarters, there was little change in the nature of their work. The *Advocate* editor wrote campaign publicity; the radio writer prepared McLain's special daily election broadcasts. Institute speakers toured the district advocating McLain's election, and the print shop turned out election material. The subheadquarters in the district were staffed with clerical employees of the Institute.

The campaign was conducted as if it were an advertising and publicity drive. Lacking a precinct organization, McLain resorted to a variety of devices to bring his name to the voters' attention: mass meetings with and without entertainment, daily radio programs, special issues of a newspaper, billboards, balloons, campaign buttons, car bumper and window stickers, doorknob reminders, and cocktail napkins. This circus-like campaign seemed to justify the newspapers' accusation that he was a "promoter"; it may have hurt him for this reason.

McLain evidently conceived his election campaign as a one-way communications process. He bombarded the voters with propaganda materials; but he failed to seek information and insights which might have gained him the support of groups influential in the district or at least prevented their turning against him. He did not deem it necessary to make sure that members of his campaign staff were acceptable to the groups with which they were to work. Nine persons who had not previously been on the Institute staff were hired for the campaign. Although some of these were professionally competent, few had any standing in the groups assigned to them.

Only McLain's two Negro staff members had some roots in their community. This fact, plus McLain's willingness to delegate decisions regarding the campaign in the Negro community, showed in the results. The Negro community was the only one McLain carried, and he did so with a substantial majority over Doyle.

The lack of any mutual relationship between McLain and the CIO led to a series of expensive errors. McLain had been assiduously wooing the CIO, one of the groups which had delayed its decision. In an attempt to get CIO support, McLain, upon the recommendation of his labor adviser, proclaimed a "Philip Murray Day" in Lynwood and invited scores of CIO leaders to attend a reception in his new home to celebrate the occasion. Not a single first-rank or even secondary CIO leader appeared. The steelworkers' union felt that McLain had misused their president's name, and reacted with indignation. The district director of the union issued a statement excoriating McLain.

McLain's first "labor adviser" had been discharged by his own union for factional activities in which he had been opposed by the leaders of his union and of almost the entire CIO. McLain could hardly have found a person less likely to help him win support from the unions than this "labor liaison" man. He fired the man after the debacle of "Philip Murray Day," but the leadership of the labor movement had already been alienated. Similarly, the staff chosen by McLain for community and lodge contacts was unequipped by background or experience to deal with any organizations except fraternal orders.

McLain further antagonized the CIO by characterizing Doyle, who from labor's point of view had a perfect voting record, as a "Chamber of Commerce representative." When Doyle received the endorsement of the CIO, McLain verbally cudgeled its leaders for making the endorsement, thus forcing them to denounce him in turn. McLain then attempted to get the union membership to disown their leaders' endorsement, but succeeded only in creating open warfare between himself and the whole CIO. As a result of this lack of understanding of the "rules" of organizational life, he did not get a single important labor endorsement for his congressional campaign. It was no doubt only a small consolation that he did receive the support of the Southern California Retail Liquor Dealers' Association.

As the campaign progressed, McLain became involved in a heated controversy with the secretary of the Los Angeles CIO Council. During this controversy he asked the members to write Philip Murray, then national president of the CIO, requesting an investigation of his secretary's "anti-McLain attitude." Such letters were written by 456 members, but only 22 letters came from McLain's district, where the Institute had several thousand members. This was in sharp contrast to the response elicited from members on another occasion. In 1951, when McLain asked his followers to send telegrams to Sacramento to protest the appropriation of funds for Senator Weybret's Interim Welfare Committee, the membership sent thousands of telegrams to the Senate Appropriations Committee demanding a cut in the committee's funds.

McLain pictured himself as a champion of the labor movement "fighting for the steelworkers and challenging both the special interests and other candidates in the district to reply." He argued that "neither steel nor any branch of labor has been able to muster sufficient strength in our Congress since the inception of the famous Wagner Labor Act of 1919" (*sic*), and that his election might help to correct this situation. He berated Doyle for his opposition to President Truman's seizure of the steel mills during a national steel strike and interpreted this as an antilabor attitude. The fact that the steelworkers' union itself had opposed the seizure was disregarded by McLain; perhaps he was not even aware of the union's position.

McLain's claims for his own virtues were not modest. One of his slogans was: "McLain went to Washington as a private citizen —as a citizen he produced the possible—send him back to Washington as your Congressman—and he will produce the impossible." On one broadcast McLain interviewed Oscar Ewing, former federal Social Security administrator. Before the program was ten minutes old, McLain was claiming Ewing's support for his own candidacy. After the broadcast he sent a photograph of himself with Ewing to newspapers in Los Angeles. The only paper that published the photo was the *People's World,* the Communist daily on the west coast.

Both the Institute and McLain paid a heavy price for his attempt to win the nomination. Not only did the campaign cost the Institute a great deal of money; even more, it antagonized the very elements in the community that occasionally supported Institute activities. McLain's campaign against Doyle reinforced the image which Democratic leaders have of McLain as a marginal type, a "loner." Had he withdrawn his candidacy after Doyle's decision to run, he might well have won a commitment of support for a future election. He failed to recognize that large segments of the population, outside the Chamber of Commerce, regarded him, correctly or not, as a "pension promoter."

The CISW in Office

The passage of McLain's Proposition 4 in November, 1948, took the entire state by surprise. Only McLain and his organization had taken the campaign seriously. The newspapers had opposed the measure, but there was no major effort to defeat it.

A few days before the election, McLain had been virtually a political unknown; a few days after it he was the subject of widespread discussion. The referendum passed by the narrow margin of 37,292 votes. McLain had found it necessary to challenge the count in some counties, claiming fraud, and it was not until the disputed votes were added to the tallies that McLain's victory was certain.

The proposition, which was to go into effect on January 1, 1949, made a number of changes in the state old-age and blind-aid programs. It increased the benefits to $75, abolished relatives' responsibility, and shifted the adminstration of the program from the counties to a centralized state agency created by the measure. Myrtle Williams, a CISW official, was named director of the state welfare agency.

A widow who had gone into the real estate business, Myrtle Williams joined McLain in the early 'forties when he organized one of his first pension groups. Devoted to the interests of the Institute and McLain, she had been his trusted junior partner for years. Always content with a supporting role, she had never challenged his leadership of the organization or competed for the favor of the members.

Her election as director of the State Welfare Department was greeted with mixed emotions by the professional welfare staff. State versus county administration is an old and familiar debate in California welfare circles. Many of the state personnel supported a centralized administration, and their attitude toward the new regime necessarily reflected the fact that McLain was the instrument of achieving a desirable end. Some of the state officials were opposed to the relatives' responsibility clause and in favor of increased benefits. The new status of the department meant larger appropriations and increased responsibilities. Much of what McLain had done could legitimately call for the support of the professional staff. At the same time, the staff was apprehensive lest the department become a tool of political manipulation.

The staff's ambivalent attitude toward McLain and Myrtle Williams was heightened by almost total lack of prior contact with either of them. Until the day Mrs. Williams arrived to take over her office, accompanied by McLain and photographers, most of the civil servants had never seen her.

Soon after the election a number of conferences were held in Sacramento between Mrs. Williams and the department staff. She was accompanied to the meetings by several assistants whom she was to bring with her to Sacramento when she took office. According to one of the participants, Mrs. Williams took no active part in discussing plans for the future operation of the department.

It seems clear that the dependence that had characterized Mrs. Williams' prior relationship to McLain continued in her job as welfare director. Some of the staff have stated that Mrs. Williams would make no decision on a matter of general policy until she had had an opportunity to discuss it with McLain, who was living in a Sacramento hotel during the legislative session. On a number of occasions the civil servants conferred directly with McLain at his hotel. At least one such policy conference was held when Mrs. Williams was not present. Her role as an Institute official and the dominant position of McLain were generally recognized among staff members of the department.[5]

Walter Chambers, who had not previously been identified with the Institute but who knew McLain, was hired as chief administrative officer for Mrs. Williams' department. At one time he had been director of the state relief administration. Chambers acted as deputy director for only a few months, after which he spent his time traveling in the field; later he claimed that he had been doing political work for McLain. In July, 1949, he resigned, although his separation form states that he was dismissed. Chambers later appeared at the Senate hearings as a witness against Mrs. Williams and McLain, stating that he had left the department because he "didn't want to be a Charlie McCarthy" to McLain.

The star witness against McLain at the Senate investigation was Jack Cartwright, originally brought into the department by McLain and Mrs. Williams to fill the newly created post of publications director. Cartwright submitted his resignation in May, 1949, but, like Chambers, was listed as a dismissal on his separation form. In addition to these two staff people, six others, in some way identified with either McLain or the Institute, were hired during Mrs. Williams' tenure of office. Most of them left under conditions of strain and later appeared as witnesses against the McLain group.

Except for the old-age security and blind-aid programs, in which Mrs. Williams and McLain actively participated, the professional civil servants conducted the affairs of the department without interference. Mrs. Williams showed concern only for those aspects of the work which were relevant to the Institute and to McLain. The civil servants had little respect for her skills and competence, but found few occasions to come in direct conflict with her. She impressed some staff members with her apparently sincere desire to "humanize" the department's operations. Her attitude compared favorably with that of some old-line public assistance workers who looked upon recipients as mere financial

---

[5] The material on the relations between Myrtle Williams, McLain, and staff is based on testimony given before the Senate Interim Committee as well as interviews with personnel of the State Department of Social Welfare.

burdens. When, for technical reasons, a recipient's checks were delayed, Mrs. Williams' only interest was to get the money to the pensioner as quickly as possible, viewing administrative difficulties as obstacles to be overcome. To some of the professionals, her administration represented an improvement over previous conditions in the department. No attempt was made to replace the civil servants, although McLain had discussed changing some of the top positions from civil service to "merit" jobs.

Since Mrs. Williams felt that the quality of the work performed by her political appointees was bad, she soon replaced them with competent civil servants. During the first six months after the "take-over," Williams and McLain accepted the entire staff. But when the political fight over the control of the State Welfare Department grew sharp the staff relationships characteristic of the Institute began to appear in the department; the rapport between the welfare staff and Mrs. Williams began to break down. After the repeal of the proposition, Mrs. Williams refused to participate in implementing the new program.

Mrs. Williams' lack of interest in department affairs other than the old-age and blind-aid programs was evidenced in her handling of the two state welfare boards. Under the provisions of the proposition, responsibility for the old-age assistance and blind-aid programs was taken away from the State Social Welfare Board, whose members had been appointed by Governor Warren, at that time regarded as a political enemy by McLain. A new advisory board was created, with members appointed by the welfare director. Mrs. Williams did not attend a single meeting of the old Welfare Board, which continued to function. She did attend the meetings of the new board; but she did not take an active role except when the board sat as an appeals body.

The advisory board had no policy-making function. It did, however, serve as an appeals commission in disputes between recipients and the department. It was here that Mrs. Williams had her greatest difficulty with the board. She was unwilling to deny appeals, perhaps because of her past associations with the Institute.

The advisory board was a subject of controversy almost from its inception. Although it was authorized by the November referendum, the first appointments to it were not sent to the State

Senate for confirmation until April of the following year. Three of the April appointees resigned before their names were even submitted to the Senate. Another appointee, Hazel Hurst, prominent in work for the blind, resigned in September, 1949. William Bassett, an AFL official, although confirmed by the Senate, failed to take the oath of office or attend a single meeting. Still another appointee, Daniel Marshall, a Los Angeles lawyer, was not confirmed by the Senate.

The first board meeting was held in July, 1949; subsequent meetings took place every month until February, 1950, when the board went out of existence. Sheridan Downey, Jr., son of Senator Sheridan Downey, served as chairman after his appointment in July, 1949. Frank Gardner, head of the Institute's welfare service, and associated with McLain prior to the passage of the referendum, was appointed to the board to fill the vacancy created by Hazel Hurst's resignation.

The board was not a rubber stamp for Mrs. Williams. According to members of the professional staff, Downey conducted its affairs honestly and efficiently. Had the proposition not been repealed, relationships between Mrs. Williams and the board might have become strained, especially over the issue of recipients' appeals rejected by the board.

Nor was there any extensive use of the department for McLain's political purposes. The commitments of the professionals in the department and the civil service system would have hindered any attempt at exploiting the department. But there is no evidence that McLain ever tried to transform the department into a political machine. A rare instance of utilization of the department for political purposes occurred after the beginning of the campaign to repeal the proposition. Walter Chambers testified that, while on the state payroll, he spent much of his time attempting to organize outside support for Mrs. Williams. Other political appointees were similarly used in the campaign against the repeal of the proposition.

The civil servants in the department were generally unaffected by the campaign. Nevertheless, the rivalries, personality clashes, and power struggles which to some extent characterize any bureaucratic organization gave rise, after some months, to the beginnings of a Williams-McLain faction. In part, the conflict related to state versus county administration. The advocates of state administration tended to rally around Mrs. Williams. When the state-wide fight for the repeal of the proposition grew bitter, the pressures and conflicts within the department increased. Once again the civil service status of most staff members protected them in the political conflict.

Resistance in the counties.—During the entire regime of Mrs. Williams, the anti-McLain group carried on a bitter fight against her, against McLain, and against the concept of state administration. The formation of the repeal group began immediately after the passage of the referendum, and its activities continued throughout the year, supported by almost all California newspapers. On the administrative level, the anti-McLain group was bolstered immeasurably by the active support of county welfare directors who resented their loss of independence under state adminstration or who were so committed to county administration that they were unwilling to coöperate with the new regime.

Charges of "dictatorial rule," "chaos," and "confusion" were hurled at the State Welfare Department by some county administrations, and such attacks received wide coverage in the press. Some counties coöperated only reluctantly with the state administration during the transition period; but in spite of this and a heavy increase in the case load, the change from county to state administration appears to have been relatively smooth.

The new law sharply increased the number of eligible pensioners. The age requirements were dropped to sixty-three, personal property exemptions were increased, and the relatives' responsibility clause was abolished. As a result, thousands became eligible for assistance. In January, 1949, when the new law went into effect, the number of applicants was five times as great as in January of the previous year. This strain on the counties' facilities added to the existing bad feeling between some county administrations and the state agency.

In mid-January, 1949, the state welfare agency instructed county directors to clear all information about case-load increases and other matters through the agency before public release. To McLain's opponents this was a "gag rule."

The anti-McLain and state administration group did not restrict its fight to the press. One county director, speaking to a Lions Club, declared, "Never in the history of America has it happened! We have given a blank check to a person who doesn't know a thing about welfare work." In March, 1949, the same county director sent the following official letter to all recipients in his district:

March 1, 1949

Thomas P. Douglas, Director

DEPARTMENT OF SOCIAL WELFARE
County of Orange
Court House Annex
Santa Ana, California

TO RECIPIENTS OF SECURITY FOR THE AGED
AND FOR THE BLIND:

Since the passage of Proposition 4, known as Article XXV of the California State Constitution, we have tried to keep you informed in matters affecting your grants. At this writing we were hopeful that we could tell you something definite concerning the program as it now operates. This, however, we cannot do since so many rules and regulations coming from Myrtle Williams, Director, State Department of Social Welfare, are immediately cancelled by her and there are times when we can only guess what the future program will be.

We are receiving many copies of letters written to our clients by Myrtle Williams, which would indicate that the County is responsible for making certain decisions concerning individual cases. We wish the State Director would also send out the answers to many of those questions since we are bound by law to follow the regulations of the State Department even though it is not in agreement with our opinion.

As you know, the County of Orange entered into contracts with the State Department of Social Welfare and the State Comptroller to send you your checks. This was done for the reason that no other plan seemed feasible in order to avoid a great hardship to the security clients.

Perhaps you, too, have been reading the papers which indicate that a great deal of confusion still exists and we are sorry that at this time we are not able to give you any clear information concerning future events. You may be sure, however, that the County Board of Supervisors and this Department stand committed to serve you as best we may and to continue to process your monthly checks so long as the contracts mentioned above remain in effect.

Please bear with us as we struggle through these difficult times in the hope that the atmosphere will soon clear and we will be able to give you a true picture of the administrative problems involved.

DEPARTMENT OF SOCIAL WELFARE
THOMAS P. DOUGLAS, DIRECTOR

This letter is an extreme example of the tactics employed by the repeal forces. Many of the county directors used their office to further the political fight against McLain. Indeed, it is apparent that McLain's and Mrs. Williams' use of state officials in the fight over the repeal proposition was essentially defensive. The prediction, made in the business community and repeated by the press, that McLain would use the state welfare agency for political purposes was in the nature of a self-fulfilling prophecy.

"Old Folks' Lobby"

McLain's lobbying activities in Sacramento have been carried on during each session of the legislature since 1941. Lobbying is the most consistently pursued external activity of the Institute, and it appears to be the one which McLain himself now regards as most promising.

The representative of a pension group in California faces a legislature badly divided on issues of social policy. The Assembly tends to be more favorable to social legislation, the Senate more strongly opposed. This alignment reflects both political and regional divisions. As in most states, the Senate, whose members are nearly equally distributed among counties regardless of population, is dominated by rural interests. At the same time, the rural areas are predominantly Republican. Democratic and urban legislators tend to support welfare legislation; Republican and rural legislators tend to oppose it. As elsewhere, however, there are always a number of legislators who do not consistently vote as their party affiliation and home district would lead one to expect.

An analysis of the 1951 legislature was published by McLain in August of that year.[6] The pamphlet, which recounted McLain's "fight" on the legislative front against the "enemies" of the aged,

------

[6] George McLain, *The Story of the 1951 California Legislature*, multigraphed by the Old Folks, State Headquarters, 1031 South Grand Avenue, Los Angeles 15, California; copyright by California Institute of Social Welfare, August, 1951.

included evaluations of the legislators' attitudes on welfare issues; each legislator received a rating of good, fair, or bad. While Democrats generally fared better in the ratings than Republicans, some Republicans were endorsed in preference to Democrats.

In spite of the fairly constant party division of the legislature, the dynamics of the legislative process make lobbying worth while. McLain's ratings of the legislators reflect the fact that the vote on welfare issues is not entirely consistent with party divisions. California political parties, because of their weakness, are unable effectively to control legislative votes. This lack of party discipline increases the opportunities for interest-group pressures.

Correspondingly, lobbying procedures have become highly institutionalized. Public committee hearings are held on important bills, and the hearings are attended by all interested lobbyists as well as by reporters and many casual visitors. In the political climate of California, legislators do not strive to be known as faithful party men. On the contrary, they like to be thought of as independent servants of the people who hear and weigh all sides and then make their decisions. The often dramatic public hearings, at which lobbyist after lobbyist defends the point of view of his client, help the legislators to fix this image of themselves in the public mind.

Under these circumstances, a technique of lobbying has emerged. Any lobby must be capable of selecting the bills in which it has some interest from among the five thousand or more introduced in each general session of the legislature. It must analyze the often large number of bills which are of concern to its clients. It must follow all relevant bills through the various steps of the legislative process, particularly through the legislative committees. The lobby must have at its disposal enough competent personnel to cover several hearings on a given day, prepare information for the use of legislators, and keep up personal contact with them.

McLain's activities in Sacramento meet these needs. The routine lobbying work of the "Old Folks' Lobby" is well defined. McLain establishes his headquarters in one of the larger hotels. Two or three assistants, a secretary, and perhaps his radio writer join him there. At the start of the legislative session the pace is fairly slow, but by the conclusion of the session McLain and all his assistants will have worked extremely hard. McLain restricts himself to directing the activities of his assistants and to negotiations with other lobbyists or politicians.

Each day during the session, McLain assigns the day's work at a staff meeting. The staff knows which bills concern the aged, and they have well-defined positions on them. They cover every formal hearing and informally contact every legislator concerned. When the staff member does not make a formal presentation at a committee hearing, he often attends to check on the votes cast by committee members.

Other lobbyists whose positions on welfare issues are similar to those of the CISW have come to depend upon McLain to keep them abreast of the developments in his specialized area. These men are thus freer to concentrate their attention on other legislation, secure in the knowledge that welfare matters are being effectively watched by McLain's group. When their assistance is needed, McLain briefs them on the details of the bills. The group which has thus come to rely upon McLain for certain types of information consists chiefly of representatives of organized labor, of minority and ethnic groups, and of other groups whose political preferences ordinarily go to the Democratic party. The same lobbyists will, on occasion, make arrangements with McLain for combining forces in support of or opposition to a particular measure. Sometimes they are joined by such groups as the League of Women Voters and church organizations, or by the legislative representative of the State Department of Social Welfare. McLain's "opposition" in Sacramento includes the chamber of commerce, taxpayers' associations, and the County Supervisors Association—groups which most frequently align themselves with the Republican party.

Probably the most important aspect of McLain's lobbying is the simple fact of its existence. McLain rarely succeeds in changing a legislator's mind, since most of the senators and assemblymen have well-defined positions when they arrive for the sessions. But McLain's presence as an active lobbyist is a daily reminder that he represents an organized group of considerable strength. He has also provided the direct impetus for the introduction of bills designed to increase grants and make other changes in the welfare code. With the exception of an assemblyman who at one time was on McLain's payroll, no legislators have been so consistently identified with McLain as to warrant being called "his" people. The facts of political life deter any legislator from seeking such an identification.

A sizable number of legislators, however, are in sympathy with McLain's program. In the Assembly, McLain has little difficulty in getting approval for a bill from a majority of the Welfare Committee. His problem is to find legislators who will introduce his bills. In the 1955 legislative session, McLain reportedly could get only a single assemblyman to sponsor Institute measures.

Attitudes of legislators toward McLain.—The legislators' personal feelings about McLain contribute to their unwillingness to identify themselves too closely with him. Even those who believe his operation to be effective take little pains to hide their distrust. Nor is this sentiment limited to the senators and assemblymen who oppose his policies. Distrust is expressed even by some legislators who have supported McLain's bill. The newspapermen who, year after year, cover the legislative sessions are cynical about McLain's motives. Most of them seem to share the legislators' suspicion.

McLain's effectiveness is a subject of controversy. His own version of his ten years of activity for the aged appeared in the pamphlet published by the Institute in 1951:

The difference between $40 and $75 per month is what the aged of California have obtained from their investment [in the California Institute]. No other pension organization in the country can match this achievement. Until the time we organized in 1941, old age groups had neglected the day-to-day struggle for immediate benefits in favor of some plan that would pay a large monthly sum in the long distance future. Many politicians paid lip service to these plans because they enabled the politicians to pose as friends of the aged without doing anything positive to help meet current needs.

By July 1, 1943, the new organization had wrested a $10 monthly increase from a reluctant state legislature, boosting the maximum monthly payments to the aged to $50.

During the war years membership growth was slow, so that it was not until October 1, 1946, that $5 a month was pried out of the National Legislature.

On August 1, 1947, an additional $5 monthly increase was obtained, this time from the state, and on October 1, 1948, the grant was raised another $5, once again by Congress, bringing the maximum monthly total to $65. By then the organization had grown strong enough to take the case of the aged directly to the people of California, which it did with Prop. No. 4 . . . the new law was passed in 1948 and on January 1, 1949, old age monthly benefits were increased to $75 and blind grants went from $75 to $84 per month.

The new law also freed the aged and blind from the oppression of county administration, eliminated relatives' responsibility, liberalized property qualifications, and lowered age limits.

One of the most important features of Article XXV, as Prop. No. 4 was officially known, was that for the first time, it established pensions as a matter of right instead of as a charity and by writing the sum of $75 into the Constitution it set a floor beneath which the legislature could not reduce pensions.

Unfortunately, a year later this law was repealed by the State's big business with the most costly campaign in history. Only the $75 monthly benefit was left and this was made subject to reduction by the legislature.[7]

McLain subsequently claimed credit for a $5 increase in September, 1952, and another $5 in June, 1955.

McLain's enemies, however, have a somewhat different version of pension history.[8] One state senator with more than fifteen years in the legislature said, "McLain's a fake. He's gotten nothing for his members." Another senator who has spent many years in the legislature is somewhat less convinced. "McLain's done nothing for the aged except for the $10 he got through his [1948] initiative." Still another senator, twenty years in Sacramento, thinks that "the only thing McLain has done was to get $10 increase with Proposition 4. The reason a lot of us up here resent McLain is because he makes such extravagant claims." "I think McLain is highly overrated," says a fourth legislative enemy of McLain.

But many fellow lobbyists feel that McLain has operated an extremely effective lobby, especially in recent years: "I think McLain has done some things for the old people. They might have gotten them anyway, but I'm not sure." And another said: "McLain really does a good job for his people. Sure, the legislators don't like him personally, but he's had some good staff people who really get around. His members get their money's worth."

Increased benefits.—The change from the $40 to the $85 grant

---

[7] *Ibid.*

[8] Quotations in this section are from interviews with senators and assemblymen involved in welfare legislation, conducted in Sacramento during the special session of 1951.

was accomplished in seven stages. In 1943 a $10 increase was voted by the state legislature; in 1946, Congress increased payments by $5; 1947 saw another $5 added by the state; on October 1, 1948, Congress passed an additional $5 payment; and in November, 1948, the voters passed the initiative which increased the payments to $75. Congress added another $5 in 1952, and in 1955 the legislature raised the maximum grant to $85.

What did McLain have to do with the first increase in 1943? The claims he made at the time were somewhat more modest than they are at present. In a radio broadcast delivered on June 20, 1943, he said:

The Citizens' Committee had its representatives constantly in attendance at Sacramento during the last session of the Legislature, and I had the honor to represent our committee on the Governor's Committee on Old Age Pensions. . . . Great gains in all these respects were made through the Legislature and we believe that our representatives in Sacramento played their important part. In fact we know they did. We had not appealed to the people of the state in vain.

The background for the 1943 increase was the 1942 Olson-Warren campaign, in which McLain switched his allegiance from Olson to Warren. After Warren's election, McLain was appointed to the Governor's Committee on Old Age Pensions. In the 1942 legislative session a large number of bills making changes in the pension law were submitted. The bill finally adopted was a compromise among the various groups. Although McLain was active during the legislative session, he can in no way claim credit for the passage of the increase. Certainly he had some influence, but at that time he was not considered a major figure in pressure-group activities.

By 1947, however, McLain was beginning to make his influence felt in the state. He was present as a lobbyist and did an effective job of keeping the legislators constantly aware of his existence. Although he did not control more than a few votes directly, he was able to marshal sizable support for his program. The $5 increase granted in 1947, although not directly traceable to McLain, was a result of Institute lobbying combined with pressures exerted by labor and liberal groups.

The passage of the McLain initiative in 1948, which placed

Myrtle Williams in the office of state social welfare director and put the administration of the program in the hands of state personnel, marked the high point in McLain's operations. The $10 increase in benefits, the elimination of the relatives' responsibility clause, and the lowering of the eligibility age were direct results of the McLain initiative. Its passage made the entire legislature aware of McLain's potential strength and greatly increased his effectiveness as a lobbyist. Even the repeal measure, which put Mrs. Williams out of office, maintained the $75 level of the maximum grant.

McLain can hardly claim responsibility for the 1952 congressional increase of $5, even though he did alert many of California's congressmen to the problem. The 1955 increase, however, is more directly attributable to his efforts. His bill, introduced by Assemblyman Wilson, was adopted by the Assembly and the Senate in the very last hours of the session, after a series of parliamentary maneuvers.

McLain has thus had a hand in two of the four increases granted by either the state legislature or the voters. In at least one other increase, the fear of possible action by the Institute played a role. Of course, the additions might well have been granted without McLain's intervention.

State legislators, both friends and enemies of McLain, recognize the roots of his power. One state senator commented that "McLain without the radio and initiative wouldn't be worth a damn." An assemblyman stated, "The only reason a politician is afraid of McLain is because he knows how to use the initiative." Even the most bitter foes recognize McLain's power indirectly. One state senator said: "McLain's never done a damned thing for the old people. Why, the last time the legislature was in session we passed an increase in the pension bill four days after we opened the session just so that s.o.b. couldn't claim credit for having gotten it."

Recent Developments

McLain has frequently told his members that he is fighting their battle not only in Sacramento but also in Washington. Until recently, however, McLain spent little time in Washington. He appeared briefly in 1946 and again in 1950, but created little interest.

For "contacts" in the national capital from 1952 to 1955 he depended chiefly on James Roosevelt, representative from California, who has for some time expressed sympathy for the policies advocated by the CISW.

Move to Washington.—In 1955, for the first time, McLain appeared in Washington with a staff of assistants. The earlier casual appearances before legislative committees gave way to a systematic coverage of the congressional scene during the entire session. McLain's activities in Washington represent more than an expansion of his lobbying work in Sacramento. They are a political departure, and may in the end change the character of the CISW.

Preparations for the move to Washington began in 1954, while the campaign for the $100 maximum grant was under way. McLain expressed himself as weary of the succession of lost initiative and election campaigns which yielded benefits neither to himself nor to his members. The loss of the 1954 campaign evidently did not come as a complete surprise to him. He had already laid the groundwork for an alternative line of political action by popularizing among his members the idea of a national pension.

McLain began the move to the national capital by broadening the geographical base of his organization—at least on paper. The first state-wide conference of the California Institute of Social Welfare, held in Sacramento in August, 1954, saw the creation of a National Institute of Social Welfare. McLain achieved this result by "merging" the CISW with two other small pension organizations in Oregon and Washington whose "delegates" appeared at the conference.

A second conference, styled "Eleven Western States Conference," took place in Los Angeles on November 4 and 5, 1955. According to the leaflet reporting this conference, the Los Angeles gathering included "pension leaders representing recipients from a complete cross section of the United States." The resolution of the conference is signed by delegates from eight states, most of them western; eight other states were "represented by proxy." [9]

---

[9] The signatories of the resolution were from California, Oregon, Washington, Utah, Idaho, Oklahoma, Illinois, and Alabama. States represented by proxy were Colorado, North Dakota, Pennsylvania, New York, Massachusetts, Rhode Island,

One of the resolutions calls for the organization of a "national pension conference" before the 1956 elections.

Such a conference actually met soon after the 1956 elections, on November 10 and 11, in Chicago. According to the *National Welfare Advocate* for December, 1956, a national federation of state pension organizations was formed under the chairmanship of McLain. Five organizations in addition to the CISW—one each in Colorado, Alabama, and Oklahoma, and two in Illinois—are listed as members of the newly created National Institute of Social Welfare (NISW).[10]

The gradual development of a precarious national organization was accompanied by the steady growth of lobbying activities in Washington. Since January, 1956, the NISW has had a regular representative in the nation's capital whenever Congress was in session. A chatty monthly column by the Washington representative appears in the *Advocate*. The first column gave the following description of the beginnings of the "Old Folks' Lobby" in Washington:

. . . Who makes up the Old Folks' Lobby in Washington? Well, there's George McLain, an exacting task master if there ever was one. There's Georgia Koonce, known to most of you who attend our meetings as a most spirited, attractive, helpful red-headed junior champion of the old folks. Then there's me, and to keep me in line and see that the Old Folks get a fair break, there's my wee daughter, Jill, not yet three years old, but who already knows how to say: "Mr. Congressman, please vote for the Old Folks." . . .

As liaison with Congressman James Roosevelt's office, we have the cooperation of Attorney Warren Biscailuz, son of Los Angeles County's longtime sheriff, Eugene Biscailuz. There you have the line-up of the California contingent. We'll get the ball rolling, then when the going gets rough, several pension leaders from other states have promised to hie themselves back here and pitch in with us for the big push toward real Social Security for America's Needy.[11]

Kentucky, and Tennessee. See National Institute of Social Welfare, *Eleven Western States Conference* (leaflet, Los Angeles, 1955).

[10] The names of these organizations are: Colorado Pension Union, Inc., Donald D. Pullen, president; Alabama Pension Institute, Inc., Hon. J. H. (Jack) Kelly, president; Oklahoma Welfare Federation, O. J. Fox, president; Northside National Pension Center, James Ketcham, president (Chicago, Ill.); and Old Age and Public Assistance Union, Inc., Warren O. Lamson, president (Chicago, Ill.).

[11] *National Welfare Advocate*, February, 1956, p. 2.

Legislative program.—When Congressman James Roosevelt of California, in 1955, offered two bills designed to amend and liberalize various sections of the Social Security Act, the *National Welfare Advocate* reported the preparatory work on these bills in the following terms: "[The bills] are the first in a series designed to implement the 12-point program proposed by McLain and worked out in an exchange of long-distance phone calls between Congressman Roosevelt in Washington and the California pension leader in Sacramento during the January session of the State Legislature." [12] A careful reading of the depositions of George McLain and of James Roosevelt in the 1956 hearings of the House Ways and Means Committee indicates that the two men take identical stands and use the same arguments, although McLain's statement has a slightly more propagandistic ring.[13]

McLain's success in developing contacts with congressmen and senators may explain some broadening of his legislative program. McLain and his Washington representative have testified not merely on Public Assistance measures, but also on housing for low-income families, including the aged,[14] as well as on extension of federal unemployment compensation benefits.[15]

While McLain's legislative program has been broadened slightly it has not changed fundamentally. The "Old Folks' Lobby" in Washington as well as in Sacramento has continued to argue for increased grants across the board rather than for special programs geared to the particular needs of various segments of the aged population. During the 1956 hearings, McLain opposed the administration proposals designed to make available to the states grants-in-aid for medical care. McLain maintained that the need for additional food and other necessities was so great among the

---

[12] *Ibid.*, February, 1955, p. 1.
[13] *Hearings* on H.R. 9120, H.R. 9091, H.R. 10283, and H.R. 10284, April 12, 13, 16, 19, and 20, 1956. House Committee on Ways and Means, 84th Congr., 2d sess. (Government Printing Office, Washington, D.C., 1956), pp. 118–124, 137–145. Hereafter referred to as *1956 Hearings*.
[14] *National Welfare Advocate*, May, 1956, p. 3.
[15] *Hearings* on H.R. 11326, H.R. 11327, and H.R. 11679, March 28, March 31, and April 1, 1958, House Committee on Ways and Means, 85th Congr., 2d sess. (Government Printing Office, Washington, D.C., 1958), pp. 364–366. Hereafter referred to as *1958 Hearings*.

aged that a general increase in the grants should take precedence over any special medical expenditures.[16]

McLain's coolness to measures other than increases is further reflected in his extremely negative reaction to research projects. The 1956 Administration bill contained a section authorizing federal grants-in-aid to states and to nonprofit organizations in support of "research or demonstration projects such as those relating to the prevention and reduction of dependency" or designed to coordinate private and public agencies or to increase the effectiveness of the programs. During the hearings the only objections to this section were raised by McLain and James Roosevelt. McLain commented as follows:

This proposed amendment seeks to let the bars down completely on the public-assistance program and invite every Tom, Dick, and Harry into the act of pestering these poor unfortunate souls. It not actually invites, but actually finances private nonprofit organizations and agencies to snoop and poke around into the lives of these people.

Here again, the magic words are—

prevention and reduction of dependency
and—

help improve the administration and effectiveness of programs carried on or assisted under the Social Security Act

My heavens to Betsy, if Congress and the State legislatures aren't capable of handling this program, what in the world will happen when all of these outsiders start officially moving into the picture with utterly no responsibility to the people for their actions?

Maintaining a political base.—In shifting the scene of his lobbying operations from Sacramento to Washington, McLain took certain chances with his membership. During his primary campaign for Congress, some members had privately expressed apprehensions that "George" might abandon them. He had reason to think that it might prove difficult to convince the members of the wisdom of a lobbying campaign in Washington; accustomed to looking in the direction of Sacramento, they might consider Washington as a rather remote place to fight their battle. McLain

---

[16] *1956 Hearings,* p. 119; Representative Roosevelt's parallel statement on p. 138.

evidently feared a loss of membership, for, contrary to his previous practice of deciding on new moves without preparing his followers, he sought the members' consent to the new policy.

The campaign within the organization culminated in the endorsement of the new move by a unanimous vote of the third annual convention of the CISW in May, 1955. In a rather formal address to the convention, McLain explained to the members that the "opposition" had resources and funds of such magnitude that it was "not enough" to stop them from wrecking the California welfare programs. "That is the reason," he continued, "I have worked so hard and have worked so long on laws designed—not for state action—but for national action in the Congress back in Washington, D.C. It is most gratifying that Congressman James Roosevelt, recognizing the merit and the need for such laws to be adopted in the Federal Social Security program, introduced a bill in Congress to bring this about." [17]

The same number of the *Advocate* which carried the resolution of the annual convention related a telephone conversation between Roosevelt and McLain, in which it was agreed that McLain should come to Washington to testify before the House Ways and Means Committee. McLain is quoted as follows: "The recent state-wide convention of the California Institute of Social Welfare, held in Fresno, certainly made it clear through an approving voice vote that they wanted me to appear in these hearings in the nation's Capitol, . . . and they seemed to want me to get there just as soon as possible."

It is highly probable that a shrinkage in membership has occurred. According to a statement by McLain in the *Wall Street Journal*, the Institute's income for 1956 was $332,695—considerably less than the approximately $600,000 in previous years.[18] This figure, which is based on an official audit, comprises income from dues and contributions as well as from the sale of vitamin pills. Although the number of members is not given, it is reasonable to assume that the reduction in income reflects a smaller membership.

---

[17] *National Welfare Advocate*, June, 1955, p. 2.
[18] *Wall Street Journal*, San Francisco edition, June 10, 1957.

Evidently, McLain has been able to get along on a sharply reduced income. According to his statement in the *Wall Street Journal*, the major expense is still the radio program, which costs $9,348 per month. The cost of maintaining a lobby in Sacramento is given as $1,388, and the Washington office purportedly cost no more than $1,000 monthly (both figures are evidently exclusive of salaries). But such major expenses as the initiative and referendum campaigns and the compilation of huge address lists have disappeared from the CISW budget. It is probable that the reduction in expenses more than makes up for the loss of income.

Faced with the danger of further losses, McLain has increased his efforts to maintain and, if possible, increase his following among the pensioners. In the same speech in which he announced the move to Washington, he promised the creation of clubhouses for the pensioners. McLain's preoccupation shows rather clearly through the language he used: "We want to establish this *grass roots service* for the comfort and *interest* of the elderly in every community in California." (Emphases added.)[19]

A little later an "Old Folks Center" was ceremoniously inaugurated in the Los Angeles headquarters; but the facilities appear not to have been used much by the pensioners. Various attempts to maintain and revive the social welfare clubs and the "100-clubs" (so named for the coveted $100 pension) have met with little success. The yearly banquets and picnics for life members have been staged as in the past, and the traditional meetings with speakers from the central office have continued. It would seem that McLain's followers still have rather limited needs and capacities for sociability. However, annual conferences are now held regularly, at which the active members may have more direct contact with the officers of the organization.

The main device for maintaining membership appears to be a greatly expanded program of service to the members. The number of branch offices of the CISW, where members can obtain advice on pension problems, has steadily increased. In May, 1958, the *Advocate* listed twenty such offices. McLain was quick to see that the complexities introduced into the OAS program by the

---

[19] *National Welfare Advocate*, June, 1955, p. 2.

addition of medical services and allowances would create more confusion in the minds of the recipients and produce a greater demand for consulting services.[20]

Another service to the members is the development of rather extensive housing projects under the provisions of the National Housing Act, which authorizes FHA financing up to 90 per cent of the total cost of low-cost housing projects sponsored by nonprofit associations. The CISW has created a subsidiary called "Housing for the Elderly, Inc.," which has acquired three sizable tracts of land at Palomar near San Diego, in Fresno, and in West Covina near Los Angeles. Negotiations are under way for land near Sacramento, Bakersfield, and Salinas. The housing units to be erected are designed to accommodate a thousand or more old people on each of the tracts already acquired. According to the *Advocate*, there is great demand for these housing units, which are to rent furnished, with utilities, for approximately $25 per month. The paper states that a steady stream of applications for the future housing units reaches the headquarters and that forward-looking members who have helped with the projects will be given preference.[21]

While these service activities may have helped to maintain a level of memberships and income which permits the continued operation of the Institute, McLain seems to have become increasingly conscious of the recruitment problem. The 1957 convention of the CISW, at McLain's urging, adopted a resolution calling for the appointment of Institute "county managers" who would work with committees of members in spreading the organization's message and attracting new followers. In justification of this move, McLain pointed out to his members that the average life expectancy of a pensioner is about six years; the resulting constant turn-

---

[20] Under the current system, recipients can receive as much as $89 to cover their needs for food, shelter, and other regular expenses. They may receive as much as $105 if they have special health or other needs and if their income is less than $16; and the amount to be paid may be recomputed each month if the amount needed for health care is variable. Recipients are also entitled to medical care in the form of vendor payments to a hospital or to the treating physician, nurse, or other member of the healing professions, provided they have first exhausted available community resources. Pensioners doubtless have no easy time in trying to grasp these complex provisions.

[21] *National Welfare Advocate*, February, 1958, p. 2.

over in membership necessitates steady recruitment drives.[22] Mc-Lain's recent insistence on membership participation in organizing was a departure from his previous exclusive reliance on the radio program and paid speakers.

[22] *Ibid.*, August, 1957, p. 2.

Chapter VII | Summary and Conclusions

A NUMBER of central ideas have guided us in our study of the California Institute of Social Welfare, its leader, and its members. We have not regarded McLain's CISW as an isolated phenomenon without parallels in history. Rather, we have likened it to the organizations of other emerging and dependent social groups. Such groups have often been directed by leaders who were not representative of the constituency and who were not subject to membership control. It is apparent that the aged, newly emerging to a consciousness of distinct interests and problems, have difficulty in communicating with the institutions of the larger society. It is hard for them to develop effective leadership from within their own ranks. As a result, the aged tend to rely on outside sources of leadership.

Findings

1. *The CISW was organized by a political entrepreneur who has exercised exclusive personal control over the organization.* This old-age pressure group was established in 1941 by a man who had made many attempts to find a political base. George McLain has dominated the organization and stamped it with his personality. This control has been markedly personal in character, summoning the direct loyalty and dependence of followers and staff. His leadership has been exclusive, reinforced by conscious efforts to fore-

265

the emergence of strong secondary leaders who might stand between him and the members. The members' relation to McLain is not filtered through or modified by loyalties to intermediate groups and leaders.

2. *Exclusive control has afforded the leader limited opportunities to use organizational resources for personal political advancement.* In most organizations, officials enjoy enough discretion so that they may—if they so desire—gain incidental personal advantages for themselves and their friends. This is particularly true of organizations subject to one-man control. Of what advantage to McLain is his control over the CISW? His gain is not primarily financial, for, despite the organization's large income, it does not appear that McLain has taken a significantly disproportionate share. On occasion he has attempted to use the movement to serve his own political ambitions. In doing so, he was able to take advantage of the power which society ordinarily attributes to one who has an apparently large following; and he was able to use the organizational machinery of the CISW, especially its funds, staff, and physical plant. The single important instance of such an effort was McLain's bid for Congress in 1952. These attempts have yielded no positive results; it is possible that they are not to be repeated. At the same time, it is clear that the members of the organization are not readily disposable for aims beyond the narrow sphere of pension politics. They will work hard and give large sums to further their direct interests by political means, and they will sacrifice much to maintain the organization, but they will not respond to appeals for other objectives, including the political advancement of the leader.

3. *The CISW is not an integrated part of the community; hence its actions tend to be lacking in responsibility and effectiveness.* Members of a functioning community are in many ways dependent on each other. Because of this, each member must weigh the effect of his own conduct on other members lest he find himself isolated and deprived of needed coöperation. To be a member of a community is to accept its restrictions as to aims that may be pursued and means that may be used. An isolated group has greater freedom in its choice of activities, but by the same token it cannot expect the sustained support of others. McLain and the

CISW have been isolated, not only from the general political community but also from the community of welfare-oriented individuals and groups. This isolation has made it easier for McLain to "go it alone" organizationally. He has paid a rather high price for this advantage, however. At critical times he has been unable to win the support he needed from like-minded persons, and, indeed, has alienated influential groups that might have been on his side. Some of this alienation has resulted from lack of insight into the likely responses of groups and their leaders, an ignorance associated with isolation from the community. The isolation of McLain personally and of the CISW as an organization does not mean that individual members lack normal social contacts. The emphasis here is on the relations among influential individuals and groups.

4. *The old-age assistance recipients we studied showed evidences of status-anxiety.* Californians on the old-age assistance rolls, both members and nonmembers of the McLain organization, are concerned about the position they occupy in the social world. Being "on the pension" is a mixed blessing, for it suggests a loss of status in the eyes of others, a diminished claim upon the respect of the community. The pensioners are less concerned with improving their day-to-day personal relations with others, including their children, than they are with remedying this felt loss of status. Self-justification is important to them; they feel impelled to prove that they have lived thrifty, hard-working, respectable lives. Because of their anxiety over status, with its keynotes of respect and respectability, the pensioners are basically conservative. They are not radicals seeking to espouse new values, but people who want the means to live according to established social norms. McLain's members rate somewhat higher in status-anxiety than do nonmember pensioners. This probably reflects a selective factor: strong feelings about loss of status stir resentments which make them more readily available for political participation. In addition, membership in the organization strengthens views about the pension, society, and self which show up as increased concern for social status.

5. *California's old-age security laws permit some pensioners to enjoy a "slightly privileged" status, and this group supplies a disproportionate share of CISW members.* Although all the recipients

must satisfy a legal criterion of need, some are nevertheless better off than others. The slightly privileged include modest home-owners, people with spouses still living and therefore benefiting from combined grants, and those having allowable additional income. These distinct social and economic advantages facilitate political and social participation in community life. McLain's members tend to be among the slightly privileged; the more deeply involved the member, the more likely he is to share these advantages. Thus the membership is not a movement of the utterly dispossessed. This fact is consistent with our general knowledge that extreme poverty is more likely to be associated with apathetic withdrawal than with activist protest. The slightly privileged status of the McLain members is consistent with the related conclusion that this group shows a relatively greater amount of status-anxiety. Those who have some hold upon the material foundations of respectability are more likely to sustain the aspiration and resent the loss.

6. *Membership in the CISW does not offer new and satisfying personal ties.* There is little evidence that McLain members are drawn to the organization by the need for new friendships or a new community; nor do such relationships emerge. Some satisfactions probably do accrue from the sense of protection offered by McLain and from the sacrifices that membership entails. The dedication of many members is too great to be explained as normal interest-group participation. This high involvement does not mean, however, that the member has been deeply absorbed into a new, if isolated, community. The connections among the members are too weak, and the group structure of the organization too attenuated. Rather this is an atomized "mass" group, marked by direct relations to a leader and weak relations among members.

7. *Participation in the CISW leads members to focus preëxisting negative feelings upon specific targets and increases their isolation from the community.* Among the old-age assistance recipients, the McLain members differ from nonmembers in degree rather than in kind. There is more resentment and distrust among members. And the more deeply involved members express the greatest sense of alienation from the community. Some of this negativism apparently results from the complexity of the welfare administration

and the bewilderment it induces. As the pensioner's interest in the law rises, his awareness of its complexity also increases. A member is more likely to speak of the pension law as "full of red tape," "humiliating," "confused," and "tricky." This is probably related to status-anxiety, to resentment that the law does not do more to define and secure his position in society. Although participation in the CISW increases the pensioner's negative feelings toward some of the *institutions* of society, his negativism is not necessarily focused on *persons*, such as social workers.

Members are more prone than nonmembers to regard groups or individuals as enemies of the pensioners and other old people. Their negative attitudes clearly reflect McLain's propaganda targets. However, the "enemies" of the CISW members are not entirely of McLain's making. Nor does this negativism and distrust lead to unrestrained forms of hostility. The CISW is not, in this or any other sense, an extremist group.

8. *Communication within the organization runs from the energizing leader to the receptive, passive audience; but the members in turn communicate their dependency, admiration, and guilt.* McLain's members resemble customers, the more or less stable clientele of a product or service. Like television viewers and similar publics, they are held together by a public relations program carried on by an outside source for its own reasons. The members have no independent role, nor do they expect to have one. If they lost faith in the organization they would not think of intervening to change it, but would merely cease to support it, much as they might stop buying a product. This explains and perhaps justifies the fact that McLain acts as if he "owned" the organization. That it is "his" organization is generally accepted and understood. This organized audience is highly responsive, not to the CISW but to the leader as an individual. They send their money to him personally and shower him with expressions of gratitude and admiration, usually in letters which also show marked feelings of guilt when the contributions lag.

9. *There are wide variations in the degree of involvement of McLain followers; and the organization is sustained by a fluctuating core of devoted, self-sacrificing members.* From an organizational standpoint, one of the most impressive features of McLain's

movement is the substantial core of devoted followers he has been able to create. These include life members (who contribute at least $75), people paying installments on life memberships, club presidents, and other high contributors. The measure of involvement is chiefly financial. On the scale of slight privilege, the more involved members are better off than the rest of the members, just as the members as a whole have more advantages than nonmembers. In their attitudes toward pensions and pension politics, there is a similar gradation. Club presidents represent the organization's point of view most extremely; they are also the least sentimental and the most political-minded, being more willing than other core-group members to regard McLain as a political leader rather than as "good shepherd" or protector. As expected, the more involved members are most likely to be antagonistic toward those defined as enemies of the organization.

There is some evidence that increased participation as measured by activity rather than money contribution is accompanied by estrangement from McLain. The members who do the political work of collecting signatures are not necessarily uncritical of their leader. They are aware of the community's negative opinion and share it to some extent, but they feel that this lack of respectability is a necessary cost of political action, especially when no other channel is available.

10. *McLain has been readily able to mobilize the strength to place his initiative measures on the ballot, but his ability to influence the voters is low.* In a series of campaigns the members have provided the funds and the manpower to collect the necessary signatures for qualifying initiative measures. This response has been large enough to obviate the necessity of using paid petition circulators—a considerable achievement for a California organization. But the members are less readily mobilized for the campaign to pass the measure. McLain has not been able to create a political machine, that is, a network of effective local political clubs and precinct workers. It may well be that the members sense the importance of working to get a measure on the ballot but feel that the final outcome is beyond their power to affect. There is no evidence that McLain propaganda directed toward the general public has had any significant influence on the vote. Rather, it appears

that the movement's partial success with the voters rests on widespread support for social welfare measures. The organization implicitly assumes that such support exists and that its main task is to present the issue for decision at the polls. The CISW's margin of victory or defeat depends more on the intensity of the campaign against a proposition than on its own campaign in favor of it.

11. *The McLain organization is basically unstable, dependent upon continuous exhortation by an indispensable leader.* Although it is based upon the pensioners' common interests, the CISW is not a securely established form of organization. It is highly dependent on the person of McLain himself and would very likely disintegrate if he were no longer at its head. Moreover, the common economic interests of the aged are not so strongly felt as to lead easily to effective organization. Psychological appeals are important, and the task of organizing the pensioner constituency absorbs a very large part of the leader's energies and of the funds collected. Of course, most organizations dependent on voluntary contributions from members spend much time, money, and energy on internal mobilization; they have difficulty in showing a "profit" that can be spent on external activities. However, while no accurate comparison with other groups can be made, the internal orientation of McLain's propaganda seems especially great. Lacking a secure source of funds, the leader must have continuous access to his following and must unceasingly exhort them to remember their "true" interests by supporting the organization. This reinforces the leader's role as agitator and tends to force him into ways of speaking and acting that isolate him and his group from the larger political community. If we are correct in detecting a somewhat more conservative tendency in McLain's behavior, it may be because the agitational role is less urgently called for after the organization has achieved a certain continuity and stability. But it is safe to assume that the organizing of pensioners into a political pressure group will continue to be accompanied by agitational techniques and leadership.

12. *The McLain program does not involve basic opposition to the existing social and legal order.* The CISW is distinguished from earlier pension movements by an emphasis on specific changes within the existing framework of welfare legislation. McLain has

272 | Summary and Conclusions

not offered any general scheme for financing pensions or contributing to the national prosperity, with the exception of a plan to use surplus agricultural products for pensioners. The movement has no broad ideology or general critique of the social order. McLain's use of the initiative machinery, while constitutional, has tended to challenge the existing structure of power in the community. For that machinery permits political "assaults" which bypass established leaders and institutions and are not necessarily restrained by political accommodation. Yet even in this area McLain has met defeat by restricting goals in the direction of greater respectability. His lobbying activities, especially when transferred to the national scene, offer further opportunities for restraint, since lobbying demands a large measure of coöperation and compromise. To the extent that McLain increases his commitment to effective political action for short-run goals and gives up the search for independent political office, his program will probably become increasingly restrained and respectable.

Isolation, Marginality, and Social Status

In the introductory chapter, we asserted as a fact of experience that an isolated constituency, low in status, is likely to be organized by a marginal leader. The preceding findings reveal the mechanisms which, in the instance of the CISW, explain this relationship. These mechanisms involve a complex interplay between individual behavior and attitudes on the one hand and social and institutional arrangements on the other.

Isolation of the aged constituency is, first of all, a social fact; it consists in the relative dearth and superficiality of social contacts. It is, at the same time, a fact of individual behavior: the pensioners show low interest in personal relations, and little inclination to maintain or renew them. Isolation implies that the pensioners' position in society is inadequately defined in their own minds and in those of others—social workers, legislators, and the public at large. Such lack of definition produces disorientation and status-anxiety and makes it particularly difficult for the pensioner to conceive of his relations with others as reciprocal.

The leader, also, is isolated, although not in the same way as are the recipients. It is not primarily the dearth of contacts which separates the leader from relevant groups and individuals in the community, but the instability of those contacts. "Marginality"— the particular kind of isolation characteristic of the leader— manifests itself in his long, erratic career pattern and in his lack of firm relations with those groups in the community whose interests most closely resemble his own. Associated with marginality—either as a corollary or as a reflection of some personality trait—is a certain difficulty in maintaining and visualizing reciprocal relations with others; political setbacks thus are often a consequence of having misjudged the intentions and interests of other people. A counterpart of this lack of insight into the reciprocal nature of human relations is McLain's tendency to approach most personal and social questions as problems of status. This tendency well antedates his emergence as the leader of a pension movement; it has inspired his previous attempts at organizing those deprived of their rightful place in society—the unemployed and the "native sons" of his state; it also shows up in the slightly aristocratic overtones of his autobiographical notes and in his description of the traumatic effects upon him of his father's fall from social respectability.

It is consistent with McLain's behavior patterns and with his expressed ways of thinking that the organization he founds and leads should rely upon one-way communications as the main nexus between leader and members; the proprietary form of organization makes it particularly easy for the leader to develop and proclaim policies without membership participation. It is equally consistent with the behavior and attitudes of the pensioners that they should be attracted by an organization which does not call for intensive interaction. Similarly, it is natural for McLain to phrase the pensioners' problems in status terms, and equally natural for the pensioners to accept such phrasing.

The match between the isolated constituency and the marginal leader thus appears to result from similar social experiences of relative isolation and from the typical interpretation of such experiences. Where concrete personal relations between individuals are either absent or ill defined, status orientations are likely to be strong. Deprived of meaningful experiences with other people, the individual is unable to foretell the effects of his own behavior on others and of their behavior upon him; status orientations thus serve as substitutes for a more penetrating understanding of human situations.

The form of the Institute's organization thus is the "creation" of both leader and membership in the sense that it accommodates behavior patterns and orientations of both: preferences for one-way action and status definitions. How can we account for its durability?

Any organization which achieves a degree of permanence must contain some mechanisms insuring its continuance. Many an organization is able to endure by evolving a dense network of interpersonal relations which makes membership attractive; under such conditions, even shifts in program or in leadership do not necessarily result in large membership losses. The CISW, being unable to rely for its existence upon strong interpersonal ties, persists for different reasons. In order to maintain its membership and attract new recruits, it constantly helps to recreate the social conditions of its own existence. If status-anxiety is one of the conditions for the existence of the CISW, McLain's propaganda tends to maintain and nurture it. If another condition is personal isolation, the structure of the CISW does nothing to dispel it; for some of the members, increased negativism even appears to make sustained and constructive contacts more difficult. If a third condition of the Institute's emergence is the existence of a slightly privileged group, the program of the organization fosters the maintenance and perhaps even the enhancement of social and economic differentials among pensioners.

All this is not a matter of conscious design. It may well be argued, for instance, that McLain has made deliberate efforts to increase sociability within the organization and thus to make it more attractive to a more stable membership; if he did not succeed in this, the character of his membership is at least in part to blame. Similarly, the very conditions of his existence as a leader of pensioners seem to have frustrated McLain's attempts to escape from his marginal position in the political world: in trying to mobilize his membership he is under strong compulsion to employ the same propaganda devices and political tactics which set him apart from the common run of politicians and welfare-minded lobbyists.

This does not argue that the CISW cannot undergo change; nor does it preclude the possibility that the pensioners might achieve some other kind of political representation. We can only state that changes in the objectives and methods of the CISW are not likely to arise from tensions *internal* to the organization—given an unaltered social and political environment. For, such tensions as do exist within the Institute tend to maintain the organization in its present form rather than alter it. And changes observed in recent times—increased emphasis on systematic lobbying and greater service to members and constituents—have been chiefly responses to *external* conditions; among these have been the recurring defeats of the Institute's referendum campaigns and of McLain's personal quests for political office as well as changes in the political climate in California which has become more favorable to welfare programs.

The Institute's prospects for change would thus appear to hinge on the likelihood that altered orientations in the worlds of politics and social welfare will make for greater integration of the organization and of its constituency into a larger community. If the CISW and its aged constituents were in fact likely to subvert the democratic process, the chances of such integration would be slim.

Organization and Political Change

The question whether the organization is capable of causing profound changes in the political world is one that originally motivated our research. What is the Institute's potential for effecting social change? This depends on an assessment of the nature of the organization. Is it a simple interest group or is it more nearly akin to some of the mass movements of recent times? To attempt answers to these questions, we must consider the elements of participation as they appear in different types of organizations.

There are three elements of participation: (1) *commitment,* the psychological importance to the individual of group membership and group goals; (2) *interpersonal experience,* the extent to which friendship and similar ties play an important role for the member; and (3) *rationality,* the extent to which the members take appropriate, cool-headed action to solve their problems. These elements combine in different ways in the interest group, the community, and the mass organization.

ELEMENTS OF PARTICIPATION IN ORGANIZATIONS

Type	Commitment	Interpersonal experience	Rationality
Interest groups..............	Low	Low	High
Community.................	High	High	High
Mass organization...........	High	Low	Low

In the interest group, commitment and interpersonal experience are usually low, while rationality is high. The organization is dedicated to the solution of practical problems and appears to its members as purely instrumental. A property-owners' association to protect the character of a neighborhood is one illustration. Commitment, entailing a willingness to act and sacrifice for the attainment of group goals, does not go beyond what is required by the task at hand. Interpersonal experience is low, since the members may rarely even meet; or, if they do meet, the contacts are strictly businesslike. Rationality here is high and consists in the search for the best means of attaining the single goal.

In the community, all three elements assume high values. Commitment is high because the community-type organization impinges upon the individual from many directions and binds him firmly into a network of social relations. Interpersonal experience is high because the community stimulates and builds upon friendships, informal groups, and family ties. Rationality is high, but differs from the singlemindedness of interest-group rationality in that the community participant must strike a balance among a number of goals and values. He is free, nevertheless, to make rational calculations according to his own interests.

The mass organization presents the paradox of high commitment combined with low interpersonal experience and low rationality. The members are highly responsive to directives issuing from the organization and its leaders, and they display great readiness to sacrifice for the organization. Sacrifice of economic self-interest is common. Personal relations tend to be dominated by manipulative political attitudes, and the members relate themselves directly to the leader rather than to each other. Rationality is seriously impaired by the members' inability to define their own needs and consequently to take appropriate steps for the satisfaction of such needs; the members tend to feel an inarticulate malaise which they hope the organization or its leader will relieve.

An observer of the CISW might easily conclude that this is simply an interest group. He would point to the organization's and the members' exclusive preoccupation with economic goals. And indeed, most of the political and propaganda activity is focused on obtaining larger pension payments and more liberal eligibility provisions. The observer might find additional support for the interest-group thesis in the small amount of interpersonal experience among members. Closer examination suggests, however, that mass participation is an important feature of the McLain movement. This conclusion is based on the fact that commitment to the organization is extraordinarily high among many members and on our doubts that participation is characterized by a high degree of rationality. Many members are clearly seeking psychic satisfactions through their sacrifices and their relation to the leader. While it is true that the members have a strong interest in economic betterment, their actions and attitudes betray vague, inarticulate aspirations reflecting deeper needs. The struggle for economic goals may become the vehicle for other strivings and motivations, thus transforming the meaning of participation from interest-group membership to mass involvement. But there are no signs that such strivings have been transferred from the psychological level to that of social action. And the Institute's potential for social change, and the potential of its constituency, would therefore appear to be low.

Since it is uncertain whether the CISW can be expected to undergo profound changes, and unlikely that it will be able to alter its environment appreciably, the third possibility—that of integrative action originating in the community—must be explored. So long as poverty and dependency are corollaries of retirement, we should expect and accept political pressure on behalf of the aged. On broader grounds, separate organizations of the aged may well be undersirable, if only because they sharpen the isolation created by retirement from work and family life. Yet the problem of economic privation inevitably takes precedence and must find expression in the political arena.

The CISW's program is a narrow one, attempting only to better the pensioner's condition vis-à-vis the public-assistance programs. This one-sided insistence on monetary issues may give a distorted picture to the general public as well as to the pensioners. The pensioners need a sense of status and function in society; the public needs a greater awareness of the necessity for expanded resources to solve the complex problems of aging in an industrial society. Yet pressure-group activity, when nakedly pursued, appears to many as a raid upon the public treasury; and McLain's supporters can justify the program to themselves only by vague and defensive claims to respectability. A more constructive program should be so formulated as to give both the aged and the public an understanding of the underlying problems.

Separate organizations tend to increase the isolation of the aged by creating the image of a segregated and somewhat antagonistic group. Acrimonious political struggle sharpens this antagonism, crystallizes the opposition, neutralizes potential supporters, and creates irrelevant issues which stand in the way of proposals that would otherwise gain widespread community support. Granted that decisions of public policy regarding the aged will have to be reached eventually through the political process, an isolated pressure group can bring about a *premature* drawing of political lines.

Has the marginality of the CISW brought with it any serious threat to democratic political processes? Our general answer must be no. It is true that McLain's methods have not always been above reproach. It is true also that Myrtle Williams' accession to the office of state director of social welfare had something of the quality of a coup d'état. But democracy does not presume the unfailing virtue of all participants; nor should we damn a group for taking advantage of machinery that is too readily available or too easily abused.

Furthermore, there is no convincing evidence that McLain has been able to weld his followers into a solid phalanx of disgruntled individuals ready to act according to a leader's dictates. Many of the members have developed a deep and perhaps irrational loyalty to McLain. But it is clear that he cannot enlist them for causes alien to their special interests.

If there is concern about the political health of the community, it is arguable that the CISW gives less cause for it than do some of McLain's opponents. Some of the latter have endeavored to present the whole issue of old-age security as a feud between a "pension promoter" and the people of California. If the very real issues of old-age dependency are reduced to a discussion of individual morality, they cannot receive the public hearing they deserve.

The experience of the McLain movement does show, however, that community integration is an important clue to political responsibility. Isolation from the community has undoubtedly affected the organization's way of behaving, the nature of its leadership, and the response of the electorate. This suggests that political activity on behalf of the aged ought to become part of broader social welfare programs sponsored by groups that have a secure base in the organized community. If there is to be that kind of integration, however, there must also be a broad consensus regarding the propriety of political action to relieve old-age dependency.

APPENDICES

Appendix I | Tables

(Note—For an explanation of the varying numbers of cases on which the tables are based, see Appendix II, section 2. For an explanation of the group totals within each table and the relation between percentages of groups and of total samples, see Appendix III.)

TABLE 1

RESIDENCE AT AGE OF SCHOOL ATTENDANCE
(Present residents of Los Angeles County only)

Region	Percentage
Foreign..	13
Pacific..	7
Mountain..	6
West north central..	24
West south central..	6
East north central..	19
East south central..	2
South Atlantic..	2
Middle Atlantic...	7
New England...	2
Not ascertained...	12
Total..	100
Number of cases...	305

TABLE 2

ORGANIZATIONS TO WHICH RESPONDENTS BELONG
(Exclusive of churches and church service organizations)
(Percentage)[a]

Type of organization	Totals for samples	
	Members	Nonmembers
Political...................................	1	2
Union......................................	3	2
Religious...................................	4	5
Fraternal and social.........................	17	14
Community service..........................	2	1
Recreational-rehabilitation..................	2	3
Professional................................	..	1
Townsend..................................	..	1
Not ascertained............................	24	21
No organization............................	51	53
Number of cases...........................	2,131	838

[a] Percentages total more than 100 because some respondents mentioned more than one type of organization.

TABLE 3

RELIGIOUS PREFERENCES
(Percentage)

Preference	Nonmembers		Institute members							Totals for samples	
	Have not heard of McLain	Have heard of McLain	Regular members whose participation is				Aspiring life members	Life members	Club presidents	Members	Nonmembers
			Very low	Low	Medium	High					
Baptist........	10	11	11	14	8	7	15	9	16	9	11
Evangelical and fundamentalist	9	8	11	10	14	17	23	19	19	17	8
Other Christian	59	68	53	56	60	60	51	59	47	59	65
Other..........	11	7	9	8	9	9	6	7	8	8	8
Not ascertained	11	6	16	12	9	7	5	6	10	7	8
Totals.......	100	100	100	100	100	100	100	100	100	100	100
Number of cases....	217	621	104	134	353	514	254	772	93	2,131	838

TABLE 4

Main Occupations
(Percentage)

Occupational category	OAS recipients before age of fifty (exclusive of housewives)				Longest occupation before retirement, of males, U. S. cross-section[a]	Occupation of both sexes in California, 1950[b]
	Nonmembers		Institute members			
	Do not mention McLain	Mention McLain	Sample	Club presidents		
Professionals and managers.........	19	22	11	15	14	22
Farmers and farm managers.....	4	2	3	7	27	3
Clerical and sales....	18	22	15	12	9	22
Services............	15	23	25	12	6	11
Skilled manual.......	16	12	25	31	20	16
Operatives.........	10	6	6	9	13	16
Labor.............	8	5	4	2	7	6
Agricultural labor....	6	3	3	2	4	4
Agricultural ownership status not specified	4	5	8	10	..	..
Total reporting....	100	100	100	100	100	100
Not ascertained in per cent of all cases..........	42	34	36	26		
Number of cases in sample (exclusive of housewives)...	139	439	1,547	80		

[a] Source: Robert Dorfman, "The Labor Force Status of Persons Aged Sixty-five and Over," *American Economic Review*, XLIV (May, 1954), 637.
[b] Source: U. S. Census of Populations.

TABLE 5

Last Occupation
(Percentage)

Occupational category	OAS recipients[a]				Present or last occupation of males, U. S. cross-section[b]
	Nonmembers		Institute members		
	Mention McLain	Do not mention McLain	Sample	Club presidents	
Professionals and managers..	13	17	8	12	15
Farmers and farm managers..	6	2	4	5	21
Clerical and sales..........	17	15	11	11	9
Services.................	28	29	33	23	11
Skilled manual............	14	14	22	27	17
Operatives...............	7	8	9	10	12
Labor...................	10	9	6	4	11
Agricultural labor..........	5	6	7	8	4
Total reporting..........	100	100	100	100	100
Not ascertained in per cent of all cases............	29	21	28	13	..
Number of cases (exclusive of single women without significant occupations)..	175	492	1,861	87	..

[a] For housewives, husband's last occupation was entered in this table.
[b] Source: Dorfman, *op. cit.* (see table 4).

286 | Appendix 1

TABLE 6

HOUSEWIVES' REPORT OF HUSBANDS' MAIN OCCUPATION
(Percentage)

| | OAS recipients | | | | Longest occupation[a] before retirement of males, U.S. cross-section |
| | Nonmembers | | Institute members | | |
Occupational category	Mention McLain	Do not mention McLain	Sample	Club presidents	
Professionals and managers..	20	22	9	4	14
Farmers and farm managers..	5	1	2	8	27
Clerical and sales..........	9	14	12	4	9
Services..................	4	5	8	12	6
Skilled manual.............	23	17	25	40	20
Operatives................	5	7	5	0	13
Labor....................	10	10	3	4	7
Agricultural labor.........	12	14	19	20	4
Agricultural, unspecified.....	12	10	17	8	..
Total reporting..........	100	100	100	100	100
Not ascertained in per cent of number of cases......	20	11	16	22	..
Number of cases.........	161	440	1,340	32	..

[a] SOURCE: Dorfman, *op. cit.* (see table 4).

TABLE 7

RESPONDENTS AGED SIXTY-FIVE YEARS AND OLDER
(Percentage)

| | Totals for samples | |
Age groups	Members[a]	Nonmembers
65–69...	25	22
70–74...	30	29
75–79...	26	26
80–84...	12	14
85–89...	4	5
90 and above.................................	1	1
Not ascertained...............................	2	3
	100	100
Average age............................	74.1	74.6
Number of cases........................	2,043	838

[a] Exclusive of members who had not reached their sixty-fifth birthday.

TABLE 8
Reactions to the Social Worker and the Pension Law
(Based on Adjective Check List)
(Percentage)

	Respect "Respectful" "Humiliating"	Considerateness "Efficient" "Full of red tape"	Kindness "Kind" "Cruel"	Clarity "Clear" "Confused"	Rectitude "Above-board" "Tricky"	Generosity "Generous" "Stingy"	Not ascertained	Number of cases
Social worker								
Members........	63	52	47	28	24	18	9	1,011
Nonmembers...	68	56	61	37	21	26	5	149
Pension law								
Members........	52	68	29	36	33	38	7	1,011
Nonmembers...	49	49	39	21	16	54	7	149

TABLE 9

Feelings Regarding the Pension at Present and at the Time of Application
(Percentage)

	"Glad"	"Entitled" (or "Glad" and "Entitled")	"Embarrassed" (alone or in combination with other terms)	Other negative feelings	Mixed feelings (other than "Embarrassed")	Not ascertained	Totals	Number of cases
Feelings now								
Members[a].....	29	30	13	1	27	:	100	1,795
Nonmembers.....	38	19	17	2	22	2	100	838
Feelings when applying								
Members[a].....	24	27	22	2	23	2	100	1,795
Nonmembers.....	29	16	28	4	20	3	100	838

[a] Exclusive of members not on Old Age Assistance.

TABLE 10

TYPES OF ACTIVITIES BY INVOLVEMENT[a]

Types of activities	Nonmembers			Institute members							Totals for samples	
				Regular members whose participation is				Aspiring life members	Life members	Club presidents		
	Do not mention organizations	Have not heard of McLain	Have heard of McLain	Very low	Low	Medium	High				Members	Non-members
All activities												
Per cent of respondents	77	89	92	80	87	91	95	92	92	99	91	89
Mean activity score	2.9	3.7	4.2	3.6	4.0	4.1	4.9	4.6	4.3	5.8	4.4	3.9
Solitary activities												
Per cent of respondents	54	77	83	67	78	79	85	81	81	90	81	78
Mean activity score	1.1	1.7	2.0	1.6	1.9	1.9	2.2	2.0	1.9	2.3	2.0	1.8
Activities in formal groups												
Per cent of respondents	62	58	58	58	52	60	71	68	69	86	65	68
Mean activity score	.9	.9	.9	.9	.8	.9	1.2	1.1	1.1	1.5	1.0	.9
Activities in informal groups												
Per cent of respondents	48	57	66	55	66	70	70	70	68	85	68	63
Mean activity score	.9	1.1	1.3	1.1	1.3	1.3	1.4	1.5	1.3	2.0	1.4	1.2
Recreation												
Per cent of respondents	29	37	46	44	49	49	56	72	71	80	73	72
Mean activity score	.5	.6	.7	.7	.7	.7	.9	1.3	1.2	1.5	1.3	1.3
Social participation												
Per cent of respondents	73	78	82	74	78	83	88	84	85	97	85	81
Mean activity score	1.7	1.9	2.1	1.8	2.1	2.1	2.5	2.5	2.4	3.1	2.3	2.1
Manipulation												
Per cent of respondents	49	71	76	58	71	71	80	52	53	70	52	43
Mean activity score	.8	1.3	1.3	1.1	1.2	1.2	1.5	.8	.8	1.3	.8	.6

[a] See Appendix IV for explanation of activity types.

TABLE 11

ACTUAL AND DESIRED ACTIVITIES
(Percentage)

Activity	Members		Nonmembers	
	Actual	Desired	Actual	Desired
Volunteer work	11	58	9	51
Full-time or part-time work	12	38	8	41
Hobbies and repairs	40	56	30	53
Going to meetings	37	55	24	43
Helping friends	22	43	17	34
Helping young folks	10	28	11	27
Organized recreation	4	21	4	20
Visits with family	41	58	37	52
Playing with children	16	33	15	28
Going to church	51	65	52	63
Visits with friends	52	59	47	55
Light reading	53	54	56	57
Other activities	5	12	6	5
Serious reading	47	41	46	36
Outdoor activities	58	50	52	39
Number of cases	2,131	1,120	838	383

TABLE 12

DIFFERENCES BETWEEN MEAN ACTIVITY SCORES[a] AND MEAN ACTIVITY ASPIRATION SCORES

Types of activities	Members	Nonmembers
Total activities	2.1	2.0
Solitary activities	.8	.5
Activities in formal groups	1.6	1.4
Activities in informal groups	.8	.7
Recreation	.7	.5
Social participation	.5	.4
Manipulation	1.5	1.4

[a] See Appendix IV for explanation of activity types.

TABLE 13

LIFE GOALS, AVERAGE RANKS

	Members	Nonmembers
Trust in a higher power	4.77	4.69
Respect	4.05	4.13
Friends	4.00	4.15
Active life	3.44	3.47
Money	2.35	2.16
Influence	1.95	1.71

TABLE 14

ACTIVITY ASPIRATIONS

(Activities suggested by respondents for health and welfare of a mythical older person, listed by size and direction of discrepancy between members and nonmembers)

(Percentage)

Activity	Nonmembers			Institute members							Totals for samples	
	Do not mention organizations	Have not heard of McLain	Have heard of McLain	Regular members whose participation is				Aspiring life members	Life members	Club presidents	Members	Non-members
				Very low	Low	Medium	High					
Going to meetings	18	31	49	38	39	49	63	65	61	85	55	43
Outdoor activities	30	28	43	48	37	48	55	51	48	72	50	39
Helping friends	26	26	38	38	44	38	47	43	44	46	43	34
Other activities	2	2	6	8	7	13	15	15	11	20	12	5
Visits with family	42	31	57	48	58	55	61	64	63	72	58	52
Volunteer work	38	41	55	52	46	50	64	64	65	80	58	51
Studying	21	24	40	38	28	37	46	48	45	56	41	36
Playing with children	20	20	30	26	32	32	34	33	35	33	33	28
Visits with friends	34	47	60	58	51	51	64	67	63	77	59	55
Hobbies	40	39	57	40	49	58	61	61	56	74	56	53
Going to church	58	55	65	58	63	64	66	70	70	80	65	63
Helping young folks	20	18	30	32	21	25	32	29	26	23	28	27
Organized recreation	18	10	22	12	23	18	22	23	23	23	21	20
Light reading	48	47	61	44	51	54	57	57	56	59	54	57
Full-time work	22	31	47	38	40	36	38	33	40	36	38	41
Not ascertained	30	22	13	20	17	13	9	8	8	5	12	16
Number of cases	50	51	282	50	57	179	259	150	425	39	1,120	383

TABLE 15

MEAN ACTIVITY ASPIRATION SCORES[a]

Types of activities	Nonmembers			Institute members								Totals for samples	
	Do not mention organizations	Have not heard of McLain	Have heard of McLain	Regular members whose participation is				Aspiring life members	Life members	Club presidents		Members	Non-members
				Very low	Low	Medium	High						
All activities....	4.4	4.5	6.6	5.7	5.8	6.1	7.2	7.1	7.0	8.3		6.6	6.1
Solitary activities	1.8	1.7	2.5	2.1	2.0	2.4	2.7	2.7	2.5	3.3		2.8	2.3
Activities in formal groups....	1.8	1.7	2.5	2.1	2.1	2.2	2.7	2.7	2.7	3.3		2.5	2.3
Activities in informal groups	1.4	1.4	2.2	2.0	2.1	2.0	2.4	2.4	2.3	3.5		2.8	2.0
Recreation.....	1.4	1.3	2.0	1.6	1.7	1.7	2.1	2.1	2.0	2.3		1.9	1.8
Social participation..........	1.8	1.9	2.7	2.4	2.4	2.5	3.0	3.1	3.0	3.7		2.8	2.5
Manipulation....	1.5	1.5	2.3	2.0	2.0	2.1	2.5	2.5	2.4	2.8		2.3	2.1

[a] See Appendix IV for explanation of activity types.

TABLE 16
DISSATISFACTIONS WITH VARIOUS MATTERS OF EXPERIENCE
(Percentage)

Source of dissatisfaction	Satisfied		Not quite satisfied		Dissatisfied		Not ascertained		Difference: dissatisfied members less dissatisfied nonmembers
	Members	Non-members	Members	Non-members	Members	Non-members	Members	Non-members	
Amount of money income	21	48	43	29	23	9	13	14	28
The way this country is run	20	46	34	23	26	6	20	25	31
Young people's ideas on morals and religion	18	28	34	30	25	14	23	28	15
The way the city or town is run	36	58	28	15	12	3	24	24	22
Medical attention	47	63	20	13	13	5	20	19	15
Food	60	76	22	11	9	3	9	10	17
The way people do their work nowadays	44	52	22	16	6	4	28	28	8
Housing	68	74	19	16	8	5	5	5	5
Number of family visits	55	56	15	13	6	3	24	28	5
Weather	71	79	13	7	3	1	13	13	8
Number of visits with friends and acquaintances	67	78	12	7	3	1	18	13	5
Treatment by young people	70	77	11	7	4	3	15	13	5

Total number of cases: members, 2,131; nonmembers, 838.

TABLE 17

Mean Dissatisfaction Scores (Standardized) by Involvement[a]

	Nonmembers			Institute members							Totals for samples	
				Regular members whose participation is				Aspiring life members	Life members	Club presidents		
	Do not mention organizations	Have not heard of McLain	Have heard of McLain	Very low	Low	Medium	High				Members	Non-members
Total scores on 12 items......	.1	.2	.3	.4	.4	.5	.5	.6	.5	.6	.5	.3
State aid (2 items)......	.2	.3	.4	.5	.6	.7	.7	.8	.7	.8	.7	.3
Material environment (3 items)	.1	.2	.2	.3	.3	.3	.3	.4	.3	.4	.3	.2
Material environment and state aid (above 5 items combined)......												
Social experiences (3 items)......	.2	.3	.3	.4	.4	.5	.5	.6	.5	.6	.5	.2
Ideological experiences (4 items)......	.1	.2	.3	.4	.4	.7	.6	.7	.7	.8	.6	.3

[a] Since the scores in each category are not based on the same number of items, they were "standardized" by dividing each by the number of items upon which it is based. The means of the partial scores will add to the total means, if each is weighted by the appropriate number of items.
For details concerning the indices see Appendix IV.

TABLE 18

DEMANDS FOR IMPROVED TREATMENT FOR THE AGED
(Percentage)

Demands	Nonmembers			Institute members							Totals for samples	
	Do not mention organizations	Have not heard of McLain	Have heard of McLain	Regular members whose participation is				Aspiring life members	Life members	Club presidents	Members	Nonmembers
				Very low	Low	Medium	High					
More respect from children..	53	63	63	57	71	71	75	78	79	83	72	61
Special housing..	29	38	41	45	59	53	62	67	65	55	53	39
Leadership in families......	30	30	36	38	46	50	56	60	58	69	52	34
Leadership in churches and organizations..	17	23	25	31	36	38	38	48	42	50	38	23
Low fares on public conveyances	25	20	24	33	40	34	37	49	40	43	37	24
An honor roll in each community....	13	13	15	19	26	25	27	41	35	36	27	15
High offices in government...	12	15	19	16	22	25	25	35	31	29	25	18
A special holiday to honor the aged...........	13	13	11	16	27	23	26	40	29	40	25	12
Special service in stores........	10	14	14	16	25	17	26	32	27	18	23	14
Not ascertained	27	13	8	14	9	10	5	4	5	1	8	11
Number of cases	112	105	621	104	134	353	514	254	772	93	2,131	838

TABLE 19

DEMANDS MADE BY RESPONDENTS
(Percentage of sample groups)

Number of demands	Nonmembers			Institute members							Totals for samples	
	Do not mention organizations	Have not heard of McLain	Have heard of McLain	Regular members whose participation is				Aspiring life members	Life members	Club presidents	Members	Non-members
				Very low	Low	Medium	High					
0.............	5	18	16	12	9	8	7	4	5	8	8	15
1-3...........	46	45	48	41	38	41	37	32	35	32	38	48
4-6...........	16	15	20	24	28	28	34	30	34	43	31	19
7-9...........	6	9	8	8	17	14	16	29	21	16	16	7
Not ascertained..	27	13	8	15	8	9	6	5	5	1	7	11
Totals........	100	100	100	100	100	100	100	100	100	100	100	100
Mean demand scores......	3.0	2.7	2.8	3.1	3.8	3.7	4.2	4.7	4.3	4.1	3.9	2.8
Number of cases	112	105	621	104	134	353	514	254	772	93	2,131	838

296

TABLE 20

REASONS FOR DESIRING SPECIAL ORGANIZATIONS FOR THE AGED
(Percentage)[a]

Classification	Members	Nonmembers
By nature of needs		
General need (not specified)	38	26
Economic need	28	21
Social need	31	31
Need for activity	25	25
By activity-passivity		
Active (Aged must organize and do things for themselves)	42	30
Passive (Aged need help, protection, because old, helpless)	29	35
Reactive (Aged must defend themselves against hostile world)	18	12
Not ascertained	11	23
Number of cases	70	569

[a] Percentages total more than 100 because some respondents gave more than one answer.

TABLE 21

LIVING ACCOMMODATIONS
(Percentage)

Type of accommodation	Total for samples		Club presidents
	Nonmembers	Members	
Home owned by respondent	26	47	67
Home owned by someone in respondent's family	20	14	14
Rented apartment	36	25	11
Rented room	13	9	5
Hotel or boarding house	4	2	0
Others	...	1	0
Not ascertained	1	2	3
Totals	100	100	100
Number of cases	838	2,131	93

TABLE 22

SIZE OF COMMUNITIES IN OR NEAR WHICH RESPONDENTS LIVE
(For seven counties)
(Percentage)

Population	Club presidents	Members (sample)	Nonmembers
1,000–5,000.................	41	20	14
5,000–25,000................	11	15	9
25,000–100,000...............	32	18	16
Over 100,000.................	16	47	60
Not ascertained..............	0	..	1
Totals...................	100	100	100
Number of cases..........	44	1,185	838

TABLE 23

SOURCES OF INCOME
(Percentage)

	Institute members							Totals for samples	
	Regular members whose participation is				Aspiring life members	Life members	Club presidents	Members	Nonmembers
Source of income	Very low	Low	Medium	High					
Old Age Security only	46	46	52	55	56	59	47	53	67
Old Age Security and Social Security......	19	19	29	30	22	27	38	27	26
Old Age Security and other..............	8	11	7	5	7	4	5	7	6
No Old Age Security...	28	23	11	9	13	9	9	13	0
Not ascertained.......	2	1	1	1	2	1	1	1	1
Totals.............	100	100	100	100	100	100	100	100	100
Number of cases....	104	134	353	514	254	772	93	2,131	838

TABLE 24

MARITAL STATUS

(Percentage)

Status	Nonmembers			Institute members (sample)							Totals for samples	
	Do not mention organizations	Have not heard of McLain	Have heard of McLain	Regular members whose participation is				Aspiring life members	Life members	Club presidents	Members	Non-members
				Very low	Low	Medium	High					
Single.........	8	13	9	11	5	8	9	7	10	3	9	10
Married........	29	19	32	35	45	48	49	41	45	71	47	30
Widowed........	53	57	49	46	41	37	32	39	35	19	36	50
Divorced.......	9	9	6	7	5	4	6	9	7	6	5	7
Separated......	1	1	3	1	2	2	4	4	3	1	3	3
Not ascertained..	0	1	1	0	2	1	..	0	..	0	..	0
Totals........	100	100	100	100	100	100	100	100	100	100	100	100
Number of cases	112	105	621	104	134	353	514	254	772	93	2,131	838

TABLE 25
SEX OF ALL RECIPIENTS BY INVOLVEMENT
(Percentage)

Sex	Nonmembers			Institute members							Totals for samples	
	Do not mention organizations	Have not heard of McLain	Have heard of McLain	Regular members whose participation is				Aspiring life members	Life members	Club presidents	Members	Non-members
				Very low	Low	Medium	High					
Male...........	30	32	32	38	42	45	53	35	41	64	46	32
Female.........	70	67	68	61	58	54	46	65	59	36	53	68
Not ascertained..	0	1	..	1	1	1	1	..	..	..	1	0
Totals.........	100	100	100	100	100	100	100	100	100	100	100	100
Number of cases	112	105	621	104	134	353	514	254	772	93	2,151	838

TABLE 26

Living Arrangements
(Percentage)

	Totals for samples		Club presidents
	Nonmembers	Members	
Alone............................	42	36	26
Husband and wife..............	29	46	72
Children.......................	15	7	1
Relatives or friends.............	10	8	1
Other institution...............	1	1	0
Others.........................	..	0	0
Not ascertained................	3	2	0
Totals....................	100	100	100
Number of cases...........	838	2,131	77

TABLE 27

Feelings about Pension by Comparative Advantage
(Percentage)

	No advantage	One advantage	Two advantages	Three advantages	Total no. of cases
"Glad"					
Members...............	36	33	25	17	
Nonmembers............	45	37	33	35	
"Entitled" (or "Glad" and "Entitled")					
Members...............	26	26	33	38	
Nonmembers............	15	22	17	24	
"Embarrassed" (alone or in combination with other terms)					
Members...............	12	13	15	17	
Nonmembers............	17	14	22	17	
Other negative feelings					
Members...............	3	5	5	8	
Nonmembers............	5	5	8	4	
Mixed feelings (other than "Embarrassed")					
Members...............	23	23	22	19	
Nonmembers............	18	20	15	15	
Number of cases[a]					
Members...............	354	701	615	315	1,985
Nonmembers............	240	316	196	46	798

[a] Exclusive of cases in which the number of advantages could not be ascertained.

TABLE 28

PRIVILEGES AS RELATED TO SELECTED INDICES OF ATTITUDE AND ACTIVITY

	Members		Nonmembers	
	Privileged	Not privileged	Privileged	Not privileged
Respondents with distrust indices above .2, as per cent of all respondents...................	89	71	33	12
Respondents making unfavorable[a] judgments of pension law, as per cent of all respondents..........	68	55	36	19
Respondents making unfavorable[a] judgments of social worker, as per cent of all respondents......	33	26	13	12
Respondents participating in organizations other than the CISW, as per cent of all respondents....	26	26	27	21
Number of cases[b]............	1,631	354	558	240

[a] "Unfavorable" judgments are those in which the number of negative adjectives applied to the pension law or the social worker is larger than the number of positive adjectives.

[b] Exclusive of cases in which the number of advantages could not be ascertained.

TABLE 29

PERCEPTION OF THE PENSION LAW, AS IT IS NOW, ARRANGED IN ORDER OF SIZE OF PROPORTIONS
(Percentage)[a]

Appraisal	Non-members who have heard of McLain	Institute members							Totals for samples	
		Regular members whose participation is				Aspiring life members	Life members	Club presidents	Members	Non-members
		Very low	Low	Medium	High					
Full of red tape	18	35	38	49	58	56	64	72	52	17
Humiliating	15	30	27	34	36	40	48	52	35	13
Confused	11	22	29	33	31	35	42	54	32	9
Tricky	7	15	16	21	30	36	38	44	25	6
Stingy	7	17	18	16	22	22	29	35	20	6
Generous	47	22	20	20	16	14	13	9	18	48
Kind	38	13	18	18	16	21	14	7	17	36
Respectful	32	9	16	17	18	17	12	15	16	32
Cruel	4	9	6	12	12	19	16	17	12	3
Aboveboard	10	13	9	8	8	4	5	6	8	10
Efficient	25	9	10	8	6	8	7	9	7	25
Clear	12	7	8	2	4	4	4	2	4	12
Not ascertained	4	18	13	6	4	7	5	0	7	7
Number of cases	108	54	77	174	255	104	347	54	1,011	149

[a] Percentages total more than 100 because respondents gave more than one answer.

TABLE 30

RESPONDENTS' APPRAISALS OF SOCIAL WORKER, ARRANGED IN ORDER OF SIZE OF PROPORTIONS

(Percentage)[a]

Appraisal	Non-members who have heard of McLain	Institute members							Totals for samples	
		Regular members whose participation is				Aspiring life members	Life members	Club presidents	Members	Non-members
		Very low	Low	Medium	High					
Respectful........	63	32	43	45	47	36	42	48	44	57
Kind.............	57	41	42	40	44	39	35	39	41	58
Full of red tape...	10	22	26	30	31	38	41	52	31	11
Efficient........	47	17	18	23	22	11	18	17	21	45
Humiliating......	10	13	13	21	19	29	28	30	19	11
Tricky..........	5	9	9	14	15	22	24	37	15	4
Confused........	8	7	12	16	14	20	21	35	14	7
Clear...........	32	13	14	13	15	14	12	7	14	30
Generous........	22	11	10	9	11	12	6	4	10	22
Aboveboard......	18	7	4	9	10	7	9	4	9	17
Stingy..........	6	4	5	10	7	17	14	24	8	4
Cruel...........	4	2	3	6	6	17	10	9	6	3
Not ascertained...	3	24	16	8	6	8	8	4	9	5
Number of cases...	108	54	77	174	255	104	347	54	1,011	149

[a] Percentages total more than 100 because respondents gave more than one answer.

TABLE 31

APPRAISALS OF THE PENSION LAW

(Percentage)

Appraisal	Non-members who have heard of McLain	Institute members							Totals for samples	
		Regular members whose participation is				Aspiring life members	Life members	Club presidents	Members	Non-members
		Very low	Low	Medium	High					
Very favorable (only favorable adjectives).....	61	29	31	28	23	23	18	9	26	61
Favorable (more favorable than unfavorable adjectives)............	4	2	3	5	3	2	2	4	3	4
Undecided (equal number of favorable and unfavorable adjectives)....	5	4	3	4	3	7	3	4	3	4
Unfavorable (more unfavorable than favorable adjectives)............	5	4	9	2	6	3	6	7	5	3
Very unfavorable (only unfavorable adjectives)	21	42	41	54	60	58	66	76	55	21
Not ascertained.........	4	19	13	7	5	7	5	0	8	7
Totals.................	100	100	100	100	100	100	100	100	100	100
Number of cases.......	108	54	77	174	255	104	347	54	1,011	149

TABLE 32

APPRAISALS OF THE SOCIAL WORKER

(Percentage)

Appraisal	Non-members who have heard of McLain	Institute members							Totals for samples	
		Regular members whose participation is				Aspiring life members	Life members	Club presidents	Members	Non-members
		Very low	Low	Medium	High					
Very favorable (only favorable adjectives)....	78	46	48	49	50	48	40	31	48	75
Favorable (more favorable than unfavorable adjectives)..........	3	2	5	8	6	7	5	7	6	3
Undecided (equal number of favorable and unfavorable adjectives)....	5	4	4	6	7	1	6	6	6	3
Unfavorable (more unfavorable than favorable adjectives)........	2	2	5	2	4	1	4	9	4	3
Very unfavorable (only unfavorable adjectives)	9	22	21	28	27	35	37	41	27	11
Not ascertained..........	3	24	17	7	6	9	8	6	9	5
Totals.................	100	100	100	100	100	100	100	100	100	100
Number of cases.......	108	54	77	174	255	104	347	54	1,011	149

TABLE 33

AVERAGE NUMBER OF ITEMS SELECTED ON THREE CHECK LISTS

| | Non-members who have heard of McLain | Institute members | | | | | | | Totals for samples | |
| | | Regular members whose participation is | | | | Aspiring life members | Life members | Club presidents | Members | Non-members |
		Very low	Low	Medium	High					
Groups or individuals as friends or enemies.....	9.19	9.36	10.48	12.14	12.80	12.38	13.18	13.22	12.16	8.66
Adjectives used to describe pension law.....	2.37	2.45	2.48	2.53	2.68	3.07	3.05	3.22	2.65	2.32
Adjectives used to describe social worker.....	2.90	2.34	2.38	2.52	2.55	2.88	2.83	3.15	2.55	2.83
Number of cases.......	108	54	77	174	255	104	347	54	1,011	149

TABLE 34

DISTRUST SCORES (RATIOS OF "ENEMY" TO ALL RESPONSES)
(Percentage)

	Non-members who have heard of McLain	Institute members							Totals for samples	
		Regular members whose participation is				Aspiring life members	Life members	Club presidents	Members	Non-members
		Very low	Low	Medium	High					
No "enemy" responses	31	15	12	6	5	7	3	0	7	33
More "friend" than "enemy" responses	36	15	31	24	30	18	14	15	25	35
Equal numbers of "friend" and "enemy" responses	10	13	9	22	15	16	18	18	16	7
More "enemy" than "friend" responses	7	19	31	28	35	35	51	54	33	5
Only "enemy" responses	3	5	4	7	6	4	6	4	6	4
Not ascertained	13	33	13	13	9	20	8	9	13	16
Totals	100	100	100	100	100	100	100	100	100	100
Mean ratio of "enemy" to all responses	.24	.43	.46	.51	.51	.51	.59	.60	.51	.23
Number of cases	108	54	77	124	255	104	347	54	1,011	163

TABLE 35

INDIVIDUALS AND GROUPS DESIGNATED AS "ENEMIES" OF THE PENSIONERS

(Percentage of respondents)

	Non-members who have heard of McLain	Institute members								Totals for samples	
		Regular members whose participation is				Aspiring life members	Life members	Club presidents		Members	Non-members
		Very low	Low	Medium	High						
Chamber of Commerce	24	32	57	67	73	64	82	85		67	18
Senator Weybret	13	30	51	64	72	61	85	89		65	10
Big business	24	30	52	55	62	53	74	76		57	20
Boards of supervisors	11	30	43	52	60	47	71	82		54	9
Communists	44	35	40	48	51	45	59	57		48	40
Governor Warren	6	15	22	25	35	36	54	54		31	5
State senators	7	15	18	29	27	32	34	30		26	7
Republicans	1	9	18	26	22	26	26	28		22	1
Politicians	12	9	16	20	22	19	29	20		21	10
Eisenhower	0	11	17	19	16	16	20	24		18	1
Social workers	6	11	12	14	15	18	22	22		15	5
General MacArthur	2	7	17	17	12	15	14	15		14	2
Assemblymen	4	9	12	11	16	17	15	13		14	3
President Truman	6	6	5	6	9	12	14	17		8	7
Jews	2	7	8	10	6	7	10	7		8	3
Catholics	4	9	5	6	7	16	12	11		8	4
Ham and Eggs	11	6	4	6	9	11	10	7		7	10
Dr. Townsend	4	0	1	5	7	4	13	11		6	3
Governor Stevenson	3	2	3	5	5	7	4	2		4	3
Labor unions	7	2	5	3	3	6	3	2		3	5
Democrats	2	4	3	1	4	2	5	2		3	1
Protestants	0	0	3	2	2	0	2	2		2	1
Negroes	0	2	4	1	1	2	1			1	
Not ascertained	13	33	12	13	9	20	8	9		13	16
Number of cases	108	54	77	174	255	104	347	54		1,011	149

309

TABLE 36

Response Pattern of Institute Members on Items in Friendship-Hostility Question
(Percentage)

	Regular members	Aspiring life members	Life members	Club presidents	All members
Scale types					
Weybret, Chamber of Commerce, Supervisors, Warren..............	22	31	49	51	26
Weybret, Chamber of Commerce, Supervisors..	27	20	23	33	26
Weybret, Chamber of Commerce............	10	12	7	4	10
Weybret................	5	3	3	2	5
None..................	13	14	4	0	12
Nonscale types					
Weybret, Chamber of Commerce, Warren.....	4	6	8	4	5
Supervisors, Chamber of Commerce, Warren.....	2	4	1	2	2
Supervisors, Weybret, Warren..............	1	1	1	2	1
Supervisors, Chamber of Commerce............	4	0	1	0	3
Supervisors, Weybret.....	2	1	2	2	2
Chamber of Commerce, Warren..............	1	2	0	0	1
Supervisors, Warren......	1	0	0	0	..
Weybret, Warren........	..	1	..	0	..
Chamber of Commerce....	5	4	..	0	4
Supervisors..............	2	1	0	0	1
Warren.................	1	0	..	0	1
Totals................	100	100	100	100	100
Number of cases.......	560	104	347	54	1,011

TABLE 37

HOSTILITY OF INSTITUTE MEMBERS TOWARD SENATOR WEYBRET
COMPARED WITH HOSTILITY TOWARD STATE SENATORS
(Percentage)

	Regular members	Aspiring life members	Life members	Club presidents	All members
Both enemies.............	26	38	36	33	27
Weybret enemy, state senators not enemies......	46	37	57	65	48
Weybret not enemy, senators enemies........	4	1	1	0	3
Both not enemies..........	24	24	6	2	22
Totals................	100	100	100	100	100
Number of cases........	560	104	347	54	1,011

TABLE 38

HOSTILITY TOWARD CHAMBER OF COMMERCE COMPARED WITH
HOSTILITY TOWARD BIG BUSINESS
(Percentage)

	Regular members	Aspiring life members	Life members	Club presidents	All members
Both enemies.............	58	63	77	80	61
Chamber of Commerce enemy, big business not enemy..............	17	16	12	14	16
Chamber of Commerce not enemy, big business enemy	6	2	4	4	5
Both not enemies..........	19	19	7	2	18
Totals................	100	100	100	100	100
Number of cases........	560	104	347	54	1,011

TABLE 39

Respondents' Designations of Individuals and Groups as Friends and Enemies

(Percentage)

		Friends	Enemies	Neither	Undecided	Contingency coefficients
Board of supervisors	Members.......	5	54	27	1	.51
	Nonmembers....	34	9	41	0	
Republicans	Members.......	13	22	52	..	.34
	Nonmembers....	24	1	59	0	
Chamber of Commerce	Members.......	2	67	18	0	.34
	Nonmembers....	2	18	56	0	
State senators	Members.......	23	31	33	..	.33
	Nonmembers....	55	5	24	0	
Warren	Members.......	36	15	36	..	.32
	Nonmembers....	55	5	24	0	
Social workers	Members.......	9	26	51	1	.31
	Nonmembers....	25	7	51	1	
Senator Weybret	Members.......	1	65	21	0	.29
	Nonmembers....	3	10	71	0	
Eisenhower	Members.......	22	17	48	0	.26
	Nonmembers....	51	1	32	0	
Assemblymen	Members.......	11	14	61	1	.24
	Nonmembers....	12	3	68	1	
General MacArthur	Members.......	23	14	50	0	.22
	Nonmembers....	35	2	47	0	
Labor unions	Members.......	47	3	37	..	.19
	Nonmembers....	31	5	47	1	
Ham and Eggs	Members.......	30	7	50	0	.17
	Nonmembers....	12	10	62	0	
Big business	Members.......	2	57	28	0	.15
	Nonmembers....	4	20	60	0	
Politicians	Members.......	3	20	63	1	.15
	Nonmembers....	6	10	67	1	
Catholics	Members.......	20	8	59	..	.11
	Nonmembers....	25	4	55	0	
Jews	Members.......	17	8	62	..	.08
	Nonmembers....	12	3	69	0	
Communists	Members.......	3	48	36	0	.08
	Nonmembers....	0	40	44	0	
Townsend	Members.......	47	6	34	..	.03
	Nonmembers....	30	3	51	0	
President Truman	Members.......	47	8	32	..	.03
	Nonmembers....	31	7	46	0	
Governor Stevenson	Members.......	31	4	52	0	.02
	Nonmembers....	17	3	63	1	
Democrats	Members.......	43	3	40	1	.02
	Nonmembers....	26	1	56	1	
Protestants	Members.......	28	2	57	..	.004
	Nonmembers....	29	1	54	0	
Negroes	Members.......	37	1	48	1	.0005
	Nonmembers....	25	1	58	0	

Total number of cases: members, 1,011; nonmembers, 149.
Members not ascertained, 13; nonmembers not ascertained, 16.
Counting cases not ascertained, all totals are 100.

TABLE 40

IMAGES OF GEORGE MCLAIN AMONG INSTITUTE MEMBERS
(Percentage)[a]

	Regular members whose participation is				Aspiring life members	Life members	Club presidents	All members
	Very low	Low	Medium	High				
Friend..............	37	52	55	46	38	42	39	47
Brother.............	11	8	9	20	18	22	20	15
Teacher.............	10	5	9	8	9	7	10	8
Political leader.......	14	18	13	16	11	13	20	14
Good shepherd........	24	37	37	40	48	45	43	38
Protector...........	28	31	45	48	43	49	46	44
More than three answers...........	2	2	2	2	6	3	5	2
None of these........	9	2	1	..	..	..	0	1
Not ascertained......	11	6	2	1	2	2	0	3
Number of cases....	104	134	353	514	254	772	93	2,131

[a] Percentages total more than 100 because respondents gave more than one answer.

TABLE 41

MEMBERS' IMAGES OF THE INSTITUTE OF SOCIAL WELFARE
(Percentage)[a]

	Regular members whose participation is				Aspiring life members	Life members	Club presidents	All members
	Very low	Low	Medium	High				
Club..............	9	14	9	13	14	13	30	12
Union.............	9	14	14	15	15	15	17	14
Political group.......	6	5	6	8	5	5	9	7
Religious group.......	7	11	13	13	20	15	19	12
Family.............	15	28	32	38	41	42	22	34
Service organization...	38	54	64	70	58	67	77	64
More than three answers given.......	0	0	1	..	..	1	0	..
None...............	11	7	3	3	2	2	0	4
Not ascertained.......	30	13	7	4	6	5	3	8
Number of cases....	104	134	353	514	254	772	93	2,131

[a] Percentages total more than 100 because respondents gave more than one answer.

TABLE 42

FREQUENCY OF SIGNATURE COLLECTING AMONG INSTITUTE MEMBERS
(Percentage)

Frequency	Regular members whose participation is				Aspiring life members	Life members	Club presidents	All members
	Very low	Low	Medium	High				
A lot...............	1	1	4	9	11	16	55	7
Some..............	17	25	34	45	46	49	39	38
Never any..........	41	51	47	38	29	24	4	41
Not ascertained......	41	23	15	8	14	11	2	14
Totals.............	100	100	100	100	100	100	100	100
Number of cases....	104	134	353	514	254	772	93	2,131

TABLE 43

FREQUENCY OF LISTENING TO MCLAIN'S BROADCASTS AMONG INSTITUTE MEMBERS
(Percentage)

Frequency	Regular members whose participation is				Aspiring life members	Life members	Club presidents	Totals for samples
	Very low	Low	Medium	High				
Never..............	22	10	9	7	7	4	5	9
Listen, frequency not stated............	3	4	2	2	3	3	3	2
"Occasionally".......	36	63	49	32	38	23	25	39
"Often"..............	0	2	3	2	2	3	2	2
Once a week.........	1	1	1	1	1	1	0	1
Twice a week........	2	2	2	1	1	1	1	1
Three times a week....	5	..	4	6	3	5	6	5
Four times a week.....	3	5	5	11	9	9	17	8
Five times a week.....	3	7	21	35	28	45	37	27
More than five times a week[a]...........	0	2	2	2	3	3	2	2
Not ascertained.......	25	4	2	1	5	3	1	4
Totals.............	100	100	100	100	100	100	100	100
Number of cases....	104	134	353	514	254	772	93	2,131

[a] During McLain's congressional campaign he frequently broadcast more than five time a week.

TABLE 44

ATTENDANCE OF RESPONDENTS AT INSTITUTE MEETINGS
(Percentage)

Meetings attended	Regular members whose participation is				Aspiring life members	Life members	Club presidents	All members
	Very low	Low	Medium	High				
Nearly all............	2	8	11	29	29	42	86	21
About half...........	4	11	15	24	21	15	11	18
Seldom or never......	62	67	64	40	40	35	2	50
Not ascertained.......	32	14	10	7	10	8	1	11
Totals.............	100	100	100	100	100	100	100	100
Number of cases....	104	134	353	514	254	772	93	2,131

TABLE 45

VOLUNTARY CONTRIBUTIONS TO THE INSTITUTE
(Last three months)
(Percentage)

Amount	Regular members whose participation is				Aspiring life members	Life members	Club presidents	All members
	Very low	Low	Medium	High				
None................	58	70	62	0	29	12	2	31
$ .01–1.00..........	0	4	6	0	1	2	2	2
$ 1.02–2.00..........	0	0	4	8	4	2	4	4
$ 2.01–5.00..........	0	0	0	36	19	16	25	17
$ 5.01–10.00.........	0	0	0	30	14	18	27	15
$10.01–15.00.........	0	0	0	16	8	17	11	8
$15.01–20.00.........	0	0	0	7	3	8	9	4
$20.01–50.00.........	0	0	0	6	5	14	15	4
$50.01 and over......	0	0	0	..	..	1	0	..
Unknown............	2	4	6	0	3	2	1	2
Not ascertained.......	40	22	22	0	14	8	4	13
Totals.............	100	100	100	100	100	100	100	100
Number of cases....	104	134	353	514	254	772	93	2,131

TABLE 46

RESPONDENTS' FEELINGS CONCERNING HIS OWN
AND OTHER MEMBERS' EFFORTS IN THE INSTITUTE
(Percentage)

		Institute members (sample)							
		Regular members whose participation is				Aspiring life members	Life members	Club presidents	All members
Respondent	Members	Very low	Low	Medium	High				
"Doing enough"	"Doing enough"	5	5	9	8	7	5	6	7
"Doing enough"	"Not doing enough"	2	5	9	19	16	34	28	15
"Doing enough"	Not ascertained	4	1	5	4	5	5	1	4
"Not doing enough"	"Doing enough"	5	9	4	4	4	2	1	5
"Not doing enough"	"Not doing enough"	38	50	53	54	55	43	60	51
"Not doing enough"	Not ascertained	6	11	7	3	5	3	1	5
Not ascertained	"Doing enough"	1	1	1	1	1	1	1	1
Not ascertained	"Not doing enough"	3	2	4	3	4	3	1	3
Not ascertained	Not ascertained	36	16	8	4	3	4	1	9
Totals......	....	100	100	100	100	100	100	100	100
Number of cases......	....	104	134	353	514	254	772	93	2,131

TABLE 47

RESPONDENTS ATTRIBUTING FAVORABLE CHARACTERISTICS TO THE INSTITUTE

(Percentage)[a]

	Provides recreation	Sponsors legislation favorable to pensioners	Makes country aware of old-age problems	Gives pensioners help and advice	Works for welfare of country as whole	Works selflessly for aged	Not ascertained	Number of cases
Members.........	61	71	64	71	64	51	1	77
Nonmembers......	29	62	60	46	42	35	7	589

[a] Percentages total more than 100 because respondents gave more than one answer.

TABLE 48

COMPARISONS ON SELECTED VARIABLES

	Activists	Club presidents	Members
Per cent who are "glad" to have pension	17	18	29
Mean total dissatisfaction scores.......	.71	.64	.55
Mean activity scores.................	5.66	5.98	4.47
Per cent making very unfavorable appraisals of pension law..............	85	76	55
Per cent making very unfavorable appraisals of social worker............	51	41	27
Mean total demand scores............	3.83	4.11	3.86

IMAGES OF MCLAIN

	Activists	Club presidents	Members
Friend.............................	34	39	47
Brother............................	28	20	15
Teacher............................	9	10	8
Political leader.....................	11	20	14
Good shepherd......................	49	43	38
Protector...........................	56	46	44

IMAGES OF CISW

	Activists	Club presidents	Members
Club..............................	22	30	12
Union.............................	21	17	14
Political group.....................	7	9	7
Religious group....................	17	19	12
Family............................	39	22	34
Service organization................	76	77	64
Number of cases................	110	93	2,131

TABLE 49

URBANIZATION AND CONCENTRATION OF THE AGED
IN SIX METROPOLITAN AREAS

Area	Fertility[a]	Women in labor force[b]		Single family dwellings		Concentration Index	
						1940	1950
Los Angeles.............	41.2	32.5		64.8		.26	.31
City.................		37.9		35.5	54.3		
Environs.............		44.9		29.5	74.6		
San Francisco, Oakland, and environs.........	39.1	36.8		39.1		.19	.28
San Francisco and Oakland.............		37.8		37.9	35.1		
Berkeley environs.......		39.9		33.3	52.9		
St. Louis...............	40.6	32.7		45.6		.18	.20
City.................		37.2		35.9	26.4		
Environs.............		45.9		27.5	75.6		
Minneapolis-St. Paul......	44.2	37.1		50.2			.20
City.................		41.5		38.4	45.7		
Environs.............		62.7		27.2	84.0		
Pittsburgh..............	40.1	26.1		45.6			.20
City.................		37.6		29.9	30.5		
Environs.............		42.4		22.9	45.6		
Seattle.................	47.2	33.5		66.8			.25
City.................		40.6		36.4	59.0		
Environs.............		62.0		25.8	85.2		

Appendix II | *The Questionnaires*

1. The questionnaires and interviewing guides used in this study are reproduced below. Unless otherwise specified, all statistical data concerning recipients and CISW members reported in this volume have been derived from the responses to these instruments. The only exception is the statement concerning the recipients' political party references, which was taken from the pilot study.

2. Five forms of the printed questionnaires, designated by the symbols E1, E2, G1, G2, and G3, have been used in this study. All E-forms were sent to members of the CISW; all G-forms were sent to recipients of Old Age Assistance, whose names were obtained from the departments of social welfare of seven of the largest counties. Forms 1, 2, and 3 of the same questionnaire are alike in all points, except for some questions on page 4. The differences are shown below. The reasons for using the first two forms of the questionnaire were as follows:

a. After pretests and pilot study, the number of questions which we judged indispensable was so large that the questionnaire could not have been printed on four pages, the format which had been selected for practical reasons. We therefore produced alternate forms of the questionnaire. The questions sent to only half of each sample were those which pretests had shown to be so discriminating that we could be certain of statistical reliability even with a smaller number of cases.

b. Some of the questions used with only one-half of each sample were designed to elicit the expression of feelings of distrust and hostility. It was thought that these questions might produce a "halo effect" and elicit a larger number of negative responses to other questions, particularly those dealing with the respondent's level of dissatisfaction (which precede the "distrust" questions) and those dealing with demands upon society (which follow the "distrust" questions). Comparisons between the responses to the two types of questionnaires have shown this apprehension to be unfounded; the differences are well within the confidence limits for the 1 per cent level of confidence.

The third form of the questionnaire was used in Los Angeles County only. This form was devised when the Los Angeles County Bureau of Public Assistance, under a certain amount of political pressure, declared itself unable to permit the circulation of questionnaire G1 (which included the "distrust" question).

3. Owing to the variety of forms used, not all questions were asked of all respondents. The sample totals shown in the tables reflect the numbers of respondents who answered the same form of the questionnaire.

4. The questionnaires were developed by means of extensive pretests and pilot studies. Four forms of the first draft questionnaire (Form A) were tested by means of 60 oral interviews. As a result of these pretests, a second draft, Form B, was devised and further tested in 20 oral interviews. Form C was a mail questionnaire sent to 1,000 CISW members in the pilot study. The chief purpose of the pilot study was to determine response rates and to test the feasibility of a mail questionnaire. Form D was essentially the same as Form C, except that it contained additional questions which subsequently appeared on page 4 of forms E2 and G2; this form was pretested orally in 15 cases. Forms C and D were used in preparing forms E1 and E2, the questionnaires used in the main study of the CISW membership. From this questionnaire we developed Form F, used in an oral pretest with OAS recipients in the Richmond, California, area. In the same area we also ran a mail pilot study involving 100 cases. Forms G1 and G2, the questionnaires used for the sample of OAS recipients, were developed from forms E1, E2, and F. Form G3 was developed

without pretests when it became necessary to substitute a new set of questions for those appearing on page 4 of questionnaire G1.

5. An interview guide was devised for the purpose of obtaining additional information from CISW members who had participated in the petition drive of 1954. The purpose of this instrument was not to produce data which would lend themselves to statistical treatment, but rather to provide case materials which would help us to interpret the statistical evidence gathered by means of the questionnaire. Accordingly, the interviewers were instructed not to hold too rigidly to the interview schedule, but to pursue any leads which would yield insights into the social and psychological background of the respondents. The interviewers were further instructed to gather as much biographical material from the respondents as they could obtain, although none of the formal questions specifically called for such information. The interview guide is reprinted below.

Ia. Questionnaire for Members

UNIVERSITY OF CALIFORNIA
Assisted by George McLain,
Chairman, California Institute
of Social Welfare

Form E 1a

QUESTIONNAIRE
Problems of Older People

This questionnaire was prepared for you with the greatest possible care. Please ANSWER IT CAREFULLY. READ ALL INSTRUCTIONS with the greatest attention and FILL IN ALL THE ANSWERS completely. We know you want to cooperate, and we are sure you will do your part conscientiously. THANK YOU!

I. GENERAL QUESTIONS

This first group of questions is about your health, income, and other circumstances of your life. We need to have this information in order to gain insight into the problems of older people.

1. Age.................................
   years

2. ☐¹ Male   ☐² Female

3. In or near what town do you live?

   ....
   Town   County

4. Are you ☐¹ Single   ☐² Married
            ☐³ Widowed   ☐⁴ Divorced
            or ☐⁵ Separated?

5a. What kind of living quarters do you occupy?
   ☐¹ My own home
   ☐² A home owned by someone else in my family
   ☐³ A rented apartment or flat
   ☐⁴ A rented room
   ☐⁵ A hotel or boardinghouse room
   ☐⁶ Other (explain)..................................
   ....

5b. What are your living arrangements?
   ☐¹ I have lived alone...............years
   ☐² I live with my husband or wife
   ☐³ I live with my adult children
   ☐⁴ I live with relatives or friends
   ☐⁵ Other (explain)..................................

6a. What are your present sources of income?
   ☐¹ California Old Age Pension
   ☐² Federal Old Age Insurance benefits
   ☐³ Earnings   ☐⁴ Other (explain)......................
   ....

6b. Do you share living expenses (for food and housing) with anyone else (for instance your husband or wife, children, or friends)?
   ☐¹ Yes   ☐² No

7a. How would you rate your health?
   ☐¹ Excellent   ☐² Good   ☐³ Fair
   ☐⁴ Poor   ☐⁵ Very poor

7b. Is it easy or hard for you to get around?
   ☐¹ It is easy
   ☐² Sometimes it is easy, sometimes it is hard
   ☐³ It is hard

If you are getting a PENSION now (California Old Age pension) answer these questions:

8a. How do you feel about getting the pension?
   ☐¹ I am glad I have it
   ☐² I feel entitled to it
   ☐³ I wish I could do something in return
   ☐⁴ I would prefer to work
   ☐⁵ I feel embarrassed about taking it

8b. At what age did you first apply for your pension?
   ☐¹ At 65
   ☐² Between 65 and 70
   ☐³ After 70

8c. How did you feel about applying at the time?
   ☐¹ I was glad I could apply
   ☐² I felt I was entitled to it
   ☐³ I wished I could do something in return
   ☐⁴ I really wanted to go on working
   ☐⁵ I felt embarrassed about applying

8d. Since you first applied, has your pension ever been stopped or cut?
   ☐⁰ My pension was *never* stopped or cut
   ☐² My pension was stopped for .... months
   ☐³ My pension was cut by .... dollars

II. YOUR ACTIVITIES

One of the things we need to find out is how people like to spend their time and what they like and dislike. You can see that this is important, so please don't hesitate to tell us all you can about it.

9. In general, do you feel that you are pretty well occupied, or do you often have time on your hands?
   ☐¹ I have more things to do than I can find time for
   ☐² I am mostly busy
   ☐³ I often have time on my hands

Turn to inside, please

325

10. *Here is a list of things which enter more or less into people's happiness. We would like to know how you feel about them. For EACH ONE of these things, check "satisfied" if you are satisfied with it; "not quite satisfied" if you are not quite satisfied; or "dissatisfied" if you are dissatisfied. Please be very sure to do this for EACH ONE of the things listed.*

Are you satisfied with—

	Satisfied	Not quite satisfied	Dissatisfied
the place where you live?	☐ Satisfied	☐ Not quite satisfied	☐ Dissatisfied
the way younger people treat you?	☐ Satisfied	☐ Not quite satisfied	☐ Dissatisfied
the number of visits you have with friends and acquaintances?....	☐ Satisfied	☐ Not quite satisfied	☐ Dissatisfied
the weather where you live?	☐ Satisfied	☐ Not quite satisfied	☐ Dissatisfied
the way people do their work nowadays?	☐ Satisfied	☐ Not quite satisfied	☐ Dissatisfied
the medical attention you get?	☐ Satisfied	☐ Not quite satisfied	☐ Dissatisfied
the way your city or town is run?	☐ Satisfied	☐ Not quite satisfied	☐ Dissatisfied
the number of visits you have with your family?	☐ Satisfied	☐ Not quite satisfied	☐ Dissatisfied
the amount of money you get to live on?	☐ Satisfied	☐ Not quite satisfied	☐ Dissatisfied
the young people's ideas about morals and religion?	☐ Satisfied	☐ Not quite satisfied	☐ Dissatisfied
the way this country is run?	☐ Satisfied	☐ Not quite satisfied	☐ Dissatisfied
the food you get?	☐ Satisfied	☐ Not quite satisfied	☐ Dissatisfied

11. What organizations (such as clubs, lodges, unions, and the like) do you belong to? (Please write down all of them)

....

....

....

....

12a. What is your religion or denomination?

....
Write religion or denomination

12b. Do you participate in any church activities or groups (such as service groups, missionary society, etc.)?

☐¹ Yes   ☐² No

13. *Here is a list of things that people spend time on. Please tell us how often YOU do each of these things. Check only the ones you do once a month or more often, and mark the number of times you do these things. If it is hard to figure out how often you do these things, make a rough guess.*

☐²⁴ I go to meetings .... times a month

☐²³ I go to church .... times a month

☐¹¹ I work at a hobby or repairs around the house .... times a month

☐¹⁷ I do occasional work .... times a month

☐³⁴ I visit with my family .... times a month

☐³¹ I do work or errands for friends .... times a month

☐²⁵ I play with young children .... times a month

☐³³ I visit with friends .... times a month

☐²¹ I do volunteer work .... times a month

☐¹² I do serious reading .... times a month

☐³² I help the young folks with their house and yard .... times a month

☐²⁶ I participate in organized games .... times a month

☐¹⁵ I enjoy the outdoors .... times a month

☐¹⁶ I read for pleasure .... times a month

☐⁰⁰ I don't do any of the things on this list

☐³³ I do other things (explain) ....
.... times a month

14a. How often do you go to meetings of the Institute of Social Welfare?

☐¹ I go to nearly every meeting that is held in my town

☐² I go to just about half of the meetings being held in my town

☐³ I seldom or never go to meetings of the Institute

14b. How often have you worked with the Institute in collecting signatures on petitions?

☐¹ I always collect a lot of signatures

☐² I have done some signature collecting

☐³ I never collected signatures

14c. What are your *regular dues* to the Institute of Social Welfare?

☐⁰ I am not a member

☐¹ I pay $2.00 a year for the National Welfare Advocate

☐² I pay $5.00 a year for a regular membership

☐³ I am paying on a life membership

☐⁴ I am a paid-up life member

14d. About how much did you give as *voluntary contributions* to the Institute during the last 3 months (through the mail or in meetings)?

☐⁰ Nothing

☐ About $ ....

15a. How often do you listen to George McLain's broadcasts on the radio?

☐⁰ Never

☐⁹ Occasionally

☐ .... times a week

15b. When do you pay the greatest attention to George McLain's program? (Check no more than *two*.)

☐¹ When he talks about our pensions

☐² When he asks for help and contributions

☐³ When he talks about the work of the Institute

☐⁴ When he talks about religious things

☐⁵ When he tells how the elderly people live

326

16. What does George McLain mean to you? (Check *no more than TWO words* which tell best what George McLain is like.)

To me, George McLain is like a

- [ ]⁷ Political leader
- [ ]⁸ Good shepherd
- [ ]⁹ Protector
- [ ]⁵ Teacher
- [ ]³ Friend
- [ ]⁴ Brother
- [ ]⁰ None of these

17a. Are you a member of a *Social Welfare Club?*

- [ ] Yes
- [ ] No

17b. Do you hold any office in a *Social Welfare Club?* Which one?

- [ ]⁰ None
- [ ]¹ President
- [ ]² Vice-President
- [ ]³ Secretary-Treasurer
- [ ]⁴ Chaplain
- [ ]⁵ Other (explain) ....

18. What does the Institute of Social Welfare mean to you? (Check *no more than TWO words* which tell best what the Institute of Social Welfare is like.)

To me, the Institute of Social Welfare is like a

- [ ]¹ Club
- [ ]² Union
- [ ]³ Political group
- [ ]⁴ Religious group
- [ ]⁵ Family
- [ ]⁶ Service organization
- [ ]⁰ None of these

19a. Do you feel that you are doing enough for the Institute of Social Welfare?

- [ ] Yes
- [ ] No

19b. Do you feel that most members are doing enough for the Institute of Social Welfare?

- [ ] Yes
- [ ] No

III. WORK

Now we would like to learn about your work—past and present.

20. Are you working *full time* now?

- [ ]¹ Yes
- [ ]² No

If you don't work full time now, answer these questions:

21a. What was your last full-time job or occupation?

....
Name of job or occupation

....
Kind of business

21b. Did you work for an employer or for yourself?

- [ ]¹ Employer
- [ ]² Myself

21c. How old were you when you stopped working full time?

....
Write age

21d. Why did you stop working?

- [ ]¹ I reached the age where the company made people retire
- [ ]² I was laid off
- [ ]³ I was unable to work because of ill health
- [ ]⁴ I wanted to stop working
- [ ]⁵ Other reasons (explain) ....
....

21e. How did you feel about stopping work?

- [ ]¹ I felt very bad
- [ ]² It didn't make much difference to me
- [ ]³ I was glad to stop

21f. After you stopped working did you look for work?

- [ ]¹ Yes
- [ ]² No

21g. Were you ever made to leave a job because you reached the retirement age?

- [ ]¹ Yes
- [ ]² No

21h. Were you ever refused work because of your age?

- [ ]¹ Yes
- [ ]² No

If you are (or have been) **A HOUSEWIFE answer this question.**

21i. What was your husband's main line of work?

....
Name of job

....
Kind of business

22a. What was your main line of work *before* you were *50?*

....
Name of job

....
Kind of business

22b. Were you usually satisfied with the KIND OF WORK you did, or did you often think that you would prefer a different line of work?

- [ ]¹ Usually satisfied
- [ ]² Sometimes wished for different work
- [ ]³ Often wished for different work

22c. Were you usually satisfied with your JOB RATING or BUSINESS, or did you often wish to get ahead faster?

- [ ]¹ Usually satisfied
- [ ]² Sometimes wanted to get ahead faster
- [ ]³ Often wanted to get ahead faster

22d. How often did you look around for a better job, kind of work, or business opportunity?

- [ ]¹ I rarely or never was looking for something better
- [ ]² I sometimes was looking for something better
- [ ]³ I was almost always looking for something better

327

22e. Did you usually get all the breaks you deserved for getting ahead in your job or business, or not?

☐¹ I usually got all the breaks
☐² I got some breaks
☐³ I never or seldom got a break

IV. WAYS OF LIVING

Now we would like to learn from your experience how the elderly people live and how you think they should live. Please mark all the answers that are asked for.

26a. Here are some words which some people would use to describe the pension law as it is now. Please check all the words which you think describe the present pension law.

The pension law is—

☐¹¹ Generous   ☐²⁶ Cruel
☐²⁵ Full of red tape ☐²³ Confused
☐¹⁶ Kind   ☐¹⁴ Respectful
☐¹⁵ Efficient   ☐¹³ Clear
☐²¹ Stingy   ☐²⁴ Humiliating
☐²² Tricky   ☐¹³ Above board

26b. Now here are some words which some people use to describe the average social worker. Please check all the words which you think describe the average social worker.

The average social worker is—

☐¹³ Clear   ☐¹⁶ Kind
☐²⁴ Humiliating   ☐¹⁵ Efficient
☐¹² Above board   ☐²¹ Stingy
☐²⁶ Cruel   ☐²² Tricky
☐²³ Confused   ☐¹¹ Generous
☐¹⁴ Respectful   ☐²⁵ Full of red tape

27. Who are the friends and enemies of the pensioners and of other elderly citizens?

In the list below you will find the names of persons and groups which some people regard as either friends or enemies of the pensioners. If you think a person or group is a friend of the pensioners, check the word "Friend." If you think a person or group is an enemy of the pensioners, check the word "Enemy." You don't have to check each one, just the ones which you think are mostly friends or enemies of the elderly citizens.

Boards of Supervisors	☐ Friend	☐ Enemy
State Senators	☐ Friend	☐ Enemy
Social workers	☐ Friend	☐ Enemy
Labor Unions	☐ Friend	☐ Enemy
Eisenhower	☐ Friend	☐ Enemy
Catholics	☐ Friend	☐ Enemy
Senator Weybret	☐ Friend	☐ Enemy
Communists	☐ Friend	☐ Enemy
Assemblymen	☐ Friend	☐ Enemy
President Truman	☐ Friend	☐ Enemy
Republicans	☐ Friend	☐ Enemy
Protestants	☐ Friend	☐ Enemy
Stevenson	☐ Friend	☐ Enemy
Ham 'n Eggers	☐ Friend	☐ Enemy
Jews	☐ Friend	☐ Enemy
Politicians	☐ Friend	☐ Enemy
Chambers of Commerce	☐ Friend	☐ Enemy
Dr. Townsend	☐ Friend	☐ Enemy
Governor Warren	☐ Friend	☐ Enemy
General MacArthur	☐ Friend	☐ Enemy
Big business	☐ Friend	☐ Enemy
Democrats	☐ Friend	☐ Enemy
Negroes	☐ Friend	☐ Enemy

28. How should older people be treated?

We would like to hear your ideas on how older people should be treated. Please check all those items in this question that you agree with.

☐¹ Older people should be given special housing where it is most convenient to them
☐² Children should be taught to pay special respect to older people
☐³ Older people would do the best job in high government office
☐² There should be a special national holiday to honor the older people
☐¹ Older people should get a specially low rate on railroads, streetcars, etc.
☐² Families would be better off if they listened more to their older members
☐³ In churches and clubs, older people make the best leaders
☐² Each community should express its thankfulness to their older citizens by putting their names on an honor roll
☐¹ Stores and offices should have reserved counters to take care of the special needs of older people
☐⁰ None of these things should be done

Thank you for cooperating.

We have one more question:

When did you first join the Institute of Social Welfare?...........................
Write year

If there is anything else you want to tell us, add an extra sheet.

1b. Alternative Page 4, Used with One-half of the Samples

22e. Did you usually get all the breaks you deserved for getting ahead in your job or business, or not?
- ☐¹ I usually got all the breaks
- ☐² I got some breaks
- ☐³ I never or seldom got a break

IV. WAYS OF LIVING

Now we would like to learn from your experience how the elderly people live and how you think they should live. Please mark all the answers that are asked for.

23. Loren Winter is now 65 years of age and in pretty good health. Loren has just been retired, has some income and so is not working right now.

If *you* were to give advice, what would you say Loren should do to lead a happy, contented life. Please check EACH of the things you think a person like Loren should do to make life worthwhile.
- ☐⁷⁷ Work full or part time
- ☐³³ Have frequent visits with friends
- ☐²³ Attend church very regularly
- ☐²¹ Do volunteer work for some good cause
- ☐¹⁵ Spend a lot of time on outdoor activities
- ☐¹¹ Work at hobbies or repairs at home
- ☐²⁴ Attend meetings of some good organizations
- ☐²¹ Help friends with their work and errands
- ☐¹⁶ Read for entertainment
- ☐²⁵ Participate in organized games and other recreation
- ☐¹³ Do some serious studying
- ☐³² Help the young folks with their house and yard
- ☐³⁵ Play with young children
- ☐³⁴ Have frequent visits with the family
- ☐⁸⁸ Do other things (explain)...................................
....

24. Suppose Pat Miller, an elderly person who lived next door to you, was failing in health. Pat has trouble getting around nowadays, needs a special diet and a good bit of help. To which of the following would *you* advise Pat to *turn for help?*
- ☐¹ Pat's children or other young family members
- ☐² The social worker
- ☐³ Friends of Pat's own age
- ☐⁴ The doctor
- ☐⁵ Other people (explain)...................................
- ☐⁰ Nobody

25. *What are the most important things in life?*
Now we would like some idea of your general views on life. The easiest way for you to tell us about this is to compare some of the important things in life. In the list below, you are asked to compare these important things two at a time. Please be *very sure* to make one check mark on each line. Check the thing that you think is more important. (If you really can't decide, check both things.)
Which is more important?

To have money? ☐	OR	☐ To have friends?
To trust a higher power? ☐	OR	☐ To have an active life?
To be respected? ☐	OR	☐ To have influence?
To have friends? ☐	OR	☐ To trust a higher power?
To have an active life? ☐	OR	☐ To be respected?
To have influence? ☐	OR	☐ To have friends?
To have money? ☐	OR	☐ To have an active life?
To trust a higher power? ☐	OR	☐ To have influence?
To be respected? ☐	OR	☐ To have money?
To have friends? ☐	OR	☐ To be respected?
To have influence? ☐	OR	☐ To have money?
To trust a higher power? ☐	OR	☐ To be respected?
To have an active life? ☐	OR	☐ To have friends?
To have money? ☐	OR	☐ To trust a higher power?
To have influence? ☐	OR	☐ To have an active life?

28. *How should older people be treated?*
We would like to hear *your* ideas on how older people should be treated. Please check *all* those items in this question that you agree with.
- ☐¹ Older people should be given special housing where it is most convenient to them
- ☐² Children should be taught to pay special respect to older people
- ☐³ Older people would do the best job in high government office
- ☐² There should be a special national holiday to honor the older people
- ☐³ Older people should get a specially low rate on railroads, streetcars, etc.
- ☐³ Families would be better off if they listened more to their older members
- ☐² In churches and clubs, older people make the best leaders
- ☐² Each community should express its thankfulness to their older citizens by putting their names on an honor roll
- ☐¹ Stores and offices should have reserved counters to take care of the special needs of older people
- ☐⁰ None of these things should be done

Thank you for cooperating.

We have one more question:

When did you first join the Institute of Social Welfare?...........................
Write year

If there is anything else you want to tell us, add an extra sheet.

329

IIa. Questionnaires for Nonmembers

Except for the questions reproduced below, the questionnaires for nonmembers were identical with those for members. Questions *14a–*19b, shown on this page, took the place of questions 14a–19b contained in the questionnaire for CISW members.

*14a. Do you think the older people need special groups or organizations that look out for their needs or rights?

☐¹ Yes.   ☐² No

*14b. What makes you say so?..
....
....

*14c. Which would work out *better?*

☐¹ To have *only older* people in such groups?
OR
☐² To have people of *all ages* in such groups?

*15. What do you think such groups or organizations might do for the older people?

☐¹ Provide recreation and ways for the older people to get together
☐² Speak up for the older people in getting laws passed for their benefit
☐³ Speak up for a plan to improve the welfare of the country as a whole
☐⁴ Give help and advice to older people

*16. Have you heard about the following groups or people? (Check *all* you have heard about)

☐¹ Dr. Townsend—Townsend Clubs
☐² Recreation Centers for older people
☐³ George McLain—Institute of Social Welfare
☐⁴ Ham 'n Eggs
☐⁵ Others (explain)..

*17a. Which *one* of these groups or persons (named in the last question) do you consider the *best?*

....
Write name of group or its head

*17b. *Why* do you think this group or person is *good?*

☐¹ Provides recreation and social get-togethers for older people
☐² Does a good job in getting laws passed for the benefit of older people
☐³ Makes the country aware of the problems of older people
☐⁴ Gives older people good help and advice
☐⁵ Works for the welfare of the country as a whole
☐⁶ Works selflessly for the older people
☐⁷ Does other things (explain)..............................
....

*18a. Which *one* of these groups or persons (named in question 16) do you consider the *worst?*

....
Write name of group or its head

*18b. *Why* do you think this group or person is *bad?*

☐¹ Does not provide enough recreation
☐² Spoils the older people's chances to get better laws for their benefit
☐³ Spoils the older people's reputation in the community
☐⁴ Does not give older people any real help
☐⁵ Works against the welfare of the country as a whole
☐⁶ Takes advantage of the older people
☐⁷ Does other things (explain)..............................

*19a. To which of these groups (named above) have you *ever* belonged?

....
Write name of group or its head

*19b. To which of these groups (named above) do you still belong *now?*

....
Write name of group or its head

The page reproduced below was used with one-half of the non-member sample in Los Angeles County only. This substitution became necessary because the Los Angeles County Bureau of Public Assistance was prevented from circulating the standard page 4, reproduced on page 328 of this volume.

22e. Did you usually get all the breaks you deserved for getting ahead in your job or business, or not?

- [ ]¹ I usually got all the breaks
- [ ]² I got some breaks
- [ ]³ I never or seldom got a break

IV. WAYS OF LIVING

Now we would like to learn from your experience how the elderly people live and how you think they should live. Please mark all the answers that are asked for.

26a. Here are some words which some people would use to describe the *pension law* as it is now. Please check *all the words* which *you* think describe the *present pension law.*

The pension law is—

- [ ]¹¹ Generous
- [ ]²³ Full of red tape
- [ ]¹⁶ Kind
- [ ]¹⁵ Efficient
- [ ]²¹ Stingy
- [ ]²² Tricky
- [ ]²⁶ Cruel
- [ ]²³ Confused
- [ ]¹⁴ Respectful
- [ ]¹³ Clear
- [ ]²⁴ Humiliating
- [ ]¹² Above board

26b. Now here are some words which some people use to describe the *average social worker*. Please check *all* the words which *you* think describe the average social worker.

The average social worker is—

- [ ]¹³ Clear
- [ ]²⁴ Humiliating
- [ ]¹² Above board
- [ ]²⁶ Cruel
- [ ]²³ Confused
- [ ]¹⁴ Respectful
- [ ]¹⁶ Kind
- [ ]¹⁵ Efficient
- [ ]²¹ Stingy
- [ ]²² Tricky
- [ ]¹¹ Generous
- [ ]²³ Full of red tape

27. *Who are the friends and enemies of the pensioners and of other elderly citizens?*

In the list below you will find the names of persons and groups which some people regard as either *friends* or *enemies* of the pensioners. If you think a person or group is a friend of the pensioners, check the word "Friend." If you think a person or group is an enemy of the pensioners, check the word "Enemy." You don't have to check each one, just the ones which you think are mostly friends or enemies of the elderly citizens.

	Friend	Enemy
Boards of Supervisors	[ ]	[ ]
State Senators	[ ]	[ ]
Social workers	[ ]	[ ]
Labor Unions	[ ]	[ ]
Eisenhower	[ ]	[ ]
Catholics	[ ]	[ ]
Senator Weybret	[ ]	[ ]
Communists	[ ]	[ ]
Assemblymen	[ ]	[ ]
President Truman	[ ]	[ ]
Republicans	[ ]	[ ]
Protestants	[ ]	[ ]
Stevenson	[ ]	[ ]
Ham 'n Eggers	[ ]	[ ]
Jews	[ ]	[ ]
Politicians	[ ]	[ ]
Chambers of Commerce	[ ]	[ ]
Dr. Townsend	[ ]	[ ]
Governor Warren	[ ]	[ ]
General MacArthur	[ ]	[ ]
Big business	[ ]	[ ]
Democrats	[ ]	[ ]
Negroes	[ ]	[ ]

28. *How should older people be treated?*

We would like to hear *your* ideas on how older people should be treated. Please check *all* those items in this question that you agree with.

- [ ]¹ Older people should be given special housing where it is most convenient to them
- [ ]² Children should be taught to pay special respect to older people
- [ ]³ Older people would do the best job in high government office
- [ ]² There should be a special national holiday to honor the older people
- [ ]¹ Older people should get a specially low rate on railroads, streetcars, etc.
- [ ]³ Families would be better off if they listened more to their older members
- [ ]³ In churches and clubs, older people make the best leaders
- [ ]² Each community should express its thankfulness to their older citizens by putting their names on an honor roll
- [ ]¹ Stores and offices should have reserved counters to take care of the special needs of older people
  - [ ]⁰ None of these things should be done

Thank you for cooperating.

If there is anything else you want to tell us, add an extra sheet.

III. Interview Guide

The guide reproduced below was used in oral interviews of signature collectors in Oakland and Los Angeles.

I. Introduction.

I'm from the University of California, etc. We are studying the problem of pensions, what pensions mean to older people and what Mr. McLain and the Institute of Social Welfare are doing about them.

We got your name from the headquarters of the Institute of Social Welfare. You are one of the people who have collected quite a few signatures on the petitions to qualify the initiative on this year's ballot. At Mr. McLain's headquarters, they keep a list of all the people who've been active in collecting signatures, and we got your name from one of these lists. We are trying to talk to quite a few of the people who have collected signatures this time, because we think that you folks know from your own experience about some of the things we want to study.

Of course, anything you tell me will be treated as an entirely confidential matter. We won't use or mention your name to anyone.

(Warm-up question)

1. How many signatures did you collect? Was it hard to collect them?

2. *Methods used in collecting signatures.*
   2a. How did you go about collecting the signatures?
   2b. Did you ask members of your FAMILY to sign? (If not:) Why not?
   2c. Do you have any FRIENDS who *might* have signed? Did you *try* to get their signatures?
   2d. Where did you collect most of the signatures? (e.g., church, grocery store, street corner, etc.)

332

3. *Perception of Community Attitudes Toward the Aged.*

    3a. How did people act when you asked them for their signatures?

    3b. How do you think *ordinary* people in this state feel about pensioners?

    3c. How about here in this neighborhood?

    3d. Will most of these people vote for the initiative or not?

    3e. Which ones will vote *for* it? Why?

    3f. Which ones will vote *against* it? Why?

4. *Function of Political Action.*

    4a. Do you think the initiative will go through or not?

    4b. Suppose the initiative does go through, will that make a lot of difference in the life of the pensioners or not much difference? How about yourself?

    4c. If the initiative goes through, should Mr. McLain stop or should he try to qualify other initiatives? Why?

5. *Perception of Community Attitudes Toward McLain.*

    5a. From your own experience how do people around here feel about Mr. McLain and the Institute? Which people?

    5b. Do you think *young* people feel any different about Mr. McLain and the Institute than do *older* people? In what way?

    5c. Do you think *rich* people feel any different about Mr. McLain and the Institute than do *poor* people? In what way?

    5d. What makes people feel that way about Mr. McLain?

    5e. What makes people feel that way about the Institute?

    5f. Some people say a lot of bad things about Mr. McLain . . . Have you heard that too? (If negative response—) Have you read anything bad about Mr. McLain?

    5g. Do you think there is anything to the things that are being said about Mr. McLain? Who says it? Why?

6. *Function of Institute to Members.*

    6a. Do you remember when you joined the Institute? (If R. states he is *not* a member, ask question 6bb. and skip to section 7.)

333

6bb. Did you ever think of becoming a member? (If no—) Why not? (If yes—) What made you decide against it?

6b. How did you happen to join? (Get details.)

6c. Can you recall whether you were feeling pretty good at the time—or was something bothering you?

6d. Does it mean a lot to you to be a member or is it just one of several things you are interested in?

6e. Do you think pensioners who are not in the Institute are missing out on something? What is it?

6f. Do you have any *close* friends that *are* in the Institute? (Get details.)

6g. Do you have any *close* friends that are *not* in the Institute?

7. *Participation in the Institute.*

7a. How frequently do you attend meetings of the Institute?

7b. What do you like best about the meetings?

7c. How often do you listen to Mr. McLain on the radio?

7d. What do you like best about Mr. McLain's radio broadcasts?

7e. Are you a regular member of the Institute, a life member, or paying on a life membership?

7f. About how much money did you contribute to the Institute in the last three months? (If R. can't remember, suggest some figures, starting with $1.00 and going up.)

7g. Do you think most of the members can easily spare the money they are contributing, or is it pretty hard on them?

8. *Welfare Service.*

8a. Have you heard about the welfare service of the Institute? (Be sure he knows what you are talking about.)

8b. Have you ever had occasion to use the Institute welfare service?

8c. Do you think a lot of the members are in the Institute because of the welfare service, or are they in it for other reasons?

334

9. *Perception of Self and Other Institute Members.*

  9a. How active are you in the Institute? (Give examples of activity if necessary.)

  (If R. is not a member, ask—)

  9aa. Have you done any work for the Institute before? What? (Get details.)

  9b. Do you think that you are more active than most people or less active?

  9c. Do you think it makes any difference whether a person is a life member or a regular member?

10. *Perception of Institute Structure.*

  10a. Do you think the members often make suggestions about what the Institute ought to be doing?

  10b. Have you ever done this?

  10c. Do you think headquarters listens to the members' ideas?

  10d. Some say the members ought to have more to say. What do you think about that?

11. *Organizational Participation and Experience.*

  11a. Do you belong to any other organizations—unions, lodges, social clubs?

  11b. Have you belonged to any other organizations in the past? Which organizations?

  11c. How active were you in these? (Ascertain whether there was any real organizational experience in past.)

12. *Previous Social Relationships.*

  12a. What was your main line of work before you retired? (Get details.)

  12b. What did you like about the job?

  12c. What did you dislike about it?

  12d. What were the things that you were most interested in, such as your work, family, hobbies, friends, church, clubs, etc. (Probe for function it fulfilled for respondent. Get some description of past.)

  12e. Have you been able to keep this up? Still have contacts with these people?

13. *Retirement Expectations and Experience.*

    13a. Did you look forward to retiring before you stopped working?

    13b. Did you have any ideas what it would be like?

    13c. Did things turn out the way you had expected?

14. *Feeling About Welfare Law and Service.*

    14a. How do you feel about the pension *law* as it stands now?

    14b. Is there any way in which it should be changed? How?

    14c. How about the way the welfare department is being run?

    14d. How about your own pension? Are you worrying about it? Why?

    14e. Do you think there is any danger that the State pension program may be cut down or stopped?

    14f. Do you think that you and other older people have gained from the campaign that McLain has been putting on?

    14g. Is there any other way in which people like yourself have gained from what the Institute and Mr. McLain have done? (Probe for nonpolitical and noneconomic gains.)

Sampling Procedures
and Problems

Questionnaire sample of CISW members.—The sample was drawn
from the membership roster of the CISW by taking every nth plate
in the files. The organization maintained two files: the first contained the names of all members and subscribers; the second, the
names of life members and of persons making payments on life
memberships. The first file was sampled for regular members and
subscribers only; plates of life members and of persons paying on
life memberships were rejected. The sampling ratio of 1:23 was
so calculated that the number of sample addresses should come
to approximately 2,800; the actual yield was 2,611. The life members were sampled at a rate of 1:5, which, according to Institute
statistics, should have yielded approximately 1,000 sample addresses; the actual yield was 1,089. The individuals paying on life
memberships were sampled at a rate of 5:12; the expected number
of sample addresses was approximately 1,000; the actual yield was
1,089. In addition, 201 questionnaires were mailed to persons
whose names appeared on the Institute's roster of club presidents;
these were not considered as members of the sample but as a separate group. They have not been treated as members of the sample
in our statistical manipulations.

Sample of OAS recipients.—In California, lists of Old Age Assistance recipients are kept only by the counties. In view of the
administrative and technical difficulties which would have resulted if samples had been drawn in all fifty-eight California coun-

337

ties, it was decided to restrict the nonmember sample to the ten counties having the largest recipient populations. These ten counties (Los Angeles, San Francisco, Alameda, Santa Clara, Sacramento, Fresno, Riverside, San Bernardino, San Diego, and Orange) contained approximately three-quarters of the recipient populations. As a result of political pressures, three counties (Orange, Alameda, and San Diego) withdrew from the study after an initial agreement to coöperate. A fourth county (Los Angeles) declared itself unable to circulate Form 2 of the questionnaire; in this county, Form 3 had to be substituted. As a result, the nonmember sample represents only about two-thirds of the total recipient population.

Since the two samples (of members and nonmembers) were not drawn from the same geographical area, test IBM runs were made to ascertain whether geographical factors would significantly influence the results. The CISW members in counties included in the nonmember sample were compared with those in all other counties. Such comparisons on a series of questions did not yield any statistically significant differences.

The counties' rosters of recipients were sampled at a rate of 1:50. This yielded an address list of 3,630 names.

Questionnaire responses.—The table shows response rates for samples and sample strata. In the CISW sample, response rates were directly related to membership status. It is therefore likely that, in this group, the regular members who did respond to the

	Questionnaires sent out	Questionnaires returned	Response rates (per cent)
Club presidents	201	112	56
Life members	1,068	677	63
Aspiring life members	1,089	459	42
Regular members	2,611	995	38
Nonmembers	3,630	915	26

questionnaire were those more interested and involved. Response selectivity thus has a biasing effect upon the sample in that it causes the more interested articulate and active members to be overrepresented.

In order to ascertain what bias, if any, might be introduced into the *nonmember* sample by response selectivity, a special pretest was conducted in the area of Richmond, California. After sample addresses had been selected at random from the records of the Richmond office of the Contra Costa County Social Service Department, selected clients' social workers were instructed to eliminate any addresses of people incapable of responding by mail; this included persons unable to speak English, illiterate, too sick or too senile to answer, or known to be outside the county. In this manner about 25 per cent of the addresses were excluded. Printed interviews were then sent out to 100 addresses. The questionnaires were inconspicuously marked so as to make possible the identification of addresses from which questionnaires had been returned.

Of the 100 addresses, 68 returned their questionnaires. The remaining 32 addresses were visited by our interviewers, who had been instructed to determine why the questionnaires had not been returned and to administer them orally if possible. This check showed that only 7 of the 32 nonresponding recipients could have returned their questionnaires had they wanted to do so: 25 were sick, in the hospital, out of town, or otherwise unable to answer. The 7 addressees who could have responded gave no evidence of resistance to the questionnaire: 5 apologized for having been neglectful, and readily submitted to the interview; 2 indicated that they had no interest in the subject matter covered by our questions (these were both living with their children in spacious suburban homes). In view of the small number to whom questionnaires were administered orally, it is imposible to say whether these show any distinct response pattern.

The pretest results indicate that the reasons for nonresponse among nonmembers of the CISW are the same as among members: they relate to health, literacy, and general interest in social issues. We believe, therefore, that response bias does not destroy the comparability of the two samples, since in both the same variables appear to be at work. We believe that statistically significant differences between samples reflect population differences. As further evidence we cite the fact that the distributions of nonmembers uniformly resemble more closely the distributions of the *least involved group* of members than those of *any other* group of members. This expected similarity is internal evidence for the comparability of the two samples.

Any estimates of the sizes of population statistics are unreliable, however, and must be regarded as educated guesses. Very few such estimates have been made, and they are never crucial to the interpretations given in this study.

Questionnaire sample groups.—It will be noted that the sizes of sample groups given in the tables do not correspond to the sizes of sample strata shown in the preceding section of this Appendix. After the questionnaires had been returned, the composition of the sample groups had to be changed for the following reasons:

1. It was necessary to remove the names of 77 persons from the nonmember sample because they indicated that they were members of the CISW.

2. The membership roster was not up to date. Nearly one-half of the individuals listed by the CISW as aspiring life members indicated that they were either regular members or life members. The most probable reason for this discrepancy is that some of the aspiring life members had completed their payments toward a life membership, while others had not kept up these installments and had dropped back into the ranks of regular members; corrections had not been made in the membership file. Further, a few regular members had begun to make payments on life memberships. As a result, we were forced to transfer 141 cases from the group of aspiring life members to the life-member group; 117 cases from the group of aspiring life members to the group of regular members; and 13 cases from the group of regular members to the group of aspiring life members. The 40 persons listed as life members stated that they were still making payments on their life memberships, and 6 more declared themselves regular dues-paying members. They were shifted accordingly.

Weights used in the calculation of statistics for the total sample were adjusted accordingly.

3. The roster of club presidents was greatly inflated. The number of actually functioning clubs was much smaller than the number given by the Institute. Of the 201 purported club presidents, only 112 responded (the return rate of 56 per cent is much smaller than expected in a very highly involved group); and of these, 19

indicated that they were *not* officers of any club. These 19 cases were removed.

Tests of significance.—Differences between proportions which are discussed in the text are significant on the 5 per cent level of confidence or a higher level. Significance of differences was ascertained by means of the *t*-test. For this purpose we have used the *Tables Showing Significance of Differences Between Proportion and Between Means (for Uncorrelated Data)* by Vernon Davis (Department of Rural Sociology, Washington Agricultural Experiment Station, Pullman, Washington). This table is based on the assumption that the two samples compared are of equal size; any error introduced by the use of the tables with samples of unequal size is on the conservative side. In testing significance of differences between proportions or means applying to the total samples of members and nonmembers, the fact that one of the samples was stratified has not been taken into consideration; we thus tend to overestimate sampling error.

Selection of signature collectors.—The 42 signature collectors whose interview responses have been frequently quoted in this volume were selected from lists compiled by the CISW. Within certain limitations, selection was random. In Oakland and Berkeley, lists of all signature collectors in that area were used. From these lists 17 names were drawn. In Los Angeles County, seven areas having particularly large numbers of signature collectors were utilized. Within these areas, names were drawn at random. The number of names drawn in each area was as nearly as possible proportional to the number of signature collectors. Because of limitations in time and finances, only one call-back could be made at any given address. This resulted in a large loss of sample addresses in the downtown areas of Los Angeles which have a large transient population.

It was not our intention to use the interviews with petition circulators as a sample from which statistical inferences could be drawn. The only purpose of the use of random selection procedures was to prevent the selection of repondents by interviewers or field supervisors on the basis of personal preferences.

Appendix IV | *Indices*

The indices used in this study were constructed as follows:

Dissatisfaction indices.—In computations of the index numbers, the following values were assigned to the respondent's replies: "Satisfied," 0; "Not quite satisfied," 1; "Dissatisfied," 2. The total dissatisfaction index is the sum of all items scored for a given respondent. The partial dissatisfaction indices were obtained by summing item scores as follows:

1. Dissatisfaction with material related to experiences with the welfare administration:
   "The medical attention you get"
   "The amount of money you get to live on"
2. Dissatisfaction with the material environment:
   "The place where you live"
   "The weather where you live"
   "The food you get"
3. Dissatisfaction with interpersonal experiences:
   "The way younger people treat you"
   "The number of visits you have with friends and acquaintances"
   "The number of visits you have with your family"
4. Ideological dissatisfaction:
   "The way people do their work nowadays"
   "The way your city or town is run"

343

"The young people's ideas about morals and religion"
"The way this country is run"

Indices of activity and activity aspirations.—Indices of activity or of activity aspiration were computed by counting as zero any activity not checked by a respondent, and as 1 any activity checked by him.

The total activity score or activity aspiration score is based on all items in questions 13 or 23, respectively, except for "occasional work" (Q. 13), "work full or part time" (Q. 23), and "do other things (explain)" (both questions). The reason for excluding the two "work" items is that these items are not quite comparable and tend to produce unreliable results.

In order to obtain the partial activity or activity aspiration scores, the items were grouped in two ways: by the nature of the groups within which the activities take place, and by activity-passivity. These are two overlapping classifications of the same items. The items were used for the indices as follows:

CLASSIFICATION BY NATURE OF GROUPS

1. Solitary activities:
    "Work at hobbies or repairs around the house"
    "Do serious reading"
    "Enjoy the outdoors"
    "Read for pleasure"
2. Activities in formal groups:
    "Go to meetings"
    "Go to church"
    "Do volunteer work"
    "Participate in organized games"
3. Activities in informal groups:
    "Visit with my family"
    "Do errands for friends"
    "Visit with friends"
    "Help the young folks with their house and yard"
    "Play with young children"

CLASSIFICATION BY EFFECTS UPON THE ENVIRONMENT

4. Recreation:
    "Play with young children"
    "Participate in organized games"
    "Do serious reading"
    "Read for pleasure"
    "Enjoy the outdoors"
5. Social participation:
    "Go to meetings"
    "Go to church"
    "Visit with family"
    "Visit with friends"
6. Manipulation:
    "Work at hobbies or repairs around the house"
    "Do work or errands for friends"
    "Do volunteer work"
    "Help the young folks with their house and yard"

Indices of negativism and distrust.—These indices are based on questions 26a, 26b, and 27. For each question the number of negative responses was taken as a proportion of all responses given by the same respondent. The resulting ratio is the score.

Index of ecological segregation.—This is an application of the Lorenz curve technique, frequently used for measuring concentration of incomes and similar economic and social phenomena.

For each census tract in a given metropolitan area, the proportion of people above sixty-five years of age was computed. The census tracts were then ordered by the size of these proportions of aged individuals. The metropolitan population so ordered was divided into twenty equal segments; each segment thus contained 5 per cent of the total metropolitan population. The cumulative percentages of the metropolitan population were plotted against the cumulative percentages of the aged population. If all census tracts contained equal proportions of aged individuals, all plots would lie along a straight line. If there are differences in the proportions of aged people in census tracts, the plots will follow a curve whose departure from the straight line will be larger the greater the differences in proportions. Figure 8 shows such a curve.

If the aged population were completely segregated in a ghetto-like section of the metropolitan area, the Lorenz curve would first follow the base line (since the proportions of aged people would remain zero in all but the last few census tracts) and then follow

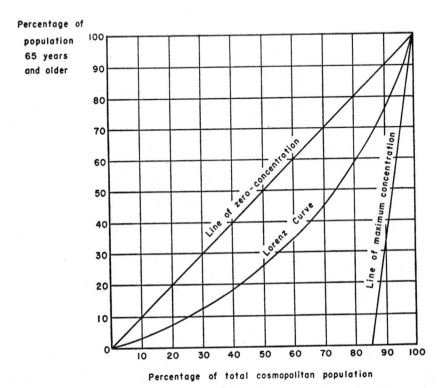

Fig. 8. Lorenz curve showing concentration of population aged sixty-five years and older.

the line of maximum concentration. This line intersects the base line at a point which represents the proportion of all people below the age of sixty-five in the total population. The area enclosed between the line of zero-concentration, the line of maximum concentration, and the base line is called the area of maximum concentration.

The index of concentration, C, is the ratio of the area enclosed by the Lorenz curve and the line of zero concentration to the area of maximum concentration. The formula used in computing this is

$$C = \cfrac{n - 1 - 2 \sum_{i=0}^{n-1} y_i}{n - 1 - \cfrac{2\left\{(n - i^*)(p - 1) + \sum_{i=i^*}^{n-1} x_i\right\}}{p}}$$

where n is the number of segments into which the population has been divided;

y_i is the ordinate of the Lorenz curve at any division point i;

i^* is the ordinal number of the division point next above $1 - p$;

p is the proportion of people aged sixty-five years and older in the total metropolitan population;

x_i is the abscissa at any division point i.

In selecting cities for comparison, the following criteria were applied: the tracted area had to include both the city proper and most of the outlying residential areas; the cities had to be as similar as possible when compared by means of conventional measures of urbanization. Table 49 (Appendix I) shows the urbanization indices together with the indices of concentration for the six cities used for this analysis.

Index